Scaffolding Reading Experiences:
Designs for Student Success

Second Edition

Scaffolding Reading Experiences: Designs for Student Success

Second Edition

by

Michael F. Graves

and Bonnie B. Graves

Christopher-Gordon Publishers, Inc.
Norwood, Massachusetts

Copyright
Acknowledgments

Chapter 2: Figure 2-1 copyright © 1976 by the National Council of Teachers of English. Reprinted by permission.

Chapter 5: Text from *Sounds All Around* by Wendy Pfeffer copyright © 1999 by Wendy Pfeffer. Reprinted by permission.

Chapter 9: Original text material for "Text Difficulty and Accessibility" copyright © 1989 by Randall J. Ryder and the International Reading Association. Reprinted by permission.

Christopher-Gordon Publishers, Inc.
1502 Providence Highway, Suite #12
Norwood, Massachusetts 02062
800-934-8322
781-762-5577

Printed in the United State of America
10 9 8 7 6 5 4 3 2 1   07 06 05 04 03 02

ISBN: 1-929024-48-7
Library of Congress Catalogue Number: 2002107846

Dedication

As with the first edition, we dedicate this second edition to our daughters, Julie and Erin, and to their teachers in the Minneapolis, Minnesota, Ouray, Colorado, and Bloomington, Minnesota, public schools, who nurtured their growing literacy. Both Julie and Erin have now completed college and graduate school, and the excellent K-12 education they received has continued to support their success in school and in their lives outside of school.

Contents

Acknowledgments

Our work with *Scaffolding Reading Experiences* goes back nearly 30 years, and as a result many people have contributed to the book's development. We wish first to thank the thousands of students and teachers who have considered our ideas about scaffolding, responded to them, added ideas of their own, and created Scaffolded Reading Experiences (SREs) for their students. We also thank Rebecca Palmer and David Furniss, who coauthored a booklet in which we introduced many of the ideas refined and elaborated here. More recently, working with Greg Sales and his Seward Leaning staff on an SRE website—www.onlinereadingresources.com—has given us an opportunity to further refine and extend our thinking about SREs. SREs written for the website by Lauren Liang and Sheri Scapple are included in this edition of the book. Additionally, research we have conducted with Cheri Cooke, Dave Fournier, Lauren Liang, and others has further confirmed the value of SREs. We were also aided by the formal reviews of Myra Vinson, Memphis City Schools; Susan Ansai, Chicago Public Schools; Dr. Kelly Chandler-Olcott, Syracuse University; Anna Hadgis, The Shipley School, PA; and Dr. Mary Regina Jett, University of Wisconsin. Our thanks to these reviewers is much more than perfunctory. Each of their reviews was thorough, insightful, and very helpful in strengthening the book. Finally, we wish to thank Hiram Howard and Susanne Canavan of Christopher-Gordon for their encouragement and assistance on both this second edition and the first edition and Kate Liston of Christopher-Gordon for her help with the myriad of details associated with publishing this edition.

Preface

Nearly a decade has passed since the first edition of this book (1994), and well over two decades have passed since the concept of instructional scaffolding was introduced into the literature by Donald Wood and his Harvard colleagues Jerome Bruner and Gail Ross (1976). Over that time period, the field of reading education has gone through some huge shifts. Psychologically and philosophically, the field has moved from behaviorism, to cognitivism, to constructivism and social constructivism. Pedagogically, it has moved from a skills orientation, to a whole language orientation, to a focus on phonemic awareness and phonics, and to a renewed interest in comprehension. Yet while so much has changed in the field, scaffolding has stood solidly as an instructional approach endorsed by virtually all reading professionals; and in recent years, scaffolding has become even more widely recommended and accepted. We think this is terrific news—for teachers, for students, and for all who realize the importance of each student achieving at the highest level possible. We believe that scaffolding students' efforts—providing them with the instructional support that allows them to accomplish tasks they could not accomplish, or could not accomplish as well, without the scaffold—serves as a bedrock for assisting young learners in reaching their fullest potential as literate members of our society.

The concept of Scaffolded Reading Experiences (SREs) has also held up very well and been increasingly accepted in the decade since the publication of the first edition. Over the period, we have presented scores of inservice workshops on SREs, taught almost that many classes focusing on SREs, published dozens of articles on SREs, and conducted several research studies on SREs. We have also created a website focusing on SREs—www.onlinereadingresources.com—which contains complete SREs for a number of widely used texts. Additionally, as this second edition goes to press, we are conducting federally funded studies of SREs in English, social studies, science, and humanities classes, as well as with special education students and English-language learners. As a result of these many and varied experiences, we know that SREs are effective in assisting students in understanding, learning from, responding to, and enjoying what they read. We know that both preservice and inservice can and will create effective SREs for their students. And we have learned how to make SREs even more powerful and how to best help teachers create powerful SREs. Consequently, our initial notions about SREs have been modified and honed in this second edition to make the book more effective and more engaging for teachers, to make the learning activities we describe more effective and more engaging for students, and to further improve students' reading and learning.

The second edition is based on the same SRE framework that served as the foundation of the first edition, but we have modified the book in keeping with the latest teaching practices, theory, and research. Chapters 1–3 present the framework and the updated information on teaching practices, theory, and research that have guided us in this new edition. Chapters 4–7 include many new pre-, during-, and postreading activities; a wealth of new children's literature; and two new comprehensive SREs, one for Kate DiCamillo's *Because of Winn-Dixie* and the other for Russell Freedman's *Eleanor Roosevelt: A Life of Discovery*. Finally, chapters 8 and 9 include new insights on integrating SREs into your classroom and the latest information on the features that make fiction and nonfiction texts comprehensible and engaging for young readers.

We believe that the approach to Scaffolded Reading Experiences we present here will make reading more enjoyable, more successful, and more understandable for students. We further believe that it will make teaching reading more manageable, more exciting, and more rewarding for teachers. We are confident that you will find this to be true. We also hope and believe that reading our book will prove to be a rewarding and successful experience, an experience that will provide you with both new insights and many very practical tools for boosting students' confidence in their reading and for nurturing their love of reading.

Chapter

1

Introduction and Overview

"I just don't get this!" Damien complains. He slams his health book shut and lays his head on his desk.

Ms. Botts, a substitute, walks over to Damien. "Did you really try to read it?" she asks.

"I did! I read all of it, but I just don't understand what they're talking about. It doesn't make sense."

After asking Damien a few questions on the chapter and having him read a few sentences aloud, Ms. Botts realizes that Damien is right. He can read the words, but he simply can't make much sense out of the chapter. Why is this the case with Damien, and why is it all too often the case with other young readers?

As you know from your own experience, either as a reader or a teacher, in order to enjoy reading and to get the most out of what you read, you need to be actively involved with the text, something that obviously wasn't happening with Damien. To be successful, a reader needs to both understand and make some connections with a text. Essential to effective reading are having the prerequisite background knowledge and strategies to deal with the selection you're reading, being motivated and prepared to read, and having some purpose for reading. Say you are glancing through the newspaper and this headline catches your attention: "New Technique Successful in Teaching All Students to Read." Right away you're motivated to read, although you may well be skeptical of the claim. You're a teacher with 28 third graders, 6 of whom are struggling readers. In a split second your brain pulls out of memory the faces of those six students, an image of your busy classroom, and the methods and materials you've used. You're more than prepared to see what this article has to tell you about teaching reading; in fact, you can't wait to get started. You want to know what this technique is and if it really can work with all students. Once you begin reading, you combine what you know about students, teaching reading, and classrooms with what is presented in the text, building meaning as you go. What the author says either refutes or confirms what you know. You might become intrigued, amused, discouraged, angered, or enlightened, but two things are certain: you are neither lost nor uninterested. After you read, you will be able to recall much of what you have read—to ponder it, to consider the author's arguments, and to apply or reject what you have learned.

How can we foster and encourage this kind of involvement in our students and at the same time bolster their competence as readers and their confidence in their reading ability so that they become committed and able lifelong readers? One key to assisting young readers in reaching these goals is to ensure that each and every reading experience they have is a successful one. We want to do everything possible to make sure that students understand what they read, learn from what they have read, and realize that they have understood and learned from what they have read. We want them to come away from their reading experiences confident in their ability to read whatever material is assigned in school and eager to read independently for the pleasure and rewards that only reading can bring.

One very powerful approach to creating these sorts of reading and learning experiences is the use of instructional scaffolding. We believe that the term *scaffolding* was first used in its educational sense by David Wood, Jerome Bruner, and Gail Ross (1976), who used it to characterize mothers' verbal interactions when reading to their your children. Thus, for example, in sharing a picture book with a child and attempting to assist the child in reading the words that label the pictures, a mother might at first simply page through the book, familiarizing the child with the pictures and the general content of the book. Then she might focus on a single picture and ask the child what it is. After this, she might point to the word below the picture, tell the child that the word names the picture, ask the child what the word is, and provide him or her with feedback on the correctness of the answer. The important point is that the mother has neither simply told the child the word nor simply asked him or her to say it. Instead, she has built an instructional structure, a scaf-

Chapters 4, 5, and 6 parallel each other. Chapter 4 describes eight types of prereading activities and gives specific examples of each. Chapter 5 describes five types of during-reading activities and gives examples of each. Chapter 6 describes and provides examples of eight types of postreading activities. Because we believe that models are extremely useful in precisely conveying our meaning, we have included many detailed examples. With each example we have included a discussion of the types of reading selections with which the activity would be useful and our reflections on the activity—our assessment of it, some of its unique features, and some general pedagogical considerations it raises.

Chapter 7 brings together the various components of an SRE and illustrates just what a complete SRE looks like by presenting detailed examples of four complete SREs selected to convey the wide range of scaffolding possible. Each example includes a detailed description of activities for the lesson, a discussion of why we included those specific activities, a discussion of other options, and some general considerations suggested by the example.

Chapter 8 addresses some considerations to keep in mind as you begin using SREs. It is divided into four sections. In the first section, we discuss some of the principal decisions you face as you move to implement SREs in your classroom. In the second section, we consider using SREs to foster higher level thinking and deep understanding. In the third section, we consider assessing students, texts, and the effects of SREs. Finally, in the fourth section, we consider the place of SREs in a comprehensive literacy program and stress that SREs are only one component of a comprehensive program.

In chapter 9 we present a qualitative approach to choosing appropriate reading selections for your students. For some time now, readability formulas, quantitative approaches to assessing text difficulty, have been severely criticized. Although we believe that quantitative approaches can serve some purposes, we also agree with the criticisms and believe that quantitative approaches can be misleading if used by themselves. The approach described here gives you an alternative or additional method to use when considering reading selections to use with your students.

The book concludes with several indexes. In order to make the book as useful and convenient to use as possible, the sample activities presented are indexed by author, title, grade-level, and subject; and the book itself is indexed by academic author and academic subject.

Along with a general description of the scaffolded reading approach and the ideas that inform it, this book contains a number of detailed samples of scaffolded reading activities. These are designed to illustrate the general ideas we discuss, to serve as models you can use in developing similar activities for your classroom, and to act as springboards for critical and creative thinking as you reflect on how these ideas might be implemented in your particular teaching situation. They are not meant to be scripts or blueprints. As you are well aware, every reading situation is slightly different. Moreover, given the dynamics of actual classrooms, even the most carefully crafted lessons have a way of taking on a life of their own. At the same time, although your plans should and will often change as they unfold in the classroom, having carefully considered plans for facilitating students' reading puts you in the best possible position to make informed, on-the-spot decisions as you scaffold and encourage students in their journeys to become competent, active, purposeful, avid, and lifelong readers.

References

Anderson, L. M. (1989). Classroom instruction. In M. C. Reynolds (Ed.), *Knowledge base for the beginning teacher* (pp. 101–115). New York: Pergamon. A succinct and insightful summary of the research on effective instruction.

Anderson, R. C., & Armbruster, B. B. (1990). Some maxims for learning and instruction. *Teachers College Record, 91,* 396–408. Scaffolding is one of nine central maxims the authors see as undergirding effective instruction.

Applebee, A. N., & Langer, J. L. (1983). Reading and writing as natural language activities. *Language Arts, 60* (2), 68–175. One of the earliest articles to examine the classroom applications of scaffolding.

Beed, P. L., Hawkins, E. M., & Roller, C. M. (1991). Moving learners toward independence: The power of scaffolded instruction. *The Reading Teacher,* 44 (9), 648–655. Discussion of the power of scaffolding in a tutoring program.

Brown, A. N., & Palincsar, A. M. (1989). Guided cooperative learning and individual knowledge acquisition. In L. B. Resnick (Ed.), *Knowing, learning, and instruction: Essays in honor of Robert Glaser* (pp. 393–451). Hillsdale, NJ: Erlbaum. A detailed consideration of reciprocal teaching, with special attention to scaffolding.

Cazden, C. B. (1992). *Whole language plus: Essays in literacy in the United States and New Zealand.* New York: Teachers College Press. Cazden endorses scaffolding as one way in which teachers can go beyond merely immersing children in rich literacy environments, something she believes must be done if all children are to reach their full potential as readers and writers.

Cooke, C. L. (2002). *The effects of scaffolding multicultural short stories on students' comprehension, response, and attitudes.* Unpublished doctoral dissertation, University of Minnesota, Minneapolis. Carefully done study, showing very positive effects of SREs.

Fournier, D. N. E., & Graves, M. F. (In press). Scaffolding adolescents' comprehension of short stories. *Journal of Adolescent and Adult Literacy.* A small experiment showing positive effects of SREs used with middle school students.

Graves, M. F., & Liang, L. A. (In press). Online resources for fostering understanding and higher-level thinking in senior high school students texts. *Fifty-first yearbook of the National Reading Conference.* Chicago: National Reading Conference.

Graves, M. F., Palmer, R. J., & Furniss, D. W. (1976). *Structuring reading activities for English classes.* Champaign, IL: National Council of Teachers of English. The roots of the thinking underlying *SREs.*

Langer, J. A. (1984). Literacy instruction in American schools: Problems and perspectives. *American Journal of Education, 93* (1), 107–132. Presents scaffolding as one very promising instructional approach.

Palincsar, A. S. (1986). The role of dialogue in providing scaffolded instruction. *Educational Psychologist, 21* (1 & 2), 73–93. A detailed look at dialogue as scaffolding.

Pearson, P. D. (1996). Reclaiming the center. In M. F. Graves, P. van den Broek, & B. M. Taylor (Eds.), *The first R: Every child's right to read* (pp. 259–274). New York: Teachers College Press. Includes a strong endorsement for scaffolding and the SRE itself.

Pearson, P. D., & Gallagher, M. (1983). The instruction of reading comprehension. *Contemporary Educational Psychology, 8,* 317–344. Source of the gradual release of responsibility figure.

Pressley, M. (2002). *Reading instruction that works: The case for balanced teaching* (2nd ed.). New York: Guilford Press. An excellent review of much of the research on reading instruction and a strong endorsement for scaffolding.

RAND Reading Study Group reference before Raphael (2000). *Reading for understanding: Toward an R&D program in reading comprehension.* Santa Monica, CA: Rand Education. Also available on-line at http://www.rand.org/multi/achievementforall/reading/.

Raphael, T. M. (2000). Balancing literature and instruction: Lessons from the Book Club project. In B. M. Taylor, M. F. Graves, & P. van den Broek (Eds.), *Reading for meaning: Fostering comprehension in the middle grades* (pp. 70–94). New York: Teachers College Press. Scaffolding is one of the cornerstones of Raphael's approach.

Resnick, L. (1987). *Education and learning to think.* Washington, DC: National Academy Press. Though written over a decade ago, this remains a seminar work on higher level thinking.

Rodgers, E. M. (2000). Language matters: When is a scaffold really a scaffold? *Forty-ninth yearbook of the National Reading Conference* (pp. 78–90). An exploration of the concept of scaffolding.

Routman, R. (2000). *Conversations.* Portsmouth, NH: Heinemann. Presents strategies for teaching, learning, and evaluating.

Snow, C. E., Burns, M. S., & Griffin, P. (Eds.). (1998). *Preventing reading difficulties in young children.* Washington, DC: National Academy Press. Seminal review of research on what makes early reading instruction and experiences effective.

Taylor, B. M., Pearson, P. D., Clark, K. F., & Walpole, S. (2000). Beating the odds in teaching all children to read. *Elementary School Journal, 101,* 121–166. A national study highlighting scaffolding as one of the most effective instructional approaches.

Vygotsky, L. S. (1978). *Mind in society: The development of higher psychological processes.* Cambridge, MA: Harvard University Press. The source of the zone of proximal development concept.

Warton-McDonald, R., Pressley, M., & Hampston, J. M. (1998). Literacy instruction in nine first-grade classrooms: Teacher characteristics and student achievement. *Elementary School Journal, 99,* 101–128. Empirical study revealing the scaffolding provided by effective teachers.

Wood, D. J., Bruner, J. S., & Ross, G. (1976). The role of tutoring in problem-solving. *Journal of Child Psychology and Psychiatry, 17* (2), 89–100. An introduction to the concept of scaffolding and an insightful examination of parent-child interactions.

Chapter

2

What Is a Scaffolded Reading Experience?

A Scaffolded Reading Experience (SRE) is a set of prereading, during-reading, and postreading activities specifically designed to assist a particular group of students in successfully reading, understanding, learning from, and enjoying a particular selection. As such, an SRE is somewhat similar to traditional instructional plans such as Emmett Betts's Directed Reading Activity (1946) and Russell Stauffer's Directed Reading-Thinking Activity (1969) and to more recent plans such as Irene Fountas and Gay Sue Pinnell's Guided Reading (1996). Robert Tierney and John Readence (2000) classify all of these plans as "lesson frameworks," and this is an appropriate classification for the SRE.

However, an SRE differs markedly from these other instructional frameworks in that it is not a preset plan for dealing with a text. Instead, an SRE is a flexible plan that you tailor to a specific situation. It has two parts. The first part, the planning phase, takes into consideration the particular group of students doing the reading, the text they are reading, and their purpose(s) for reading it. The second part, the implementation phase, provides a set of prereading, during-reading, and postreading options for those particular

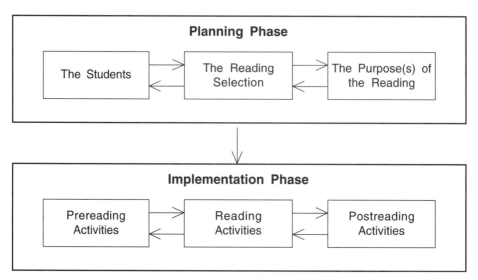

Figure 2-1.   Two Phases of an SRE

readers, the selection being read, and the purpose of the reading. The SRE framework is shown in Figure 2-1.

In the planning phase, you plan and create the entire experience. The implementation phase consists of the activities you and your students engage in as a result of your planning. This two-phase process is a vital feature of the SRE approach in that the planning phase allows you to tailor each SRE you create to the specific situation you face. Different situations call for different SREs.

Planning takes into account the students, the reading selection, and the reading purpose. Suppose you are working with average-ability sixth graders, you want them to develop some fairly deep understanding of the migration of whales, and the text you have chosen is quite demanding. Or suppose you are working with these same sixth graders, your purpose is to have them read a humorous story for the pure enjoyment of it, and you have chose a fairly easy reading selection such as Margo Sorenson's comic novel *Funny Man.*

In both of these situations, your planning leads to the creation of the SRE itself and to your implementing it, yet the two SREs will differ markedly. The components of the implementation phase are prereading, during-reading, and postreading activities. With the whale migration text, we have already suggested that you want students to develop some fairly deep knowledge and to retain much of what they learn. This means that your SRE for the whale migration text is likely to be a substantial one, with prereading activities that prepare students to read the difficult text, during-reading activities that lead them to interact and grapple with the text in ways that help them to understand and learn from it, and postreading activities that give them opportunities to check their understanding of the text and solidify their learning.

Consequently, the class might spend 4 or 5 days reading the chapter and completing the learning activities you have assembled.

Conversely, with the short, humorous novel *Funny Man* and the major goal that students simply enjoy the reading experience, your SRE is likely to be minimal. Prereading might consist of a brief motivational activity, students might read the story silently to themselves, and postreading might consist of an optional discussion. Consequently, the class might spend only a day or so reading and responding to this short book.

In addition to recognizing that the framework results in very different SREs for different situations, it is important to recognize that the components of each phase of the SRE are interrelated. Consider the three components of the planning phase: the students, the text, and the purpose. Once you decide which students you're going to work with, there are only some texts you can use and some purposes you can expect to accomplish. Once you decide which text you are going to use, there are only some students who will be able to read it and some purposes you can hope to achieve with it. Once you decide what your purposes are, there are only some texts you can use to accomplish those purposes and some students who will be able to achieve them. The same sort of interdependency applies to the three components of the implementation phase. For example, if you decide you are going to have some very challenging postreading tasks, you'll want to include prereading activities and during-reading activities that thoroughly prepare students to accomplish those challenging tasks.

The possible pre-, during-, and postreading components of an SRE are listed in Table 2-1. We emphasize that these are all the possible components of an SRE. No single SRE will include all of these activities.

In the next few pages, we briefly describe each of these pre-, during-, and postreading options. In later chapters, we discuss each of them in more depth and provide detailed examples of each.

Table 2-1.   Possible Components of an SRE

Prereading Activities
   Motivating
   Relating the reading to students' lives
   Activating or building background knowledge
   Providing text-specific knowledge
   Preteaching vocabulary
   Preteaching concepts
   Prequestioning, predicting, and direction setting
   Suggesting strategies

During-Reading Activities
   Silent reading
   Reading to students
   Guided reading
   Oral reading by students
   Modifying the text

Postreading Activities
   Questioning
   Discussion
   Writing
   Drama
   Artistic, graphic, and nonverbal activities
   Application and outreach activities
   Building connections
   Reteaching

Prereading Activities

Prereading activities prepare students to read an upcoming selection. They serve a number of functions: getting students interested in reading the selection, reminding students of things they already know that will help them understand and enjoy the selection, and preteaching aspects of the selection that may be difficult. Prereading activities are particularly important because with adequate preparation the experience of reading will be enjoyable, rewarding, and successful. Prereading activities are widely recommended (see, for example, Aebersold & Field, 1997; Ciborowski, 1992; Cunningham, Hall, & Defee, 1998; Fountas & Pinnell, 1996; Readence, Moore, & Rickelman, 2000; Schoenbach, Greenleaf, Cziko, & Hurwitz, 1999; RAND Reading Study Group, 2002; Yopp & Yopp, 1992), and a number of different types of prereading activities have been suggested. In listing the possible prereading activities for SREs, we have attempted to create a relatively small set of categories that suggest a large number of useful activities in which teachers and students can engage. We suggest eight types of prereading activities.

Motivating activities include any activities designed to interest students in the upcoming selection and entice them to read it. Although a variety of prereading activities can be motivational as well as accomplishing some other purpose, we list motivating activities as a distinct category because we believe that it is perfectly appropriate to do something solely for the purpose of motivating students. Moreover, we believe that motivating activities should be used very frequently.

Relating the Reading to Students' Lives is so self-evident a category as to leave little to say. We will, however, point out that because showing students how a selection relates to them is such a powerful motivator and promotes comprehension, it is something we like to do often.

Activating or Building Background Knowledge is always important if students are to get the most from what they read. When you activate background knowledge you prompt students to bring to consciousness already known information that will be helpful in understanding the upcoming text. For example, let us say a group of your eighth graders is researching the plight of migrant workers. Before these students read a story you have recommended from *The Circuit*, Francisco Jiménez's award-winning collection of stories based on his own experiences as a child migrant worker in California, you might encourage them to discuss what they have already learned about migrant workers from their previous reading. In addition to activating background knowledge, it is sometimes necessary to build background knowledge—knowledge the author has presupposed (probably tacitly) their readers already possess. For example, in reading the stories in *The Circuit*, you might find that Jiménez presupposes some specific knowledge of California geography that you're pretty sure this particular group of eighth graders lacks. In this case, supplying this information would make good sense. As another example of the need to build background knowledge, consider that the author of an American short story set in a movie theater is likely to assume that students are quite familiar with American movies and movie theaters and thus is not likely to explain anything about them in the story itself. For students who were raised in the United States and have been to many of movies, the assumption is correct, but you might have to explain quite a bit about movie theaters and related concepts to a Hmong student who had just arrived in this country.

As contrasted to activating or building background knowledge, **Providing Text-Specific Knowledge** gives students information that is contained in the reading selection itself. Providing students with advance information on the content of a selection—giving students the seven topics discussed in an article on whales, for example—may be justified if the selection is difficult or densely packed with information.

As used here **Preteaching Vocabulary** refers to preteaching words that are new labels for concepts that students already know. For example, you would be teaching vocabulary—a new label—if you taught fourth graders the word *crimson*, meaning "red." It often makes good sense to take 5 minutes and preteach half a dozen or so new vocabulary words before an upcoming selection.

Preteaching Concepts is a different matter. Preteaching Concepts refers to preteaching new and potentially challenging ideas, not just new labels for ideas students already understand. For example, if you wanted to teach fourth graders the full meaning of *velocity,* you would be teaching most of them a new concept. It does not make sense to attempt to preteach half a dozen new and difficult concepts in anything like 5 minutes. It takes significant amounts of time and requires powerful instruction.

We have listed **Prequestioning, Predicting, and Direction Setting** together because we believe that they are similar activities. With any of them, you are focusing students' attention and telling them what is important to look for as they read. Such focusing is often necessary, because without it students may not know what to attend to in their reading.

In the final Prereading Activity we have listed, **Suggesting Strategies,** the key word is *suggesting.* As we will explain at the end of this chapter, SREs are not designed to *teach* strategies. Teaching strategies—actually instructing students in how to do something they could not do previously—almost always requires more time than we allot to SREs. However, it is often appropriate to suggest as part of an SRE that students use strategies they already know. For example, you might suggest to seventh graders who are reading a selection that presents a complex argument that the argument found in the piece is complex and that it would be a good idea for them to summarize it in their own words. Occasionally, these strategies may be ones that students have learned on their own, but in most cases the strategies will have been deliberately taught in the past.

During-Reading Activities

During-reading activities include both things that students do themselves as they are reading and things that you do to assist them as they are reading. Like prereading activities, during-reading activities are frequently recommended (see, for example, Aebersold & Field, 1997; Bean, Valerio, & Stevens, 1999; Beck & McKeown, 2001; Beck, McKeown, Hamilton, & Kucan, 1997; Ciborowski, 1992; Fountas & Pinnell, 1996; McKeown & Beck, in press; Richardson, 2000; Schoenbach et al., 1999; Wood, Lapp, & Flood, 1992; Yopp & Yopp, 1992). However, there are probably not as many different types of during-reading activities. In creating the list of possible during-reading activities for SREs, we have again attempted to list a relatively small set of categories that suggest a large number of useful activities in which teachers and students can engage. We suggest five types of during-reading activities.

We have deliberately listed **Silent Reading** first because we believe strongly that it should be the most frequently used during-reading activity. The central long-term goal of reading instruction is to prepare students to become accomplished lifelong readers, and most of the reading students will do once they leave school—as well as in secondary school and college—will be silent reading. It is both a basic rule of learning and everyday common sense that one needs to repeatedly practice the skill he or she is attempting to master. If we choose appropriate selections for students to read and have adequately prepared them to read the selections, then students will often be able to silently read the selections on their own.

Reading to Students can serve a number of functions. Hearing a story or an expository piece read aloud is a very pleasurable experience for many youngsters and also serves as a model of good oral reading. Reading the first chapter or the first few pages of a piece can help to ease students into the material and also serve as an enticement to read the rest of the selection on their own. Reading to students can make material accessible to students who find certain texts difficult, because of their complex structure or difficult vocabulary. Some students find listening easier than reading; this is certainly the case with many less-proficient readers and with some—but by no means all—English-language learners. For these students, reading aloud—or playing an audiotape for the same purpose—is sometimes very helpful. However, in most instances, students should read silently on their own. One gets good at reading through reading.

Guided Reading refers to any activity that you use to focus students' attention on particular aspects of a text as they read it. Guided reading often begins as a prereading activity—perhaps with your setting directions for reading—and is then carried out as students are actually reading. For example, in order to help students appreciate an author's craft and to give them examples of the sort of language they might like to sometimes include in their own writing, you could have them jot down examples of particularly colorful language as they read a humorous short story. As another example, if you find that an expository piece on seashells is actually divided into half a dozen sections but contains no headings or subheadings, you might give students a semantic map that includes titles for the half dozen sections and ask them to complete the map as they are reading. Often, with guided reading activities, students' goal is to learn something from their reading rather than just read for enjoyment. Thus, guided reading activities are frequently used with expository material. However, it is also possible to guide students in understanding and responding to narratives—for example, to help ninth graders recognize the plot structure of the Newbery award-winning novel *A Single Shard* by Linda Sue Park, or to help fourth graders empathize with the beleaguered protagonist Joel in *Taking Care of Trouble* by one of us (Bonnie).

Of course, one long-term goal is to motivate and empower students to learn from and respond to selections without your assistance. Thus, with less-challenging selections and as students become increasingly competent, your support can and should be less specific and less directive, and sometimes consist only of a prereading suggestion: "After you read the first chapter in Kathleen Krull's *Lives of the Presidents*, I have a suggestion for you. Try reading it with a partner and stopping after each section to take notes. This should help you understand and remember the material better." Or, if these same fifth-grade students are reading a narrative such as Elizabeth Levy's *My Life as a Fifth-Grade Comedian*, you might say, "You'll find that Bobby is quite a character and that he changes a lot during the story. Using a journal to record the changes he undergoes and writing down how you feel about the changes may help you better appreciate what he's going through."

In some classrooms, **Oral Reading by Students** is a relatively frequent activity, while in others it is a relatively infrequent one. As we have noted, most of the reading that students do once they leave elementary school is silent reading; thus doing a lot of silent reading is important. Nonetheless, oral reading has its place. Certainly, poetry is often best and most effective when read orally. Also, poignant or particularly well written passages of prose are often appropriate for oral reading. Reading orally can be helpful when the class or a group of students is studying a passage and trying to decide on alternate interpretations or on just what is and is not explicitly stated in the passage. Students often like to read their own writing orally, and having individual students read orally can provide you with very valuable diagnostic information. Thus, oral reading is something to include among the many alternatives you offer students.

Modifying the Text is sometimes necessary to make the reading material more accessible to students. Modifying the text can involve presenting the material on audio- or videotapes, changing the format of a selection, simplifying a text, or in effect shortening a text by telling students that they need to read only certain parts of it. Modifying the text is called for in situations in which reading selections present too much of a challenge because of their length or their difficulty. Assuming that students can and will read the original selection, will they get as much out of reading a modified version of it or from listening to it on tape? Almost certainly not! But if they cannot or will not read all of the original selection, hearing it or successfully reading part of it is certainly preferable to failing to read at all.

Postreading Activities

Postreading activities serve a variety of purposes. They provide opportunities for students to synthesize and organize information gleaned from the text so that they can understand and recall important points. They provide opportunities for students to evaluate an author's message, his or her stance in presenting the message, and the quality of the text itself. They provide opportunities for you and your students to evaluate their understanding of the text. They also provide opportunities for students to respond to a text in a variety of ways—to reflect on the meaning of the text, to compare different texts and ideas, to imagine themselves as one of the characters in the text, to synthesize information from different sources, to engage in a variety of creative activities, and to apply what they have learned in the classroom and in the world beyond the classroom. Not surprisingly, given their many functions, postreading activities are also widely recommended (see, for example, Aebersold & Field, 1997; Alverman, 2000; Bean et al., 1999; Ciborowski, 1992; Fountas & Pinnell, 1996; Gambrell & Almasi, 1996; Schoenbach et al., 1999; Wood et al., 1992; Yopp & Yopp, 1992), and in most classrooms they are very frequently used. In listing the possible postreading activities for SREs, we have once again attempted to create a relatively small set of categories that suggest a large number of useful activities. We include eight types of postreading activities.

Questioning, either orally or in writting, is a frequently used and frequently warranted activity. Questioning activities give you an opportunity to encourage and promote higher order thinking—to nudge students to interpret, analyze, and evaluate what they read. Questions can also elicit creative and personal responses: "How did you feel when . . . ?" "What do you think the main character would have done if . . .?" Sometimes, of course, it is appropriate for students to read something and not be faced with some sort of accountability afterwards. However, in many cases, neither you nor your students will be sure that they gained what they needed to gain from the reading unless they answer some questions. Of course, teachers are not the only ones who should be asking questions after reading. Students can ask questions of each other, they can ask you questions, and they can ask questions they plan to answer through further reading or by searching the Internet.

Some sort of **Discussion**—whether it is done in pairs, in small groups, or with the entire class—is also very frequent and often very appropriate. If there is a chance that some students did not understand as much of a selection as they need to—and there is often this chance—then discussion is definitely warranted. Equally important, discussion gives students a chance to offer their personal interpretations of and responses to a text and to hear those of others. Discussion is also a vehicle for assessing whether reading goals have been achieved—to evaluate what went right with the reading experience, what went wrong, and what might be done differently in the future.

Writing is a postreading task that probably ought to be used more frequently than it is. In recent years, there has been a good deal of well-warranted emphasis on the fact that reading and writing are complementary activities and ought to be dealt with together. We certainly agree. However, we want to stress that writing is often a challenging activity, and it is important to be sure that students are adequately prepared for writing. Among other things, this means that if students are expected to write about a selection, you usually need to be sure that they have comprehended the selection well. We say *usually* because sometimes students can write to discover what they have comprehended in a selection or to deepen their understanding of it.

Drama offers a range of opportunities for students to get actively involved in responding to what they have read. By drama we mean any sort of production involving action and movement. Given this definition, short plays, skits, pantomimes, and Readers Theatre are among the many possibilities.

Artistic, Graphic, and Nonverbal Activities constitute additional possibilities for postreading endeavors. In this broad category we include visual art, graphics, music, dance, and media productions such as videos, slide shows, and audiotapes, as well as constructive activities that you might not typically think of as artistic. Probably the most frequent activities in this category involve creating graphics of some sort: maps, charts, trees, diagrams, schematics, and the like. Other possibilities include constructing models or bringing in artifacts that are responses to the selection read. Artistic and nonverbal activities may be particularly useful because they are fun, they are often a little different from typical school tasks, and they provide opportunities for students to express themselves in a variety of ways, thus creating situations in which students of varying talents and abilities can excel. This is not to say that such activities are frills, something to be done just to provide variety. In many situations and for many students, artistic and nonverbal activities offer the greatest potential for learning information and for responding to what has been read.

Application and Outreach Activities. Here we include both concrete and direct applications (e.g., cooking something after reading a recipe) as well as less direct ones (e.g., attempting to change some aspect of student government after reading something about state government that suggests the possibility). Here we also include activities that extend beyond the campus, such as planning a drive to collect used coats and sweaters after reading a news article on people in need of winter clothing, or taking a field trip to a local art museum after reading about one of the artists represented there. Obviously, there is a great range of application and outreach options.

Building Connections. Although there is some overlap between this postreading activity and the previous one, we have chosen to list this as its own category because building connections is so important. Only by helping students to build connections between the ideas they encounter in reading and the other parts of their lives can we ensure that they come to really value reading, that they read enough to become truly proficient readers, that they see the relevance of reading, and that they remember and apply important learnings from their reading. Several sorts of connections are important. First, we want students to connect the wealth of out-of-school experiences they bring to school with their reading—for example, to relate the pride they felt in learning to ride a two wheeler with the pride a story character feels when she meets a difficult challenge. Second, we want students to connect what they learn in one subject with what they learn in others—for example, to realize that their understanding of the motives of Johnny in Esther Forbes's *Johnny Tremain* can help them to appreciate the feelings of children they read about as they study the American Revolution. Third, we want them to realize that concepts they learn from reading can apply well beyond the classroom—for example, that just as a fictional character's perseverance brought her success, so too might their perseverance at real-life tasks they face bring them success.

The final postreading activity we consider is **Reteaching.** When it becomes apparent that students have not achieved their reading goals or the level of understanding you deem necessary, reteaching is often in order, and the best time for reteaching is usually as soon as possible after students first encounter the material. In some cases, reteaching may consist simply of asking students to reread parts of a selection. In other cases, you may want to present a minilesson on some part of the text that has caused students' problems. In yet other cases, students who have understood a particular aspect of the text may assist other students in achieving similar understanding.

Planning SREs

We have described a fairly lengthy list of possible activities, far too many to be used with any single selection. Again, this is simply a list of options. From this set of possibilities, you choose only those that are appropriate for your particular students reading a particular text for a particular purpose. Suppose, for example, you are working with a class of sixth graders on social studies. The class is reading the first chapter of Michael L. Cooper's *Indian School,* and their goal is to learn the most important information presented in this chapter. In this situation, you might decide to provide prereading instruction that includes a motivational activity, the preteaching of some difficult vocabulary words such as *interpreter* and *proposition,* and a questioning activity in which students pose who, what, when, where, how, and why, questions that they expect to be answered in the chapter. Next, for the during-reading portion of the lesson, you might decide to read part of the chapter orally and then have students read the rest silently, looking for answers to their questions. Finally, after students have finished the chapter, you might decide to have them break into discussion groups of three or four and answer the questions they posed during prereading. After this, the groups might come together as a class and share their answers. Here is a list of the activities for this SRE for sixth graders reading the first chapter of *Indian School.*

Prereading:	Motivating
	Preteaching vocabulary
	Questioning
During-Reading:	Reading to students
	Silent reading
Postreading:	Small-group discussion
	Answering questions
	Large-group discussion

There are two characteristics of this example that are particularly worth emphasizing at this point. For one thing, this combination of prereading, during-reading, and postreading activities is only one of a number of combinations you could have selected. For another, you selected the activities you did based on your assessment of the students, the selection they were reading, and their purpose in reading the selection.

We can again highlight the fact that SREs vary considerably by giving another example. Suppose the same sixth graders are reading a simple and straightforward narrative, something like Andrew Clements's award-winning *Frindle.* Suppose also that their primary purpose in reading the story is simply to enjoy this thought-provoking yet fast-paced, humorous tale. In this case, prereading instruction might consist of only a brief motivational activity, the during-reading portion might consist entirely of students reading the novel silently, and the postreading portion might consist of their voluntarily discussing the parts of the story they found most humorous or interesting. Here is the list of activities for this SRE for *Frindle.*

Prereading:	Motivating
During-Reading:	Silent reading
Postreading:	Optional small-group discussion

It is, as you can see, much shorter than the one for *Indian School.* It is short because neither your students, the story itself, nor the purpose for reading the story requires a longer and more supportive SRE.

A Sample Planning Experience

Now shift gears a bit and consider the planning you might do and another SRE you might construct, in this case for a chapter on waves in a seventh-grade science text. Your students are seventh graders of average to high ability, and the class includes two English language learners for whom reading English is still a challenge. After reading the chapter, you decide the important reading purposes are for students to understand the concept of waves, to note some of the properties of waves, to describe several different types of waves, and to come away with the understanding that waves are important physical phenomena, a scientific topic they will learn more about in later grades.

Thinking again about your class, you decide that they can handle the chapter with your help. You identify the concepts you want to stress, and you note that the chapter contains some material that students do not need to deal with at the present time. You also note that the chapter is 10 pages and about 3,000 words long, and you estimate that it will take students 20–30 minutes to read through it once.

All of this thinking—these considerations about your students, the chapter, and the reading purposes—are in your mind as you plan the SRE. (As a matter of fact, in actually planning an SRE, you would probably consider more factors than we have listed in this brief example.) With those considerations firmly in mind, you come up with pre-, during-, and postreading activities. Table 2-2 shows an outline of what the SRE might look like.

For prereading, you decide to include a motivational activity that will relate the topic of waves to students' lives and preteach the concept. You include motivation because you believe that some sort of motivation is almost always a good idea and because students will not automatically be interested in waves. You have students demonstrate a wave by arranging themselves in a line across the front of the room and then successively standing up and sitting down—much as fans do at a football game. After this demonstration (students will probably have to practice the wave several times before it becomes rhythmic and looks very much like a wave), you point out the various attributes of their wave and of waves generally. For example, their wave and all waves are rhythmic and have amplitude and frequency. You might go on to explain these related concepts and then have students again demonstrate several different wave forms, changing the amplitude by raising both hands rather than standing up, and changing the duration by standing up and sitting down or raising and lowering their hands at different rates. Finally, you might draw several wave forms on the board to illustrate the rhythmic patterns and the different amplitudes and durations that waves can have.

Motivating students might also include stressing that waves are an important science topic, reminding them that they are already familiar with some

Table 2-2. SRE for "Waves" Chapter

Planning		
Students	Selection	Purpose
Fifth graders of average to high ability; the class includes two English language learners.	Chapter titled "Waves" in fifth-grade science text.	To understand and recall concept of waves, some wave properties, and types of waves.

Implementation		
Prereading Activities	During-Reading Activities	Postreading Activities
Motivating: Act out the motion of a wave.	**Reading Aloud**: Read first section aloud to students.	**Discussion**: Small groups discuss chapter and add information to outline.
Preteaching a Concept: Teach the concepts of amplitude and frequency.	**Manipulating Medium**: Tape chapter and make tape available to ESL students.	**Reteaching**: Reteach and extend central concepts as necessary.
Building Text-Specific Knowledge: Use the headings in the chapter to preview and predict its contents.	**Silent Reading**: Students read chapter on their own.	**Writing**: Have students write an imaginative tale in which a wave goes berserk.

sorts of waves (such as those in oceans or lakes) and asking them what other sorts of waves play a part in their daily lives (microwaves and TV waves are likely responses).

Next, because the chapter contains several difficult concepts—more, actually, than you would like—you decide to preteach two of the most important ones. These are the concepts of amplitude and frequency as they apply to waves. You begin by defining each of the concepts. The amplitude of a wave is the height of the wave from its origin to its crest. The frequency of a wave is the number of cycles of the wave that pass through a given point in a certain amount of time. You then remind students that their own wave had amplitude and frequency; its amplitude was perhaps a foot or two, and its frequency might have been 10 cycles a minute. After this, you might show a video that illustrates the two concepts. Finally, you could ask students if they know of other words or phrases that express concepts similar to amplitude and frequency—*height, size,* and *how often something happens* are possible responses. Of course, these brief activities have not fully taught the concepts, but students will be better prepared to understand them when they come up in the chapter.

As the next activity, in order to prepare students to deal with both the content and the organization of the chapter, you write the headings and subheadings from the chapter on the board, being sure to preserve the features of the text used to show subordination—for example, the major topics might be in all capital letters and flush left, while the subordinate topics might have just the first letter of each word capitalized and be indented. Then you ask students to identify the major and subordinate topics by noting their placement and the type of letters used. Finally, you ask students to brainstorm on what they can learn just from the headings. For example, the first heading, "HOW DO WAVES TRANSFER ENERGY?" clearly indicates that one thing waves do is transfer energy. You write this on the board and continue through the rest of the outline with the class, jotting down similar information that students glean from the outline.

For during-reading activities, you decide to make an audiotape of the chapter for your English language learners. Your plan also includes reading the first section of the chapter aloud to all students to ease them into the chapter. After the first section, the English language learners will listen to the tape, and the rest of the class will finish the chapter by reading silently to themselves. Before students begin their listening or reading, however, you remind them that they shouldn't try to learn everything in the chapter but should focus their attention on the topics discussed in the outline: the properties of waves and the different sorts of waves described.

In deciding on postreading activities, you would probably take into account the fact that the chapter is challenging and that you definitely want students to remember the major concepts dealt with in the chapter. You might, therefore, hand out a discussion guide that parallels the chapter outline you wrote on the board and give students 20 minutes to discuss these concepts in small groups. After that, the class could come back together, and each group could report one piece of information they discovered about waves. Also, it is likely that some of your students will need extra work with concepts such as amplitude and frequency, and you might offer to join a group of students if there are any who would like to further consider these ideas. Finally, because many of your students have a creative bent and because you believe that waves and related concepts might prompt interesting fantasy tales, you suggest that students work alone or in small groups to create stories, sketches, or poems in which a wave goes berserk. Then, once students have completed their creations, they can either present them orally or post them around the room.

All in all, your students might spend 3 or 4 days with this SRE. Your purpose in designing these activities—and the purpose in planning and carrying out any SRE—is a straightforward one: You want to do everything possible to ensure that students have a successful reading experience. As we suggested earlier, we believe that a successful reading experience is one in which students understand the selection, learn from it, and enjoy it. Moreover, our goal includes students realizing that they have been successful, recognizing that they have dealt competently with the selection because that is exactly what they have done. If students are to become successful lifelong readers—people who voluntarily choose to read in order to better understand themselves and their world, gain information, and experience the joy of reading—then the vast majority of their reading experiences must be successful ones.

What an SRE Is Not

In order to conclude our explanation of an SRE, we must clearly explain what an SRE is *not,* and what goals SREs are not designed to achieve.

We will begin with the obvious. The SRE framework is not a plan for a comprehensive reading program. It does not deal at all with fostering emergent literacy—building phonemic awareness, teaching children to track print, teaching the alphabet, and the like—or with word identification skills— phonics, syllabication, blending, word parts, use of context, and similar skills. It does not provide a systematic program of vocabulary instruction. It does not take the place of literature circles or of recreational reading, independent reading, or free reading programs. Nor does it provide instruction in reading comprehension strategies, a topic that Michael Pressley has extensively investigated and written about (2000, 2002). This does not mean that providing comprehensive and balanced reading programs is not vitally important. One of us (Graves, 1998) has directly addressed the importance of providing balanced reading instruction, and both of us are co-authors of an elementary reading-methods text, *Teaching Reading in the 21st Century,* that lays out a comprehensive and balanced reading program (Graves, Juel, & Graves, 2001).

The purpose of this book, however, is not to describe a comprehensive reading program. Our purpose here is to describe SREs and how to use them. Although SREs are only one part of a reading program, they are an extremely important part. They assist students in understanding, enjoying, and learning from the selections they read. These successful experiences will produce more avid readers and better readers. Success breeds success! The SRE is our attempt to provide you with an instructional framework that will lead all students to the success they need and deserve.

Concluding Comments

In this chapter, we have attempted to explain the SRE. In doing so, we have discussed the purpose of SREs, described the SRE framework, listed the components of SREs and briefly described each of them, given examples of SRE activities and how we would go about planning them, and directly explained what SREs are not designed to do. The next chapter examines the thinking that prompted us to develop the SRE as we have.

References

Aebersold, J. A., & Field, M. L. (1997). *From reader to reading teacher: Issues and strategies for second language classrooms.* Cambridge, UK: Cambridge University Press. This very useful text on teaching reading to second-language learners deals largely with a prereading, during-reading, and postreading framework.

Alverman, D. E. (2000). Classroom talk about texts: Is it dear, cheap, or a bargain at any price? In B. M. Taylor, M. F. Graves, & P. van den Broek (Eds.), *Reading for meaning: Fostering comprehension in the middle grades* (pp. 136–151). New York: Teachers College Press. Highlights the strengths and some possible weaknesses of small group discussion.

Bean, T. W., Valerio, P. C., & Stevens, L. (1999). Content area literacy instruction. In L. B. Gambrell, L. M. Morrow, S. Newman, & M. Pressley (Eds.), *Best practices in literacy instruction* (pp. 175–192). New York: Guilford Press. Advocates a before-reading, during-reading, and after-reading framework to provide students with assistance as they read in various content areas.

Beck, I. L., & McKeown, M. G. (2001). Text talk: Capturing the benefits of read-aloud experiences for young children. *The Reading Teacher, 55,* 10–20. Suggests a read-aloud procedure that scaffolds children's efforts and keeps the focus on important text ideas.

Beck, I. L., McKeown, M. G., Hamilton, R., & Kucan, L. (1997). *Questioning the author: An approach for enhancing student engagement with text.* Newark, DE: International Reading Association. Detailed description of a during-reading discussion technique designed to yield deep understanding of a text.

Betts, E. (1946). *Foundations of reading.* New York: American Books. General methods text containing the original presentation of the "Directed Reading Activity," a plan that once served as the lesson framework for basal readers.

Ciborowski, J. (1992). *Textbooks and the students who can't read them: A guide to teaching content.* Cambridge, MA: Brookline Books. Describes an approach to teaching less able readers that employs a before-reading, during-reading, and after-reading format.

Cunningham, P. A., Hall, D. P., & Defee, M. (1998). Nonability-grouped multilevel instruction: Eight years later. *Reading Teacher, 51,* 652–664. An update on Cunningham's "Four Blocks" approach, which includes prereading activities as part of guided reading.

Fountas, I. C., & Pinnell, G. S. (1996). *Guided reading: Good first teaching for all students*. Portsmouth, NH: Heinemann. Describes a lesson framework for small group instruction of primary-grade readers. Like the SRE, guided reading is one part of a reading program.

Gambrell, L. B., & Almasi, J. E. (1996). *Lively discussions! Fostering engaged reading*. Newark, DE: International Reading Association. This collection contains 18 chapters focusing on discussion.

Graves, M. F. (1998, October/November). Beyond balance. *Reading Today*, p. 16. This brief essay describes what balance is and why it is important.

Graves, M. F., Juel, C., & Graves, B. B. (2001). *Teaching reading in the 21st century* (2nd ed.). Boston: Allyn & Bacon. In this elementary reading methods text, we describe the components of a comprehensive and balanced reading program in detail.

McKeown, M. G., & Beck, I. L. (In press). Taking advantage of read alouds to help children make sense of decontextualized language. In A. van Kleeck, S. A. Stahl, & E. B. Bauer (Eds.), *Storybook reading*. Mahwah, NJ: Erlbaum. A description of the "Text Talk" approach to scaffolding and focusing children's efforts during read-alouds.

Pressley, M. (2000). What should reading comprehension instruction be the instruction of? In M. Kamil, P. Mosenthal, P. D. Pearson, & R. Barr (Eds.), *Handbook of reading research* (vol. 3, pp. 545–561). Mahwah, NJ: Erlbaum. Consideration of a variety of component parts that constitute a comprehensive instructional program aimed at developing reading comprehension.

Pressley, M. (2002). *Reading instruction that works: The case for balanced teaching* (2nd ed.). New York: Guilford Press. Chapter 7 presents an excellent history of research on teaching reading comprehension strategies.

RAND Reading Study Group. (2002). *Reading for understanding: Toward an R&D program in reading comprehension*. Santa Monica, CA: Rand Education. Also available on-line at http://www.rand.org/multi/achievementforall/reading/. A well done and widely respected summary of what we know about reading comprehension and a plan for further research.

Readence, J. E., Moore, D. W., & Rickelman, R. J. (2000). *Prereading activities for content area reading and learning* (3rd ed.). Newark, DE: International Reading Association. This useful resource presents a variety of activities for preparing students to read as well as strategies students can use independently as they approach content area reading selections.

Richardson, J. S. (2000). *Read it aloud: Using literature in the secondary content classroom.* Newark, DE: International Reading Association. Suggests the value of reading literature aloud in various content areas, with the major goal of spreading the joy of reading.

Schoenbach, R., Greenleaf, C., Cziko, C., & Hurwitz, L. (1999). *Reading for understanding: A guide to improving reading in middle and high school classes.* San Francisco: Jossey-Bass. Here two teachers and two staff developers describe their approach to a reading course designed for urban middle school and high school students.

Stauffer, R. G. (1969). *Directing reading maturity as a cognitive process.* New York: Harper & Row. Contains the original presentation of the "Directed Reading-Thinking Activity." Still a valuable resource.

Tierney, R. J., & Readence, J. E. (2000). *Reading strategies and practices: A compendium* (5th ed.). Boston: Allyn & Bacon. This very valuable and extensive compendium—more than 500 pages in length—describes and evaluates at least 60 reading strategies and practices.

Wood, K. D., Lapp, D., & Flood, J. (1992). *Guiding readers through text: A review of study guides.* Newark, DE: International Reading Association. A detailed, lucid, and very useful description of 17 types of study guides that teachers can use to focus students' attention and guide them toward learning and understanding as they are reading.

Yopp, R. H., & Yopp, H. K. (1992). *Literature-based reading activities.* Boston: Allyn & Bacon. Describes pre-, during-, and postreading activities for literary selections.

Children's Literature

Clements, A. (1998). *Frindle.* New York: Aladdin. 104 pages

Cooper, M. L. (1999). *Indian school: Teaching the white man's way.* New York: Clerion Books. 103 pages.

Graves, B. (2002). *Taking care of trouble.* New York: Dutton. 70 pages.

Hackett, J. K., & Moyer, R. H. (1991). "Waves." In *Science in your world,* Level 6. New York: Macmillan/McGraw-Hill. 10 pages.

Jiménez, F. (1999). *The circuit.* Boston: Houghton. 144 pages.

Krull, K. (1994). *Lives of the presidents: Fame, shame (and what the neighbors thought).* San Diego: Harcourt. 96 pages.

Levy, E. (1997). *My life as a fifth-grade comedian.* New York: Harper-Collins. 192 pages.

Park, L. S. (2001). *A single shard.* New York: Clarion. 152 pages.

Sorenson, M. (2002). *Funny Man.* Logan, IA: Perfection Learning. 95 pages.

Chapter

3

The Thinking Behind
Scaffolded Reading

The past 30 years has been an enormously exciting and productive time in the field of reading. Theoreticians, teachers, and researchers representing a variety of perspectives have helped us to better understand the reading process, readers, reading instruction, and the contexts that surround children learning to read. Contributions to this understanding have come from cognitive psychologists, linguists, constructivist scholars, whole-language theorists, and a host of others. These contributions are rich and varied and include: understanding the mental processes underlying skilled reading and learning to read; appreciating the active and constructive nature of reading and learning; understanding the importance of using authentic texts and tasks in the classroom; and understanding the power of quality literature, to name just a few. We could list many more contributions of the past three decades, but our main point is that we now have rich and deep knowledge about the reading process and the teaching of reading (Bransford, Brown, & Cocking, 2000; Kamil, Mosenthal, Pearson, & Barr, 2000; National Reading Panel, 2000; RAND Reading Study Group, 2002; Snow, Burns, & Griffin, 1998).

In this chapter, we discuss the ideas that most influenced us as we developed the scaffolded reading approach. Some of these ideas, as the above paragraph suggests, are new; others have existed for some time. Some of the ideas are rather formal and properly deserve the term *theories*; others are much less formal and are better termed *notions*. Some are complex and require serious study; others are simple and easily grasped. Some are supported by a great deal of research; others have more modest research support. All in all, it is a diverse set of ideas, linked by a single unifying theme: Each of these ideas makes a direct and practical statement about what can and should be done to assist students in reading and enjoying what they read.

We have already introduced some of these ideas—the concept of scaffolding and the related concepts of the zone of proximal development and the gradual release of responsibility model. The concept of scaffolding is at the center of the plan we are presenting, and here we want to amplify what we said earlier. Later in the chapter, we'll say more about the zone of proximal development and the gradual release of responsibility model.

In chapter 1, we defined a scaffold as a temporary supportive structure that enables a child to successfully complete a task that he or she could not complete without the aid of the scaffold. Here we want to modify that definition slightly by adding that in addition to helping children complete tasks they could not otherwise complete, scaffolding can aid students by helping them to better complete a task, to complete a task with less stress or in less time, or to learn more fully than they would have otherwise.

Training wheels for young children's bicycles are an excellent example of a scaffold used to assist youngsters in mastering a challenging physical task. Training wheels are temporary, they are supportive, they can be adjusted up or down to provide more or less support, and they allow a child to learn to ride a bicycle with fewer falls, with less stress, and in a shorter amount of time than they would be able to do without the scaffold. This is very similar to the function that the Scaffolded Reading Experience (SRE) serves in supporting students' reading. An SRE maximizes the chances that students will understand the reading, learn from it, experience it as nonthreatening, and enjoy both what they read and the experience of reading it.

In the remainder of this chapter, we have grouped the other ideas underlying the scaffolded reading approach under four headings: Student Engagement, Cognitive and Constructivist Learning Concepts, Instructional Concepts, and Pedagogical Orientations. We have grouped our ideas under these four headings to avoid giving you one long list of topics. We stress, however, that the topics included in one of these areas could in some cases have been placed in another, and that the collection of topics within a single area is sometimes quite diverse. Grouping the topics is in fact a form of scaffolding that should aid you in understanding and remembering them.

Student Engagement

The theme of this section is that students' reading abilities will grow in direct proportion to the extent to which they see reading as an activity that they succeed at, that is under their control, that they can improve at, and that is worthwhile and enjoyable. In elaborating on this theme, we consider three topics: the critical importance of success, attribution theory and learned helplessness, and the significance of creating a literate environment that will nurture children's reading and writing development.

Success

The dominant thought motivating not just this section of the hcapter but this entire book is the overwhelming importance of success. As the professional judgments of both teachers and researchers has repeatedly verified (Brophy, 1986; Guthrie & Alvermann, 1999; Guthrie & Wigfield, 2000; Pressley, 2002), if students are going to learn to read effectively, they need to succeed at the vast majority of reading tasks they undertake. Moreover, if students are going to become not only proficient readers but also avid readers—children and later adults who voluntarily seek out reading as a road to information, enjoyment, and personal fulfillment—then successful reading experiences are even more important.

There are a variety of ways in which reading experiences can be successful. Several of them are particularly important. First, and most important, a successful reading experience is one in which the reader understands what he or she has read. Of course, understanding may take more than one reading, it may require your assistance or that of other students, and it will sometimes require the reader to actively manipulate the ideas in the text: summarize them, discuss them with classmates, or compare them to other ideas. Second, a successful reading experience is one that the reader finds enjoyable, entertaining, informative, or thought provoking. Certainly, not every reading experience will yield all of these benefits, but every experience should yield at least one of them. Finally, a successful reading experience is one that prepares the student to complete whatever task follows the reading.

To a great extent, children's success in reading is directly under your control. You can select and allow your students to select materials that they can read. To the extent that the material they read presents challenges, you can provide support before, during, and after they read that will enable them to meet those challenges. You can also select and help them to select postreading activities at which they can succeed.

Doing this—choosing selections, arranging activities, and selecting doable postreading tasks so that students are successful in their reading—is the essence of the scaffolded reading approach, of this entire book. Here we give three brief examples of ways in which you can help to ensure student success. Suppose you have a group of students who read at about 100 words a minute and have a 15-minute period in which they will be reading. Giving students a selection slightly shorter than 1,500 words will ensure that they at least have time to complete it, while giving them a selection much longer than 1,500 words is very likely to leave them frustrated and all but ensure failure.

As another example, suppose you have a group of fourth-grade students who will be reading a science chapter on the ecology of freshwater lakes but who have virtually no concept of ecology, who have never even thought about the relationships among organisms and their environment. Preteaching the concept of ecology—quite possibly in a fairly extensive lesson—will greatly increase the possibilities that students will understand the chapter and not simply flounder in a sea of new ideas. Or suppose that you have a group of ninth-grade students for whom the questions at the end of a social studies chapter on Reconstruction are likely to present too great a challenge. In such a case, you might cue students to the places where the questions are answered in the text, or you might work through the first few questions as a group to get students off to a good start. The point, once again, is to do everything possible to ensure success.

In concluding this discussion of success, we want to point out an extremely important qualification. Saying that students should succeed at the reading tasks you ask them to complete and that you should do everything possible to ensure success does not mean spoon-feeding them. Unless readers undertake some challenging tasks, unless they are willing to take some risks and make some attempts they are not certain of and get feedback on their efforts, there is little room for learning to take place. Moreover, as Mihaly Csikszentmihalyi (1990) has discovered in more than three decades of research, facing significant challenges and meeting them is one of the most fulfilling and rewarding experiences a person can have. In order to develop as readers, children need to be given some challenges. However, it is vitally important for teachers to arrange and scaffold reading activities so that students can meet these challenges.

Attribution Theory and Learned Helplessness

Attribution theory deals with students' perceptions of the causes of their successes and failures in learning. As Michael Pressley (2002) explains, in deciding why they succeed or fail in reading tasks, students can attribute their performance to ability, effort, luck, the difficulty of the reading task, or a variety of other causes. All too often, children who have repeatedly failed in reading attribute their failure to factors that are beyond their control: an unchangeable factor, such as their innate ability, or a factor that they can do nothing about, such as luck. Once this happens, children are likely to lose their motivation to learn to read in general, and they are likely to doubt their capacity to success-fully read and comprehend specific selections. From their perspective, there is no reason to try because there is nothing they can do about it. Moreover, as long as they do not try, they can't fail; you can't lose a race if you don't enter it.

As Peter Johnston and Peter Winograd (1985) have pointed out, one long-term outcome of children repeatedly attributing reading failure to forces be-yond their control is falling into a "passive failure" syndrome. Children who exhibit passive failure in reading are apt to be nervous, irritable, withdrawn, and discouraged when they are faced with a reading task. They are unlikely to be actively engaged in reading, to have goals and plans when they read, to monitor themselves when they are reading to see if the reading makes sense, or to check themselves after reading and see if they have accomplished their reading goal. Finally, even when they are successful—and this is not likely to be very often—children who are passive failures are likely to attribute their success to luck, to their teacher's skill, or to some other factor over which they have no control.

Obviously, we need to break this cycle of negative attributions and learned helplessness. Here we suggest three approaches. The first, and almost cer-tainly the most powerful, is something we just stressed: Make reading a suc-cessful experience; make it so frequently successful for students that they will be compelled to realize that it is themselves and not some outside force that is responsible for their success. Second, tell students that their efforts make a dif-ference, and when they are successful in a reading task, talk to them about the activities they engaged in to make them successful. If, for example, after sec-ond graders read an informational piece about dinosaurs, students success-fully answer several questions about dinosaurs that they generated before reading the selection, discuss how generating those questions beforehand helped them to focus their attention so they could find the answers to the questions as they read. Third, try to avoid competitive situations in which students compare how well they read a selection to how well others read it; instead, focus students' attention on what they personally gained from the se-lection. Some coaches are particularly adept at creating such a focus, teaching young athletes to continually strive for their "personal best," a goal that is al-ways in sight and that can realistically be achieved. Finally, provide a number of reading activities in which the goal is to enjoy reading, have fun, and expe-rience something interesting and exciting rather than offering only reading activities that are followed by answering questions or some other sort of ex-ternal accountability.

A Literate Environment

The phrase *literate environment* has been used to describe a classroom, school, and home environment in which literacy will be fostered and nurtured (Goodman, 1986; Graves, Juel, & Graves, 2001). Probably the most important component of a literate environment is the modeling done by people children respect and love. In the best possible literate environment, children's teachers, principals, parents, brothers and sisters, and friends read a lot and openly display the pleasure that reading gives them, the fact that reading opens up a world of information to them, the value they place on reading, and the satisfaction they gain from reading. To be most effective, this modeling should occur not just once but repeatedly—all the time, really. Also, this modeling should include repeated demonstrations on your part—reading along with students during a sustained silent reading period, looking up an answer to a question children have in a book, and sharing a favorite poem with your class—as well as direct testimonials—"Wow! What a story." "I never knew what fun river rafting could be till I read this article; I sure wish I'd read it sooner." "Sometimes I think the library is just about my favorite place."

Another important component of a literate environment is the physical setting in which children read; for teachers, this generally means the classroom. In the best possible literate environment, the classroom is filled with books that are readily accessible for students to read in school or to take home. The walls are covered with colorful posters that advertise books and the treasures they offer. And there are several comfortable and inviting places to read: a carpeted corner of the room where children can sit on the floor and read without interruption, beanbags or other comfortable chairs that entice young readers to immerse themselves in a book, places where students can gather in groups to read to each other or discuss their reading, and tables for students to use when reading prompts them to write.

Still another component of a literate environment is the content of the books, magazines, and other reading materials that are available to students. These materials should reflect the diversity of your classroom—the range of abilities, interests, and cultural, linguistic, and social backgrounds of your students—as well as the diversity of the larger society outside the classroom. What students read must connect with their individual experiences if reading is to have meaning for them; what students read must connect them to the larger society if both students and the larger society are to prosper.

A final and equally important component of a literate environment is the atmosphere in which children read; for teachers, this again means the classroom. In the best possible literate environment, everything that happens in the classroom sends the message that reading—learning from what you read, having personal responses to what you read, talking about what you read, and writing about what you read—is fantastic! In such a classroom, children are given plenty of time to read; they are given ample opportunities to share the information they learn and their responses to what they have read with each other; they are taught to listen to and respect the ideas of others; and they learn that others will listen to and respect their ideas. A literate atmosphere is a thoughtful atmosphere in which values and ideas are respected—a book's values and ideas, one's own values and ideas, and other people's values and ideas.

In concluding this section on student engagement, we emphasize that the concepts described here—success, attribution theory and learned helplessness, and literate environment—are interrelated. Frequent success is crucial, and one of the most fulfilling sorts of success is achieving at challenging tasks. One reason that success is crucial is that it precludes learned helplessness; successful students are simply not faced with the repeated failures that lead them to attribute failure to factors beyond their control. Finally, a literate environment nurtures success and provides students with a secure place that enables them to deal positively with the small failures they will inevitably encounter from time to time.

Cognitive-Constructivist Learning Concepts

From about 1930 to about 1970, the dominant psychological orientation in the United States was behaviorism. Behaviorist psychologists viewed people as rather passive respondents to their environment and gave little attention to the mind and its role in learning. Beginning in the 1960s, behaviorism began to be replaced by the cognitive orientation, and up until about 1990 cognitive psychology reigned supreme as the dominant psychological orientation in this country. Cognitive psychologists view the mind as central to learning and the study of learners' thought processes as a central focus of their work. They also view learners as active participants who act on rather than simply respond to their external environment as they learn. More recently, certainly by the 1980s, constructivism became a prominent force in psychology, particularly educational psychology, and as we begin the 21st century many educators see themselves as constructivists. Five concepts have emerged from what might be called the cognitive-constructivist orientation: schema theory, the interactive model of reading, automaticity, constructivism, and reader response theory. These are particularly important to understanding the reading process, reading instruction, and the scaffolded reading approach.

Schema Theory

Schema theory is concerned with knowledge, particularly with the way knowledge is represented in our minds and its importance to learning. As described by schema theory, knowledge is packaged in organized structures termed *schemata*. According to David Rumelhart (1980), schemata constitute our knowledge about "objects, situations, events, sequences of events, actions, and sequences of actions" (p. 34). We have schemata for objects such as a house, for situations such as being in a class, for events such as going to a football game, and for sequences of events such as getting up, eating, showering, and going to work. We interpret our experiences—whether they are direct encounters with the world or vicarious experiences gained through reading—by comparing and in most cases matching those experiences to an existing schema. In other words, we make sense of what we read and of our experiences more generally by a tacit process that in essence tells us, "Ah-ha. This is an instance of such and such."

Obviously, both what we learn and the ease or difficulty of the learning are heavily influenced by our schemata. The more we know about something, the easier it will be to deal with that topic and learn more about it. Three sorts of schemata that children possess to varyious degrees are particularly important to consider as we plan reading instruction. One of these is knowledge of the world and its conventions: the makeup of families; daily routines of children going to school and adults going to work; institutions such as churches and the government; holidays such as Memorial Day and Martin Luther King Day; places such as zoos and the beach; and a myriad of other events, places, institutions, objects, and patterns of behavior. Children acquire a good deal of this knowledge simply by growing up in and experiencing the world. This knowledge will generally serve students well in understanding narratives (stories, plays, and novels) because this is the principal sort of knowledge that narratives require. However, if children grew up in a culture different from that depicted in the narrative, then the world and the conventions they understand may be different from those depicted in the narrative, and they will need some help developing appropriate schemata for the narrative. If your classroom includes students from several different cultural backgrounds, you will want to take these backgrounds into account when you consider reading selections and deliberately choose some selections that are particularly appropriate for each of the cultural groups represented in the class.

Another sort of schema that children possess to various degrees concerns the ways in which different types of texts are organized. Most children have relatively well-developed schemata for the organization of narratives because most narratives mirror the temporal order of the world in which they live and have a similar structure. Most narratives have a beginning, a middle, and an end; most have characters that are involved in a plot that includes some sort of complication; and most end with some sort of resolution to the complication. Moreover, most children have had numerous experiences with narratives both in school and at home. Unfortunately, most children do not have well-developed schemata for the structure of expository material, the informational material they encounter in social studies, math, science, health, and the like. This is true because children often have not had much experience with expository material, because it can have a number of different structures, and because a good deal of the expository material children read is not very well structured (Chambliss & Calfee, 1998). Students often benefit from additional help in dealing with expository material.

The third sort of schemata that children possess to varyious degrees are schemata for the content of various subjects: knowledge about science, history, and geography. Most of this knowledge does not come from simply living in the world; most of it comes from formal schooling. Each year, teachers help students to build their knowledge in such areas as history, health, math, and science. Until students develop their schemata for various content areas, they will often need assistance in successfully reading in these areas.

As a final comment on the importance of schemata in reading, we quote a particularly eloquent statement by Marilyn Adams and Bertrand Bruce (1982): "Without prior knowledge, a complex object such as a text is not just difficult to interpret; strictly speaking, it is meaningless" (p. 23).

The Interactive Model of Reading

Schema theory emphasizes the importance of the reader's knowledge in understanding a text. The interactive model of reading, on the other hand, serves to remind us that both the reader and the text play important roles in reading. In arriving at the meaning of a text, Rumelhart (1977) has explained, readers use both their schemata and the letters, words, phrases, sentences, and longer units in a text. Moreover, they use these various sources simultaneously and in an interactive fashion. They do not, for example, look at a sentence with no idea what it will be about, zero in on the first word, first recognize the letter *t* and then the letter *h* and then the letter *e*, decide that the word is *the*, and then move on to do the same thing with the next word. Instead, readers begin a passage with some idea of what it will be about; encounter the letter string *t-h-e* and decide that it is the word *the* partly because it's followed by the noun *cat* and partly because *the* is frequently the first word in a sentence; and determine that the third word in the sentence is *meow* partly because that's what cats do, partly because of its spelling, and partly because it makes sense in the sentence.

The authors of the RAND Reading Study Group report (2002) capture the notion of reading as an interactive process when they define reading comprehension as "the process of simultaneously extracting and constructing meaning through interaction and involvement with written language" (p. 11). Good readers need to rely appropriately on the texts they are reading and on their background knowledge to arrive at meaning, and teachers need to provide them with the sorts of texts and tasks that promote their doing so. For example, giving students a selection that deals with a largely unfamiliar topic and that includes too much difficult vocabulary may force them to give undue attention to the individual words they encounter and to neglect summoning up their prior knowledge to bear on their understanding of the text. Even worse, having students do a lot of oral reading, emphasizing their being 100 percent correct in it, and putting them in a position where they face a penalty for being incorrect will almost certainly force them to give undue attention to the text and focus on words and letters rather than on sentences, paragraphs, and ideas. For example, having less able students read orally in front of their peers without adequate preparation for doing so is likely to lead them to focus almost all their attention on correctly pronouncing individual words and thus giving little attention to meaning.

Conversely, having children only read silently and providing no follow-up to what they read, or having them repeatedly engage in postreading discussions that are only vaguely related to what they read, may encourage them to give too little attention to the text itself. In such situations, some students may largely ignore the words and sentences on the page, frequently guess at the meaning of what they are reading, and make little use of the text in confirming their guesses. For example, giving students a steady diet of individualized reading may not provide them with sufficient opportunities to check their understanding of what they have read with you or with other students, and without such checks they may fall into a habit of guessing a great deal. Again, the goal is an appropriate balance of attention to the text itself and to prior knowledge.

Automaticity

An automatic activity is one that we can perform instantly and with very little attention. As David LaBerge and S. Jay Samuels (1974) point out in their pioneering work on automaticity in reading, the mind's attentional capacity is severely limited; in fact, we can attend to only about one thing at a time. If we are faced with a task in which we are forced to attend to too many things at once, we will fail. For example, a number of people have reached a level of automaticity in driving a stick-shift car. They can automatically push in the clutch, let up on the accelerator, shift gears, let out the clutch, and press on the accelerator; and they can do all this while driving in rush-hour traffic. Beginning drivers cannot do all of this at once; they have not yet automated the various subprocesses, and it would be foolish and dangerous for them to attempt to drive a stick-shift car in rush-hour traffic.

Reading includes a number of subprocesses that need to take place at the same time: recognizing words, assigning meanings to words, constructing the meanings of sentences and larger units, and relating the information gleaned from the text to information we already have. Unless some of these processes are automated, readers simply cannot do all of this at once. Specifically, readers need to perform two processes automatically: recognizing words and assigning meanings to words. For example, if a seventh grader is reading and comes across the word *imperative*, he or she needs to automatically recognize the word and automatically—immediately and without conscious attention—know that it means "absolutely necessary." If the student needs to pause very often and go through some sort of mental process to recognize and assign meanings to words, reading will be difficult and laborious, and the student will not understand much of what he or she is reading. Note that achieving automaticity can be a particular challenge for English language learners.

Fortunately, the road to automaticity is a very straight one. In order to become automatic at an activity, we need to practice the activity frequently in nontaxing situations. To become automatic in reading, students need to do a lot of reading in materials that they find relatively easy, understandable, interesting, and enjoyable. Furthermore, they need to do that reading in situations that are nontaxing; that is, in situations in which they can read for enjoyment and not be faced with difficult questions or requirements based on the reading. In short, you need to encourage students and give them frequent opportunities for independent reading of material that they find interesting and enjoyable (Pressley, 2002).

Constructivism

Constructivism is a philosophical and psychological position that holds that much of the meaning an individual gleans from a text is constructed by the individual. As Dennis Phillips (1995) notes and as his edited volume on constructivism (2000) makes very clear, constructivism is a diverse construct with a number of roots, and exactly how much texts shape and constrain meaning is a matter of debate. However, most constructivists place a good deal of emphasis on the reader's contribution. Many constructivists also hold that the social world in which we live heavily influences our interpretations (Gergen, 1985). These two views—that much of the meaning a reader arrives at when reading a text is actually constructed by the reader and that social interactions heavily influence a reader's constructions—have important implications for reading instruction. Here we discuss three of them.

Constructivism serves as a direct reminder that comprehending a text is an active, constructive process. Constructivists often use the phrase *making meaning* to emphasize the reader's active role in comprehending texts. Students cannot just passively absorb meaning from texts. A truly passive reading would mean that the reader simply turned the pages. Instead, readers must actively engage with the text, consider what they are reading, and link the information they are gleaning from the text with ideas, topics, and events they already know. Moreover, the more difficult a text becomes for students— the more new and challenging information it presents—the more actively engaged readers must be.

In addition to emphasizing the active nature of reading, constructivism adds a new point to the view of the reading process we are describing: The meaning that one constructs from a text is subjective, the result of that particular reader's processing of the text. Just as no two builders will construct exactly the same house from a blueprint, so no two readers will construct exactly the same meaning from a text. A particular reader's processing is influenced by the sum total of her experience as well as by her unique intellectual makeup. Because of this, each reader constructs a somewhat different interpretation of the text—the text as he or she conceptualizes it (Glaserfeld, 1984). One reader's conceptualization of a text will never be precisely that of another.

Finally, the constructivist tenet that gleaning meaning from texts is a social process supports the use of group projects and group discussion. Students need to be given opportunities to work together in preparing to read texts, in considering alternate interpretations of texts, in writing about what they read, in preparing and delivering oral presentations on their reading, and in completing projects prompted by the reading. Group work gives students the chance to talk through and gradually build up their interpretations of a text in a nonthreatening setting. Group work also gives students opportunities to teach each other, to learn from each other, to get actively involved in learning, and to learn that others often have different interpretations of texts. More generally, as many educators are currently noting (e.g., Aronson & Patnoe, 1997; Johnson, Johnson, & Holubec, 1994; Slavin, 1987), group work gives students the opportunity to learn to work together, a skill that is becoming increasingly important in today's interdependent world. At the same time that we endorse group work, we want to note that not all group work is constructivist (Marlowe & Page, 1998) and not all group work is productive (Anderson, Reder, & Simon, 1998). The Johnson's *The New Circles of Learning* (1994) contains a number of sound ideas for orchestrating effective group work.

Reader Response Theory

Reader response theory, the last element of the cognitive-constructivist view of reading, has much in common with constructivism. However, reader response theory has different roots and deals specifically with reading, particularly with reading literature. Although there are many varieties of reader response theory (Beach, 1993), the most influential originated in the work of I. A. Richards (1929) and Louise Rosenblatt (1938) more than half a century ago. The theory was slow to influence classroom instruction, but over the past 30 years it has become a very prominent influence in literature instruction (Beach, 1993; Galda & Guice, 1997; Marshall, 2000). Reader response theory puts a good deal of emphasis on the reader. It stresses that the meaning one gains from a text is the result of a transaction between the reader and the text and that readers will have a range of responses to literary works (Rosenblatt, 1938, 1978). When reading complex literary texts, students will derive a variety of interpretations. Many literary texts simply do not have a single correct interpretation, and readers should be allowed and encouraged to construct a variety of interpretations if they can support them.

At this point, a caution is in order: One very important fact to keep in mind when considering reader response theory is that it applies primarily to certain types of texts and certain purposes for reading. As part of explaining when and where reader response theory applies, Rosenblatt (1978) points out that there are two primary types of reading: *efferent,* or informational, reading and *aesthetic* reading. In efferent reading, the reader's attention is focused primarily on what he or she will take from the reading—what information will be learned. Much of the reading that both students and adults do is done for the sake of learning new information, answering questions, discovering how to complete a procedure, or gleaning knowledge that can be used in solving a particular problem. Much of the reading done in such subjects as health, science, math, and geography is informational reading. These texts, unlike many literary texts, often constrain meaning substantially, do not invite a variety of interpretations, and should yield quite similar interpretations for various readers (Stanovich, 1994).

The other sort of reading that Rosenblatt considers, *aesthetic* reading, is quite different. In aesthetic reading, the primary concern is not with what students remember about a text after they have read it but with what happens to them as they are reading. The primary purpose when reading aesthetically is not to gain information but to experience the text. Although the aesthetic reader, like the reader whose goal is gaining information, must understand the text, he or she must "also pay attention to associations, feelings, attitudes, and ideas" (Rosenblatt, 1978, p. 25) that the text arouses. For the most part, literature is written to provide an aesthetic experience. Most adults read literature for enjoyment; they do not read literature to learn it. Students need to be given opportunities to do the same.

In considering how this distinction between aesthetic and informational reading affects what you do in the classroom, several points should be kept in mind. First, reader response theory does not imply that one sort of reading is superior to the other. Students need to and deserve to become adept at reading as an aesthetic experience as well as to gain information. Second, although much of the reading students do in textbooks and in other material used in content areas is informational reading, and much of the reading they do in the novels and short stories they encounter is aesthetic reading, literary texts often contain useful information and informational texts can often yield aesthetic enjoyment and pleasure. Finally, in order to have an appropriate aesthetic response, some understanding of a text is necessary; if a group of ninth grade students read John Steinbeck's *The Red Pony* and do not understand that Jody feels partly responsible for the pony's death, it would be very difficult for them to have a full response to the piece. Moreover, if students are to learn about literary texts, to learn how they are constructed and how to better understand and more fully enjoy them, they need to sometimes treat literary texts as information to be studied.

In concluding this section on cognitive-constructivist learning concepts, we very briefly review the major educational implications of each concept. Schema theory emphasizes the importance of making sure that students have the background knowledge to read the texts you assign. The interactive model is a reminder that the reader needs to use both the text and his or her background knowledge to understand the selections. The notion of automaticity stresses the importance of students doing a lot of reading that is relatively easy for them—the sort of reading that we as adults do when we read the newspaper, a magazine, or a popular novel—so that they can become automatic. Constructivist theory highlights the fact that reading is an active constructive process, explains that constructing meaning for a text is a subjective process, and underscores the value of group work. Finally, reader response theory stresses the value and appropriateness of personal responses to literature.

Instructional Concepts

In addition to producing some rather general concepts such as those described in the previous section, the past three decades of educational theory and research have produced a number of more specific concepts that have very direct implications for instruction. In this section of the chapter, we consider four of them: active teaching, active learning, the zone of proximal development, and the gradual release of responsibility model. Together, these ideas suggest some very powerful approaches to instruction.

Active Teaching

The term *active teaching* refers to a set of principles and teaching behaviors that teacher effectiveness research has shown to be particularly effective. As noted by Brophy (1986), teachers who engage in active teaching are the instructional leaders of their classrooms; they are fully knowledgeable about the contents and purposes of the instruction they present and about the instructional goals they wish to accomplish. Active teachers do a lot of teaching. Although they use discovery learning for some purposes, they do not generally rely on students discovering what it is they are supposed to learn. Similarly, although they use a variety of materials as part of their teaching, they do not rely on materials to do the teaching. Often, they directly carry the content to be learned to students in short presentations, discussions, and demonstrations. When active teachers use cooperative groups, they make certain that each group is made up of students who can and will work together, that students have the training necessary to work cooperatively, that group members have clearly defined goals, and that each group has definite goals. When active teachers have students work on projects, whether in groups or alone, they make certain that students understand their goals at the onset, monitor students' work, and give them periodic feedback as they work to accomplish those goals.

Active Learning

In discussing constructivism, we noted that comprehending text is an active, constructivist process. Here we want to stress that all learning is the result of an active, constructive process. Just as it is vital that the teacher be actively involved in teaching, it is also vital that the learner be actively involved in learning (Brophy & Good, 2000). The learner must do something with the material he or she is studying if he or she is to truly learn from it. As David Perkins (1992) points out, "Learning is a consequence of thinking." The learner must somehow think about—mentally manipulate—the material to be learned. This mental manipulation can take a variety of forms: The learner might apply the new information, such as a science student does when he or she develops a theory about the flow of electrical energy and designs a circuit to test that theory. The learner might compare or contrast the information to already known information, or might use the new information in a creative endeavor such as writing a story. These are just a few of the myriad possibilities for active learning; there are countless others. But some type of involved mental activity is absolutely necessary. As Ernest Boyer (1988) put it, after observing that not much active learning was talking place in the classrooms he observed:

> If students are to excel, they must be actively engaged in learning. The mastery of subject matter is essential. But unless students are creative, independent thinkers, unless they acquire the tools and motivation to go on learning, the prospects for excellence will be enormously diminished.

The Zone of Proximal Development

The concept of the zone of proximal development is primarily attributed to the Russian psychologist Lev Vygotsky (1978). It places major emphasis on the social nature of learning, stressing the fact that learning is very much a social phenomenon. We learn much from our social interchanges with others. The notion is therefore very consistent with constructivist theory; in fact, it is one of the ideas that stimulated social constructivist thinking. According to Vygotsky, at any particular point in time children have a circumscribed zone of development, a range within which they can learn. At one end of this range are learning tasks that they can complete independently; at the other end are learning tasks that they cannot complete even with assistance. In between these two extremes is the zone most productive for learning, the range of tasks at which children can achieve *if* they are assisted by someone more knowledgeable or more competent.

If left on their own, for example, many third graders might learn very little from a *National Geographic World* article on the formation of thunderstorms. Conversely, with your help—with your spending some time getting them interested in the topic, focusing their attention, preteaching some of the critical concepts such as the effects of rising heat, arranging small groups to discuss and answer questions on certain parts of the article—these same students may be able to learn a good deal from the article. However, with other topics and other texts—for example, with a chapter on gravity in a high school text—no reasonable amount of outside help will foster much learning for these third graders. The topic of gravity and its presentation in the high school text is simply outside the third graders' zone of proximal development.

Outside school, many people can and do serve as more knowledgeable or more competent guides—parents and foster parents, brothers and sisters, relatives, friends, and clergy. As a teacher creating scaffolded reading activities, you may occasionally be able to bring in outside resources to assist students. More often, however, you will arrange reading situations so that you serve as the more knowledgeable person who assists students in successfully reading selections they could not read on their own. In many cases, students will be able to pool their resources and assist each other in dealing with reading selections they could not successfully deal with alone.

The Gradual Release of Responsibility

The gradual release of responsibility involves a progression in which students gradually assume increased responsibility for their learning from the teacher. The model was first suggested by Joseph Campione in 1981, and since that time it has had a very significant effect on reading instruction. David Pearson and Margaret Gallagher (1983) present a particularly informative visual representation of the model, and we have included a slightly modified version in Figure 3-1.

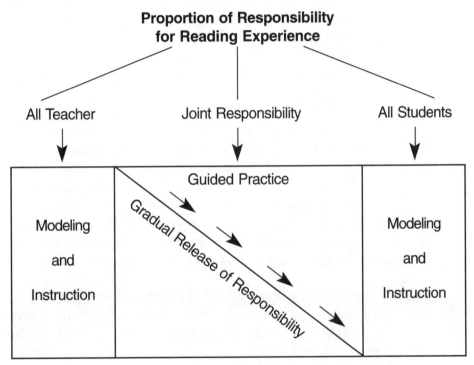

Figure 3-1. Proportion of Repsonsibility for Reading Experience

What the model depicts is a temporal sequence in which students gradually progress from situations in which the teacher takes the majority of the responsibility for their successfully completing a reading task (in other words, does most of the work for them), to situations in which students assume increasing responsibility for reading tasks, and finally to situations in which students take total or nearly total responsibility for reading tasks. In considering the model as it applies to scaffolding reading activities, we emphasize three notions: the meaning and importance of gradual release; the role that the text and student development play in deciding how much responsibility is appropriate for teachers and how much is appropriate for students; and the view that the model depicts a recursive process, one that students will cycle through many times throughout their schooling.

Here, we give several concrete examples to illustrate these notions. Consider first a kindergarten or first-grade teacher in early October seated in a circle with a group of children and displaying a big book, one large enough that a group of children can all see the pictures and the print. The book has a colorful cover, with a picture providing some good clues as to what the book is about, and a similarly revealing title. The teacher reads the title aloud and talks a little about what it and the picture on the cover make him think of. Then he asks the children what the title and picture make them think of and what the book might be about. After listening to students' responses and trying to emphasize and highlight those that are likely to help students understand the story, the teacher begins reading. Even though there are only a handful of words on each page and the story is a very simple one, the teacher stops every two or three pages, asks students what has happened, summarizes the story up to that point if children's responses suggest that a summary is necessary, and perhaps asks students what they think will happen next. After completing the story, the teacher may ask students a few questions to see if they understood it. He may also get some other sorts of responses from them: how they felt about one of the characters, if they have had any experiences similar to those in the story, or what emotions the story aroused in them. He might also share his understanding of the story and some of his personal responses to it. But whatever he does afterwards, he will try to ensure that each student has gotten something from the story and leaves the experience feeling good about it.

At home, many of the children will tell their parents what they did in school, and many will say that they read a story. Of course they really didn't read a story. The teacher selected the book, gathered the children together, previewed the story and built their interest in it, read it to them, checked on their understanding and summarized events when necessary, and engaged them in postreading tasks they could accomplish. Appropriately, the teacher took a huge proportion of the responsibility for their "reading" the story.

Now consider this same teacher and class in January. Over the past three months, the teacher has continued to take much of responsibility for the students' reading. He has built interest, read to students, checked on their understanding, and the like. Over this same period, he has gradually introduced children to longer and more challenging books. At this point, when students go to read something like the very simple picture book they read in October, he will let them handle it largely on their own—perhaps having children self-select books and then pair off to read and share them. With the more challenging books, however, the teacher will continue to scaffold activities.

This same process of gradually releasing responsibility holds for older students—fourth graders, eighth graders, high school students, and even college students. As students progress through school, they assume increased responsibility for their learning. The gradual release of responsibility model emphasizes that over time the goal is to dismantle the scaffolds we have built to ensure children's success. However, children do not repeatedly deal with the same sorts of text over time. Instead, over time students deal with increasingly challenging texts and with a broader range of topics. At any particular point in time, they are likely to be (and should be) dealing with some texts that are more challenging and some that are less challenging. Many fourth graders will be able to take full responsibility for reading an easy novel such as *One Lucky Summer* by Laura McGee Kvasnosky. These same students may need you to assume some of the responsibility for their successfully dealing with a historical novel such as *Esperanza Rising* by Pam Muñoz Ryan, and they may require you to assume a great deal of responsibility for their successfully dealing with an expository article on acid rain. Eighth graders may be able to take full responsibility for dealing with an article on acid rain that is much like the one fourth graders needed your help with. However, eighth graders may need you to assume some of the responsibility for their successfully dealing with a thought-provoking novel such as John Steinbeck's *The Red Pony*, and they may require you to assume a great deal of the responsibility for their successfully dealing with a challenging short story such as Ray Bradbury's "The Foghorn."

High school students may be quite capable of reading "The Foghorn" without assistance, but they will require the teacher's help in reading F. Scott Fitzgerald's *The Great Gatsby* or to achieve a basic understanding of the United Nations *Universal Declaration of Human Rights*. Most college students are unlikely to understand the full meaning of the *Universal Declaration of Human Rights* or understand much of anything about a difficult and technical topic like the genetic code without a skilled teacher to scaffold their efforts.

The Centrality of Word Knowledge

As is all too often the case with educational topics, emphasis on vocabulary periodically waxes and wanes. Luckily, at the present time there is considerable interest in the topic. This has been spurred by several factors: a compelling study showing the very small vocabularies of children growing up in poverty (Hart & Risley, 1995), the importance of a basic vocabulary to both native-speaking students and English language learners (Biemiller, 2001; Nation, 2001), the importance of vocabulary to reading comprehension (National Reading Panel, 2000; RAND Reading Study Group, 2002), the possibility of enriching students' vocabularies through robust vocabulary instruction (Beck, McKeown, & Kucan, 2002), and the possibility of getting students interested and excited about words by fostering word consciousness (Graves & Watts, 2002). One of us (Graves, 2000) has recently outlined the components of a comprehensive vocabulary program, but it is not our purpose to describe such a program here. We do want to emphasize, however, that teaching vocabulary is one possible and very important component of SREs. In chapter 4, we describe teaching new words and new concepts as possibilities for prereading instruction. However, vocabulary instruction can also be a useful component of during-reading and postreading activities.

We will conclude this section by briefly reviewing the instructional implications of each of the concepts presented. The concept of active teaching makes it clear that teaching is not a passive endeavor; teachers frequently need to carry the content to be learned to students. The concept of active learning makes it similarly clear that learning is not a passive process; the learner needs to be involved in the learning process and mentally manipulate the material to be learned. The concept of the zone of proximal development indicates that there is a circumscribed range within which children can learn, that the assistance of a more knowledgeable or competent other person extends this range, and that instruction should be targeted to present learning tasks that are within this range. The gradual release of responsibility model indicates that we can think of instruction of new and difficult material as beginning with the teacher doing all or most of the work and ending with students doing all or most of the work. The gradual release of responsibility model also indicates that when the learning task becomes really difficult, virtually any learner will benefit from the aid of a skillful teacher. Finally, the emphasis on the centrality of word knowledge suggests that vocabulary should be a frequent concern as you plan SREs.

Pedagogical Orientations

In this last section of the chapter, we discuss four pedagogical orientations, four contemporary stances toward teaching and learning. These include reflective teaching and teacher decision making, whole-language and literature-based instruction, making use of the relationship between reading and writing, and teaching for understanding.

Reflective Teaching and Teacher Decision Making

The concept of teacher reflection was first introduced by John Dewey (1909), who saw the reflective teacher as a person who deliberately and consciously reflects on his or her instruction and its effects on students. Somewhat more recently, the concept of reflection was revived and elaborated on by Donald

Schön (1983), who examined the role of reflection among professionals such as engineers, architects, and managers. The concept continues to be an influential one today (Eby, Herrill, & Hicks, 2002).

As applied to teaching, reflection is a cyclical process in which teachers repeatedly view their ongoing instruction and the results of that instruction as a series of problems to be examined and temporarily solved. We say *temporarily* solved because a central tenet of reflective teaching is that there is no single or ultimate solution to instructional questions; the context in which instruction takes place will heavily influence what is appropriate in any particular case. In reaching these temporary solutions, reflective teachers use the knowledge they have acquired formally, their experience and intuitions, and the ongoing events of the classroom. A reflective teacher consciously reflects on all aspects of the learning situation: the students, the materials, the learning activities, and what is learned. These are the aspects of learning considered in the scaffolded reading approach. Additionally, one very important object of reflection is the values inherent in what is being taught and in the teaching itself (Calderhead, 1992).

Considering all aspects of the learning situation in planning a particular reading experience, in observing the experience as it unfolds in the classroom, and in evaluating that experience is essential to optimizing your ability to create the best possible reading experiences for students. Moreover, to the extent that you share your reflections with students, you will not only be honing your own teaching but also assisting them in becoming more conscious about what does and does not work for them as they are reading.

Suppose, for example, that a group of your ninth grade social studies class is reading *The Black Soldier: 1492 to the Present* by Catherine Clinton, a selection that you judged to be fairly easy for these students and something that would easily gain their attention and for which you consequently did little prereading preparation. A few minutes after students begin reading, however, you notice that some of them are not engaged in the reading. A few students are talking, a few heads are nodding, and quite a few pairs of eyes look a bit glazed. A reflective teacher would first notice the situation and then decide what to do about it. The decision, of course, could be made only in the context of a specific class reading a specific selection. One alternative, would be interrupting the class at that point and attempting to kindle or rekindle interest in and commitment to the topic. Another would be deciding that an interruption at that point would be counterproductive and so instead making alternative plans for students' next encounter with a similar topic. If the latter were your choice, further reflection might focus on whether you could find texts that were intrinsically more interesting, or whether with such topics you need to include more motivational and interest-building activities as part of prereading instruction. Finally, the fact that the topic of Black soldiers, and the materials and approach used in presenting the topic, did not result in much engagement on the part of students would itself be a matter for reflection.

As another example, suppose you plan a set of activities for a lesson on mental health for your fourth graders, who will be reading books such as *Anger Management* by Judith Peacock. As you read through the books, you decide that many of the concepts are difficult ones and that you will need to do a great deal of preteaching of concepts and building background knowledge before they read. Consequently, you prepare a substantial set of prereading activities. However, when you begin the prereading activities, you quickly learn that your initial assessment of students' knowledge of mental health was incorrect; your students actually know a lot about the topic. Of course, one appropriate step here is to truncate the planned prereading instruction and let students get on with the reading itself. Beyond that, however, as a reflective teacher you would want to consider what led you to underestimate the students' knowledge in the first place so you could make a conscious effort to avoid doing so in the future.

What we know about teacher decision making indicates that teachers must make complex decisions like this all the time (Shavelson, 1983). Recent research on effective reading instruction shows that the best reading teachers do make them all the time, and that constantly reflecting on your work and deciding what to do based on that reflection is absolutely crucial (Taylor, Pearson, Clark, & Walpole, 2000). The SRE model provides you with a framework for systematically making these decisions.

A central tenet of reflective teaching and teacher decision making is that such reflection and decision making should be a continuing process for all teachers. It is not something that you do only until you get it "right," or something that only new teachers do. The complexities of the classroom—the ever changing combination of students, texts, learning activities, and goals—require that reflection be an ongoing part of teaching.

Whole-Language and Literature-Based Instruction

The influence of the whole-language movement has waned in recent years, to the extent that at least one very prominent reading educator (Pearson, 2000) has formally announced its demise. Nevertheless, a number of the tenets of whole language continue to be useful and widely accepted. Here we concentrate on those aspects of whole language that inform the scaffolded reading approach.

Two very prominent whole-language principles are that children ought to enjoy reading and that becoming lifelong, dedicated readers who view reading as a rich source of information, insight, and enjoyment is every bit as important as becoming competent in the cognitive practice of reading. We strongly endorse both of these principles; students succeeding at reading and realizing that they have succeeded are major goals of every SRE.

Another whole-language principle is that the situation in which children learn and use their literacy skills is crucial to their success. The supportive and encouraging "literate environment" described earlier in the chapter is the type of setting in which literacy flourishes.

Still another whole-language principle is that risk taking is a necessary part of learning to read. We have already noted the importance of risk taking in qualifying our emphasis on the importance of success with the caution that students need to face some challenges if their reading and other literacy skills are to grow. Also, considering students' zone of proximal development and providing the support they need to achieve at the outer limits of their competence is one method of encouraging and supporting risk taking.

The final whole-language principle that we highlight, and one we will return to, is that reading and writing are supportive skills that should often be integrated with each other. We discuss the close relationship between reading and writing in the next section.

Some of the same forces that have led to the demise of the whole-language movement have lessened the influence of the literature-based approach to reading instruction in some classrooms. The most notable of these forces are probably reports such as *Preventing Reading Difficulties in Young Children* (Snow et al.,1998), *Teaching Reading Is Rocket Science* (American Federation of Teachers, 1999), and the Report of the *National Reading Panel* report (National Reading Panel, 2000). Each of these reports lays great stress on the alphabetic code and on children's mastering the code during the first few years of school. As a consequence, there is less emphasis on using children's literature in initial reading instruction than there was few years ago. However, one central construct of the literature-based approach continues to be (and should be) very powerful. Advocates of literature-based instruction such as Leslie Morrow and Linda Gambrell (2000), children's literature scholars such as Lee Galda, Gwynne Ash, and Bernice Cullinin (2000), and the vast majority of reading educators continue to put special emphasis on the value and importance of quality children's literature in the reading program. Good literature is seen as particularly valuable and supportive of children's growing competency in reading because it deals with important and widely applicable themes. Good literature often has great emotional appeal and thus has the potential to foster students' love of reading—to create readers who are both competent in reading and motivated to read. Good literature also presents sentence structures and vocabulary that can stretch children's growing competence with language and serve as models for their own writing.

Finally, it is worth noting that quality children's literature includes both narratives and exposition. To be sure, a lot of good literature consists of narratives, or stories. Narratives offer a particular advantage to beginning readers because they follow an organizational structure that children are already familiar with. They involve a setting, a cast of characters, a plot with some sort of complications, and a resolution to those complications. Such familiar structures nourish children's understanding and memory for what is read and thus make the task of learning to read easier. However, children also need to read and learn from expository material—informational materials, including textbooks, magazine articles, and nonfiction trade books. Scaffolded reading activities are designed to support reading both narrative literature and expository material.

Making Use of the Relationship Between Reading and Writing

Not too long ago, reading and writing were taught as separate subjects, divorced from each other, almost as if by law. Today, as the wide use of texts such as Nancy Atwell's *In the Middle* (1998), Lucy Calkins's *The Art of Teaching Reading* (2001), and Regie Routman's *Conversations* (2000) attest, instruction in these two facets of language is very frequently integrated.

There are a number of excellent reasons for linking reading and writing (Nelson & Calfee, 1998). One reason is that doing so is economical for both you and your students. There is no need to present reading during one segment of the day and writing during another; doing so is bound to take more time than integrating the two.

Another reason is that reading is an excellent prompt for writing. Frequently, one of the biggest problems facing students as they begin to write is having something to write about, but reading often solves that problem. The fifth- or sixth-grade student who has just finished Avi's *The True Confessions of Charlotte Doyle* is likely to have an easy time writing about how he would feel if he suddenly found himself in Charlotte's shoes, alone on a ship with a cruel and murderous captain and a crew bent on reaping their revenge before the voyage ends. Fiction is not the only sort of reading that can stimulate writing. The third grade student who has read *Spiders* by Theresa Greenaway from the series *Mini Pets* has gained a lot of information that could be used in writing a descriptive piece about some creepy-crawly creature she has encountered or a fanciful story about a pet spider.

Of course, it is not just that reading provides a good stimulus for writing; writing also complements and aids students with their reading (Fitzgerald & Shanahan, 2000). The student who writes about how he would feel if he were in Charlotte's place is learning to relate to fictional characters, empathize with them, and consider how their experiences are similar to and different from his own. The student who writes a descriptive piece prompted by what she has read about black widow spiders is engaged in generative learning, establishing a relationship between information in a text and her existing knowledge and experiences. The writing should improve both her understanding of what she has read and her memory for the information. More generally, writing is an excellent study technique, one that is by its nature active and constructive.

Still another advantage of linking reading and writing is that students can learn a lot about reading from writing. As Robert Tierney and David Pearson (1983) have explained, it is useful to view reading as a composing process, as a situation in which a reader must actively construct meaning. Particularly for students who are not active readers, the process of composing may serve as a cue to the importance of getting actively involved in their reading. Students can also learn a lot about reading from writing because both processes employ the same organizational structures. A student who has just written a narrative and has found that organizing the piece was almost automatic is in an excellent position to discuss just what constitutes the narrative form and to realize that most narratives follow a prototypic form. Conversely, a student who has just written an informational piece and found that he or she had to struggle with a number of different ways of organizing the piece is in a good position to recognize the fact that expository writing can have many structures and that dealing with the organization of expository materials when reading them may be a demanding task.

Finally, reading, writing about what they read, and sharing that writing with others allows students to appreciate a host of complex features of reading and writing. Writers usually write for some purpose; they have information they want to communicate, a position they want to support, or an idea or feeling they wish to convey. Readers usually read for some purpose; they may want to learn something, they may wish to be entertained, or they may seek an aesthetic experience from reading. Writers often have to strive to convey their message, and despite the attempt, not all messages are successfully conveyed. Authors must write in different ways for different readers; what will inform or please one reader will not necessarily satisfy another. Different readers of the same text will come away with quite different messages and quite different responses. The list of subtleties to be learned is nearly endless, and such subtleties will not be learned simply because reading and writing are taught and practiced together; however, combining experiences in reading and writing can certainly help to promote such learning.

Teaching for Understanding

Over the past decade or so, a number of educators and researchers have given considerable attention to teaching for understanding (Graves, 1999). Particularly useful from a classroom teacher's perspective is the work of Fred Newmann (Newmann, Secada, & Wehlage, 1995), Grant Wiggins (Wiggins & McTighe, 1998), and David Perkins and his colleagues (Blythe, 1998; Perkins, 1992; Wiske, 1998). Perkins's approach is the one that has been described most completely in the literature and the one we describe here. However, we stress that each of these approaches has a number of exciting and innovative features and that you might want to look at the work of all three of these authorities.

An important prelude to understanding Perkins's notion of teaching for understanding and its importance is the realization that in some ways schooling is not going well even for our best students, that all too few students attain the deep level of understanding critical in today's world (Bransford et al., 2000; National Research Council, 1999). Recent National Assessment of Educational Progress data on high school seniors, for example, show that only 6 percent reached the advanced level in reading, only 3 percent reached the advanced level in science, and only 1 percent reached the advanced level in history (Graves, 1999). Such results bode extremely poorly for students' success in the information age.

Students need to be able to deeply understand what they read. They must, for example, be able "to explain, muster evidence, find examples, generalize, apply concepts, analogize, represent in a new way, and so on" (Perkins, 1992, p. 13). To teach for understanding, Perkins explains, we must go beyond simply presenting students with information and ensure that they accomplish three tasks:

- They must understand topics deeply.
- They must retain important information.
- They must actively use the knowledge they gain.

Not all SREs can or should be designed to lead students to such deep understanding. Sometimes your purpose for reading a selection will be for students to simply enjoy it. At other times, however, you definitely want to foster deep understanding, and SREs can help to do that. Appropriate prereading, during-reading, and postreading activities can help students to understand topics deeply. Appropriate postreading activities—particularly activities in which students actively investigate, manipulate, and transform the information they have learned—will lead to retention of important information. Other appropriate postreading activities—particularly activities that give students the opportunity to apply what they have learned from reading to their lives and the world they live in—will prepare them to actively use the knowledge they gain from reading.

We end this section with educational implications. Because the four notions—reflective teaching, whole-language and literature-based instruction, making use of the relationship between reading and writing, and teaching for understanding—are pedagogical concepts, the implications are straightforward. Teachers should be reflective; we should continually examine our teaching and its results and attempt to make our instruction and our students' learning more and more effective. Although whole language no longer occupies the position it once did, a number of whole-language principles are still worthy of consideration; the importance of developing committed lifelong readers is one of the most worthy. First-rate literature, exposition as well as narratives, should be a major component of every reading program. Reading and writing belong together and mutually support each other, and the two should frequently be intertwined in SREs and other classroom activities. Finally, although the goals of SREs are as varied as your students and the texts they read, teaching for deep understanding is one particularly important goal.

Concluding Comments

In this chapter, we have described much of the thinking that prompted us to develop the scaffolded reading approach and that has continued to shape the approach. The ideas that motivated us have been diverse. They include affective concerns such as the importance of success, concepts from cognitive psychology such as the importance of prior knowledge, general instructional concepts such as the gradual release of responsibility, and current ideas about teaching and learning such as the value of integrating reading and writing instruction. Although somewhat less diversity might at first seem desirable, we have decided that this is not the case, for two reasons. First, the scaffolded reading approach is itself diverse and multifaceted because it is designed so that you can tailor activities to a wide array of students, texts, and purposes of reading. It is not surprising that a diverse set of concepts is needed to underpin such a flexible plan. Second, we very much believe that a variety of perspectives offers useful ideas about teaching and learning and that no single perspective or small set of perspectives can offer all the background that teachers need to meet the challenging goal of SREs, to make each and every reading experience a successful one for each and every student.

References

Adams, M., & Bruce, B. (1982). Background knowledge and reading comprehension. In J. A. Langer & T. M. Smith-Burke (Eds.), *Reader meets author: Bridging the Gap* (pp. 2–25). Newark, DE: International Reading Association. A brief and very readable discussion of the importance of background knowledge to reading comprehension.

American Federation of Teachers. (1999). *Teaching reading is rocket science: What expert teachers of reading should know and be able to do.* Washington, DC: Author. The AFT position on beginning reading instruction, heavily influenced by Snow's *Preventing Reading Difficulties* report cited below.

Anderson, J. R., Reder, L., & Simon, H. A. (1998). Radical constructivism and cognitive psychology. In D. Ravich (Ed.), *Brookings papers on educational policy, 1998* (pp. 227–278). Washington, DC: Brookings Institution Press. Three eminent psychologists' carefully crafted response to what they see as the excesses of radical constructivism.

Aronson, E., & Patnoe, S. (1997). *The jigsaw classroom* (2nd ed.). New York: HarperCollins. A update of Aronson's work on the jigsaw approach to cooperative learning.

Atwell, N. (1998). *In the middle: Writing, reading, and learning with adolescents* (2nd ed.). Portsmouth, NH: Heinemann. Focuses on teaching young adolescents through integrating reading and writing.

Beach, R. W. (1993). *A teacher's introduction to reader-response theories.* Urbana, IL: National Council of Teachers of English. A thorough and quite sophisticated introduction to reader response.

Beck, I. L., McKeown, M. G., & Kucan, L. (2002). *Bringing words to life: Robust vocabulary instruction.* New York: Guilford Press. As the title indicates, this describes a program of robust vocabulary instruction.

Biemiller, A. (2001, Spring). Teaching vocabulary: Early, direct, and sequential. *American Educator,* pp. 24–28, 47. Argument for systematically and directly teaching a small number of words to disadvantaged students.

Blythe, T. (1998). *The teaching for understanding guide.* San Francisco: Jossey-Bass. A very practical, teacher-oriented guide to teaching for understanding as developed by David Perkins and his colleagues.

Boyer, E. L. (1988). *College: The undergraduate experience in America.* New York: Perennial Library. Influential report on undergraduate education.

Bransford, J. D., Brown, A. L., & Cocking, R. R. (Eds.). (2000). *How people learn: Brain, mind, experience, and school (expanded edition)*. Washington, DC: National Academy Press. A major synthesis of what we know about teaching and learning based on work commissioned by the National Research Council.

Brophy, J. (1986). Teacher influences on student achievement. *American Psychologist, 41,* 1069–1077. Concise summary of the findings of the teacher effectiveness research.

Brophy, J., & Good. T. (2000*). Looking into classrooms* (8th ed.). New York: HarperCollins. Chapters 3 and 4 provide detailed information on the authors' position on active teaching and effective instruction generally.

Calderhead, J. (1992). The role of reflection in learning to teach. In L. Vali (Ed.), *Reflective teacher education: Cases and critiques* (pp. 139–146). New York: SUNY Press. A lucid treatment of the importance of reflection in becoming an effective teacher.

Calkins, L. M. (2001). *The art of teaching reading.* New York: Longman. This inservice text on teaching reading includes a great deal of attention to writing.

Campione, J. (1981, April). Learning, academic achievement, and instruction. Paper presented at the second annual Conference on Reading Research of the Center for the Study of Reading, New Orleans, LA. The original source of Campione's widely endorsed and very useful gradual release of responsibility model.

Chambliss, M. J., & Calfee, R. S. (1998). *Textbooks for learning: Nurturing children's minds.* London: Blackwell. A truly insightful book on improving learning by improving textbooks.

Csikszentmihalyi, M. (1990). *Flow: The psychology of optimal experience.* New York: Harper & Row. This popular book summarizes Csikszentmihalyi's three decades of work on optimal human experiences—the joy, creativity, and total involvement he calls *flow.*

Dewey, J. (1909). *How we think.* Lexington, MA: Heath. Dewey's classic text on the relationship of reflective thinking to effective teaching.

Eby, J. W., Herrell, A. L., & Hicks, J. L. (2002). *Reflective planning, teaching, and evaluation, K–12* (3rd ed.). Upper Saddle River, NJ: Merrill. Well-known text with reflection as a central theme.

Fitzgerald, J., & Shanahan, T. (2000). Reading and writing relations and their development. *Educational Psychologist, 35,* 39–50. Very careful analysis of this relationship.

Galda, L., Ash, G. E., & Cullinin, B. E. (2000). Children's literature. In M. Kamil, P. Mosenthal, P. D. Pearson, & R. Barr (Eds.), *Handbook of reading research* (Vol. 3, pp. 361–379). New York: Longman. Major review of the research on children's literature.

Galda, L., & Guice, S. (1997). Response-based reading instruction in the elementary grades. In S. A. Stahl & David A. Hayes (Eds.), *Instructional models in reading* (pp. 311–330). Mahwah, NJ: Erlbaum. An overview of the reader-response approach.

Gergen, K. J. (1985). The social constructionist movement in modern psychology. *American Psychologist, 40,* 266–275. One of the most readable introductions to social constructionist thinking.

Glaserfeld, E. von. (1984). An introduction to radical constructivism. In P. Watzlawick (Ed.), *The invented reality* (pp. 17–40). New York: Norton. An introduction to radical constructivism and a defense of it.

Goodman, K. (1986). *What's whole in whole language?* Toronto, Canada: Scholastic TAB. A concise overview of the whole language approach by one of the founders of the movement.

Graves, M. F. (1999). Fostering high levels of reading and learning in secondary schools. *Reading Online.* Available: http://www.readingonline.org/articles/graves/. Argument for teaching for understanding.

Graves, M. F. (2000). A vocabulary program to complement and bolster a middle-grade comprehension program. In B. M. Taylor, M. F. Graves, & P. van den Broek (Eds.), *Reading for meaning: Fostering comprehension in the middle grades.* New York: Teachers College Press. Description of a comprehensive vocabulary program.

Graves, M. F., Juel, C., & Graves, B. B. (2001). *Teaching reading in the 21st century* (2nd ed.). Boston: Allyn & Bacon. Chapter 2 of this comprehensive elementary reading methods text includes a description of what constitutes a literate environment.

Graves, M. F., & Watts, S. M. (2002). The place of word consciousness in a research-based vocabulary program. In S. J. Samuels & A. E. Farstrup (Eds.), *What research has to say about reading instruction* (3rd ed.). Newark, DE: International Reading Association. An exploration of word consciousness as an important part of a comprehensive vocabulary program.

Guthrie, J. T., & Alvermann, D. E. (1999). *Engaged reading: Processes, practices, and policy implications.* Newark, DE: International Reading Association. An edited collection of chapters on reading engagement and related topics.

Guthrie, J. T., & Wigfield, A. (2000). Engagement and motivation in reading. In M. Kamil, P. Mosenthal, P. D. Pearson, & R. Barr (Eds.), *Handbook of reading research* (Vol. 3, pp. 403–422). Mahwah, NJ: Erlbaum. A contemporary review of research on engagement, motivation, and related factors.

Hart, B., & Risley, T. R. (1995). *Meaningful differences in the everyday experiences of young American children.* Baltimore: Brookes. Solid, dramatic, and very readable report of a study showing that students raised in deep poverty may develop small vocabularies and arguing that these small vocabularies hugely hamper them in school.

Johnson, D. W., Johnson, R. T., & Holubec, E. J. (1994). The *new circles of learning: Cooperation in the classroom and school.* Alexandria, VA: Association for Supervision and Curriculum Development. A brief, informative, and extremely readable description of the Johnsons' approach to cooperative learning. Highly recommended.

Johnston, P. H., & Winograd, P. N. (1985). Passive failure in reading. *Journal of Reading Behavior, 17,* 279–301. A powerful and important explanation of this very destructive phenomenon.

Kamil, M., Mosenthal, P., Pearson, P. D., & Barr, R. (Eds.). (2000). *Handbook of reading research* (Vol. 3). New York: Longman. The third and newest edition of this major handbook of reading research.

LaBerge D., & Samuels, S. J. (1974). Toward a theory of automatic information processing in reading. *Cognitive Psychology, 6,* 293–323. The original description of this simple yet powerful concept.

Marlowe, B. H., & Page, M. L. (1998). *Creating and sustaining the constructivist classroom.* Thousand Oaks, CA: Corwin Press. One view of a constructivist classroom.

Marshall, J. (2000). Response to literature. In M. Kamil, P. Mosenthal, P. D. Pearson, & R. Barr (Eds.), *Handbook of reading research* (Vol. 3, pp. 381–402). Mahwah, NJ: Erlbaum. A thoughtful overview and analysis of reader-response research.

Morrow, L. M., & Gambrell, L. B. (2000). Literature-based reading instruction. In M. Kamil, P. Mosenthal, P. D. Pearson, & R. Barr (Eds.), *Handbook of reading research* (Vol. 3, pp. 563–586). New York: Longman. Major review of literature-based instruction.

Nation, I. S. P. (2001). *Learning vocabulary in another language.* Cambridge, UK: Cambridge University Press. A comprehensive look at learning vocabulary in a second (or other) language.

National Reading Panel. (2000). *Teaching children to read.* Bethesda, MD: National Institute of Child Health and Human Development. A nationally commissioned review of research on reading.

National Research Council. (1999). *Improving student learning.* Washington, DC: National Academy Press. Presents a comprehensive plan for educational research.

Nelson, N., & Calfee, R. C. (1998). *The reading-writing connection.* Chicago: National Society for the Study of Education. Major collection on reading and writing.

Newmann, F. M., Secada, W. G., & Wehlage, G. G. (1995). *A guide to authentic instruction and assessment: Vision, standards and scoring.* Madison, WI: Wisconsin Center for Educational Research. An overview of Newmann's authentic instruction approach.

Pearson, P. D. (2000). Reading in the 20th century. In T. L. Good (Ed.), *American education yesterday, today, and tomorrow* (Vol. 2, pp. 152–208). Chicago: National Society for the Study of Education. A well-known reading educator and researcher's account of reading instruction during the last century.

Pearson, P. D., & Gallagher, M. C. (1983). The instruction of reading comprehension. *Contemporary Educational Psychology, 8,* 317–344. Still a useful summary of the research on teaching reading comprehension.

Perkins, D. (1992). *Smart schools: From training memories to educating minds.* New York: Free Press. A well-written, engaging, and comprehensive consideration of teaching for understanding.

Phillips, D. E. (1995). The good, the bad, and the ugly: The many faces of constructivism. *Educational Researcher, 24* (7), 5–12. Explores several meanings of this complex and often difficult concept.

Phillips, D. E. (Ed.). (2000). *Constructivism in education.* Chicago: National Society for the Study of Education. A recent major collection on constructivism as it applies to education.

Pressley, M. (2002). *Reading instruction that works: The case for balanced teaching.* New York: Guilford Press. An extremely thorough review of the research on elementary reading instruction. Chapter 8 deals specifically with motivation.

RAND Reading Study Group. (2002). *Reading for understanding: Toward an R & D program in reading comprehension.* Santa Monica, CA: RAND Education. Excellent summary of our knowledge about teaching reading comprehension.

Richards, I. A. (1929). *Practical criticism.* New York: Harcourt Brace. An early influence on contemporary response theory.

Rosenblatt, L. (1938). *Literature as exploration.* New York: Appleton-Century. Rosenblatt's original presentation of her response theory.

Rosenblatt, L. (1978). *The reader, the text, the poem: The transactional theory of the literary work.* Carbondale, IL: Southern Illinois Press. Another presentation of Rosenblatt's response theory; both this and her 1938 book have had enormous influence on the teaching of literature.

Routman, R. (2000). *Conversations.* Portsmouth, NH: Heinemann. Very popular text featuring integration of the language arts.

Rumelhart, D. E. (1977). Toward an interactive model of reading. In S. Dornic (Ed.), *Attention and performance* (Vol. 6, pp. 573–603). Hillsdale, NJ: Erlbaum. The original description of the interactive model, done by one of the major researchers in the area.

Rumelhart, D. E. (1980). Schemata: The building blocks of cognition. In R. J. Spiro, B. C. Bruce, & W. F. Brewer (Eds.), *Theoretical issues in reading comprehension* (pp. 33–58). Hillsdale, NJ: Erlbaum. One of the original descriptions of schema theory, done by a pioneer researcher on the topic.

Schön, D. (1983). *The reflective practitioner.* New York: Basic Books. The book that first prompted current interest in the importance of teacher reflection.

Shavelson, R. J. (1983). Review of research on teachers' pedagogical judgements, plans and decisions. *Elementary School Journal, 83,* 392–413. A concise review of the research on teacher decision making by a prominent researcher in the area.

Slavin, R. E. (1987). *Cooperative learning: Student teams* (2nd ed.). Washington, DC: National Education Association. A brief overview of several of Slavin's approaches to cooperative learning.

Snow, C. E., Burns, M. S., & Griffin, P. (Eds.). (1998). *Preventing reading difficulties in young children.* Washington, DC: National Academy Press. Seminal review of research on what makes early reading instruction and experiences effective.

Stanovich, K. E. (1994). Constructivism in reading education. *Journal of Special Education, 28,* 259–274. Notes that texts vary markedly in the extent to which they constrain meaning.

Taylor, B. M., Pearson, P. D., Clark, K. F., & Walpole, S. (2000). Beating the odds in teaching all children to read. *Elementary School Journal, 101,* 121–166. A national study highlighting teacher reflection as one of the most important components of effective instruction.

Tierney, R. J., & Pearson, P. D. (1983). Toward a composing model of reading. *Language Arts, 60,* 568–580. A cogent perspective on reading as an active, constructive process.

Vygotsky, L. S. (1978). *Mind in society.* Cambridge, MA: Harvard University Press. One of Vygotsky's classic texts, probably best known for its description of the zone of proximal development.

Wiggins, G., & McTighe, J. (1998). *Understanding by design.* Alexandria, VA: Association for Supervision and Curriculum Development. The basic description of Wiggins's approach to teaching for understanding.

Wiske, M. S. (Ed.). (1998). *Teaching for understanding: Linking research with practice.* San Francisco: Jossey-Bass. A detailed look at teaching for understanding by the participants of the Harvard Teaching for Understanding research group.

Children's Literature

Avi. (1990). *The true confessions of Charlotte Doyle.* New York: Orchard. 215 pages.

Bradbury, R. (1990). The foghorn. In *The stories of Ray Bradbury.* New York: Knopf. 12 pages.

Clinton, C. (2000). *The black soldier: 1492 to the present.* Boston: Houghton Mifflin. 128 pages.

Fitzgerald, F. S. (1925) *The great Gatsby.* New York: Scribner. 182 pages.

Greenaway, T. (1999). *Spiders.* Austin, TX: Steck-Vaughn. 32 pages.

Kvasnosky, L. M. (2002). *One lucky summer.* New York: Dutton. 112 pages.

Peacock, J. (1999). *Anger management.* Mankato, MN: Capstone. 64 pages.

Ryan, P. M. (2001). *Esperanza rising.* New York: Scholastic. 262 pages.

Steinbeck, J. (1955). *The red pony.* New York: Bantam. 100 pages.

United Nations. (1948). *Universal declaration of human rights.* New York: Author. 5 pages.

Chapter

4

Prereading
Activities

The place to start students on the road to a successful reading experience is at the beginning. Prereading activities, the first set of optional activities in an SRE, prepare students to read, making sure that they get off to a good start. Taking time to adequately prepare students before they read will greatly increase their ability to read fluently, understand what they read, learn from what they read, enjoy reading, and find it a rewarding experience. In chapter 2, we described the following eight categories of prereading activities:

1. Motivating
2. Relating the reading to students' lives
3. Building or activating background knowledge
4. Providing text-specific knowledge
5. Preteaching vocabulary
6. Preteaching concepts
7. Prequestioning, predicting, and direction setting
8. Suggesting strategies

Here we elaborate on these descriptions and give examples of activities in each of these categories. Before doing so, we should point out that it may be useful to think of these categories as serving four different purposes. Activities in the first two categories—Motivating and Relating the Reading to Students' lives—serve primarily to get students interested and enthusiastic about reading the upcoming selection. Activities in the next four categories—Building or Activating Background Knowledge, Providing Text-Specific Knowledge, Preteaching Vocabulary, and Preteaching Concepts—build students' knowledge, providing them with a sturdy base for understanding the text. Activities in the next category—Prequestioning, Predicting, and Direction Setting—key students to what they are to attend to as they read. Finally, the last category—Suggesting Strategies—gives you an opportunity to remind students of strategies they already know that will be particularly useful in reading the upcoming selection.

The different types of prereading activities described here are intended to prompt you to consider a wide array of activities as you plan effective prereading instruction. As you consider the various types of activities, you will find that a number of them overlap. That's fine. We created the categories to suggest the range of options available, not because there is a need to classify each activity. What's important is that the activities you choose assist your students in achieving the purposes you and they have for a particular reading experience.

As we explained in chapter 2, in planning a Scaffolded Reading Experience (SRE) you initially consider three factors: the students, the selection, and the purpose or purposes for which students are reading. After either you or your students have selected the text to read, and after you have read through it and identified topics, themes, potentially difficult vocabulary, and other salient features of the material, you begin to map out the entire SRE. What is your students' overall goal for reading—is it primarily for an aesthetic experience, or is it to gain information or insights? Will getting the jist of the material be sufficient, or do students need to gain a deep and thorough understanding of it? The kinds of activities students will be involved in before, during, and after reading will reflect these goals.

As you continue planning prereading activities, ask yourself questions like the following: How can I get these students really interested in this selection? What sort of background knowledge do they have on this topic? What might they need to know to profit most from their reading? Is there anything in the material I can relate to their lives? Are there any concepts or vocabulary in the selection that students might benefit from working with? Could they use any of their repertoire of reading strategies to help them better understand the material? The answers to these questions will guide you in planning an effective SRE for your class.

Table 4-1 outlines the prereading activities described in this chapter.

Table 4-1. Prereading Activities

Motivating	*Frindle* (p. 66) *Survival Kit* (p. 68)
Relating Reading to Students' Lives	*Common Threads* (p. 70)
Building Background Knowledge	*Places, Events, and Times* (p. 74)
Activating Background Knowledge	*Think About It!* (p. 76)
Providing Text-Specific Knowledge	*In a Nutshell* (p. 78)
Preteaching Vocabulary	*Paired Questions* (p. 82) *Word Clues* (p. 84)
Preteaching Concepts	*Living Words* (p. 88) *Is It, or Isn't It?* (p. 90)
Prequestioning	*What Do You Want to Know?* (p. 95)
Predicting	*I Predict* (p. 96)
Direction Setting	*Looking for Old, Looking for New* (p. 97) *Looking for Answers* (p. 99)
Suggesting Strategies	*A Quick Look* (p. 101)

Motivating

A big part of preparing students to read is motivating them. Whatever the task, it is always more interesting, exciting, and meaningful if we have a good reason for wanting to do it. Think about yourself and your own reading. What motivates you to pick up the evening newspaper, to read an article in *The Instructor*, or to read a mystery novel? Is there a particular purpose you have in mind? Do you read to be informed, enlightened, inspired, entertained? We all read for a combination of reasons, but usually because we expect the text to give us something we need or want—information, enlightenment, inspiration, or entertainment. In order to ensure a successful reading experience for students, we need to be sure that they have this sort of motivation to read.

Motivational activities are just that—activities that incite enthusiasm, an eagerness to delve into the material. Sometimes you will use activities that serve primarily to motivate students. However, motivational activities frequently overlap with other kinds of prereading activities, such as activating background knowledge, relating reading to students' lives, and preteaching concepts. In general, motivational activities will draw upon the interests and concerns of the particular group doing the reading. Puppets and puppies might be part of a motivating activity for first and second graders; a rap song or challenging puzzle for fourth to sixth graders; and perhaps a real-world problem for seventh to ninth graders. You know what kinds of things interest and excite your students. Use these to help motivate their reading.

Motivational activities often involve hands-on experiences, active student participation, drama, and intrigue:

> "Feel this fabric and tell me what it makes you think of and how it makes you feel."

> "Think of your favorite color. Walk around the room and touch three things that have that color in them."

> "Guess what's in this box?"

> "Look at this picture. Imagine you are there. What are you doing? How are you feeling?"

Once the students' interest is piqued, the next step is to transfer that interest to the reading material:

> "Robbie, the little boy in the story you will read today has a special blanket made of the fabrics you were feeling—flannel and satin."

> "*Hailstones and Halibut Bones* is a poem all about colors."

> "I guess my clues were good ones, and you're pretty good detectives. What was in the box is pumice, and we'll be reading about it and other kinds of igneous rocks in our science chapter today."

> "The picture you were looking at shows the village of Sân Paulo in Brazil. Pedro, the main character in the story you will be reading, lives in a village very much like it."

Motivating Sample Activity for Frindle

This motivational activity was used by Lauren Moser with a group fourth graders in a Midwestern suburb. The selection students were about to read was *Frindle* by Andrew Clements. In this award-winning middle grade novel, Nick is intrigued by how words are created and decides to create a new word for a pen. He calls it a "frindle" and tries to get others to call it that as well. Soon the new word spreads from the school, to the town, and across the country. Mrs. Moser's purpose in this prereading activity was to pique her students' interest and to build upon their concept of how objects get named, a central theme in the novel.

Mrs. Moser began by taking several items out of a bag and placing them on a table in front of her students: a chalkboard eraser, a book, an orange, a painter's cap, and a pen. Without saying anything, she wrote the word *lollop* on the board. She pointed to the word and said to her students, "What if I told you one of these things is a lollop. Which one do you think it is?"

The students looked puzzled but intrigued and offered their guesses. Then she said to the students, "What if I told you this is a lollop? [She holds up the chalkboard eraser.] This is a vole. [She holds up the book.] This is a grinderfife. [She holds up the orange.] This is a weedlewizenbracker. [She puts on the cap.] And this one, my friends, is a frindle! [She holds up the pen.] What would you say?"

"Maybe you're talking in another language," one student offered.

"You're trying to trick us," said another.

After a few more students gave their opinions, Mrs. Moser asked, "How do things get the names we give them, anyway? Why do we call an orange an *orange* and not a *grinderfife*?" After students gave a few suggestions, Mrs. Moser pulled a dictionary from her bag and began to thumb through it, reading a few words and their definitions. "There are thousands of words in the English language that are found in this dictionary. How did they get there?"

After a brief discussion, Mrs. Moser wrote *frindle* on the board. "Could you invent a new word for pen, could you call it a frindle and get it in the dictionary?" She then pulled another book from her bag—*Frindle*—and showed the students the cover illustration, which shows the hand of a boy holding a pen. "That's just what Nick, the fifth grader in this story, wanted to find out. He wanted to call a pen a frindle, and see if he could get his new word in the dictionary. Do you think he was able to do it? When you read the book *Frindle*, you'll find out!"

As Mrs. Moser's technique aptly illustrates, motivating activities should be fun. They get students interested and involved. They also direct students' thinking toward the themes, topics, and concepts of the material you are preparing them to read, and they relate to the types of during- and postreading activities that students will do, as well.

We present another sample motivational activity below, this time using the format we will use for the rest of the sample activities. Each description begins with a heading showing the type of activity and giving the specific activity a name. Then comes a brief description of the activity. Next there are sections on the selection, the students for whom the activity was written, a rationale for the activity, the procedures to be followed, and a note on adapting the activity.

The final section in each sample activity is called "Reflection." This serves a function somewhat similar to that of dialogue journals. Dialogue journals, as you know, are used to share a common interest or to work out a common problem with someone else. Unfortunately, a book format doesn't allow us to hear your responses. However, what these sections do allow is for us to expand, in a conversational style, on ideas and issues that emerge from the activities. In these informal remarks, we have tended to do two different things. Most of the time, we comment on the activity itself: what it did, what it did not do, how it might be changed. Less frequently, we comment on a general principle the activity reminds us of. We hope you find these informal reflections helpful and that they encourage your own reflection.

Motivating Sample Activity 2: *Survival Kit*

Survival Kit motivates students to think about the items they would need to survive in the Arctic wilderness.

Selection: *Frozen Fire* by James Houston. This exciting adventure novel tells the story of Matthew Morgan and his Eskimo friend Kayak, who battle to stay alive while attempting to rescue Matthew's father and a helicopter pilot who are lost in the Canadian wilderness.

Students: Sixth and seventh graders of low to average ability.

Reading Purpose: To understand and enjoy an exciting survival story.

Goal of the Activity: To movitate students to want to read this novel, to activate their prior knowledge about the Arctic, to consider what items might be needed for survival in the Arctic wilderness, and to gain practice in making decisions.

Rationale: Planning for an imaginary journey to a potentially dangerous and exciting locale is an activity that students are very likely to find engaging. Also, having students think about what items they might need to survive in a frozen wilderness will help to focus their attention on one of the main themes of this story—survival.

Procedure: Ask students to imagine that they are going to take a trip to the northern Canadian wilderness. Locate northern Canada and Frobisar Bay on a map or globe. (The story's setting is in the vicinity of Frobisar Bay in northeastern Canada.) Discuss what the climate might be like and what sort of terrain they can expect to find there.

Ask students to think about what kinds of things they might need to take in order to survive in an extremely cold and isolated environment. Beginning with the letter *A,* have students suggest one item that begins with that letter to take on their trip, then continue through the rest of the alphabet (*ax, bedding, can opener,* etc.). After 26 items have been named, tell the students that you are going to ask them to think about which 10 items they would most want to have if stranded in the Arctic wilderness. Organize students into groups of three or four to decide which 10 items they would choose. Appoint a facilitator and a recorder for each group. Allow students about 10 minutes to meet and discuss their choices.

When students have finished making their choices, call on the recorders to name the choices their groups made. Write these on the chalkboard. Compare and contrast the items in each group's list.

After students finish the book, it would be worthwhile to repeat this activity. Students may have quite a different perspective on the most important things necessary for survival in the Arctic after their reading. It will be interesting for them to see how their perceptions have changed.

Adapting the Activity: *Survival Kit* can be adapted to any reading selection in which the protagonists find themselves in a setting away from home. For example, this activity can be used before reading in a story about kids going to camp (What sorts of items might they want most at camp?), kids visiting grandparents and/or a dad or mom they don't live with. It can also be used before reading a social studies text such as the expeditions of Lewis and Clark or pioneers on the Santa Fe Trail (What sorts of items might Lewis and Clark or the pioneers take?). *Survival Kit* can also be adapted as a motivational activity for any selection in which the protagonist is trying to achieve a goal or solve a problem. For example, if the main character wants to win a new friend, students can think of what he or she might need in a "survival kit" to make that happen. Students might suggest qualities such as friendliness, honesty, or cooperativeness. *Survival Kit* could also be used as a postreading activity in science. After reading about various careers in science, students might pack survival kits for geologists, oceanographers, or astronomers.

You can also reverse the *Survival Kit* activity. Instead of having students suggest items for a survival kit, you do the selecting and present these to the students. For example, let us say that second- and third-grade students are going to read *Charro: The Mexican Cowboy* by George Anacona. You can identify words that name things that are critical for a Mexican cowboy to have—for example, *rope, horse, muscles,* and *courage.* Write your words on cards, use pictures, or even supply the real things and put them in a prop such as a saddlebag or backpack to add interest. Then let students guess who might need these things in a survival kit and why.

Reflection: As you may have noticed, in addition to motivating students to want to read a selection, this activity builds and activates students' background knowledge of its content and themes. It also challenges their thinking. Considering just what someone might need to survive, endure, or triumph in various life situations requires higher order thinking.

Note that it isn't always necessary that students come up with a word for every letter of the alphabet. Better to keep the activity lively and focused than to have students labor over a letter or offer inappropriate words. It's important to keep in mind that the idea of the activity is to motivate students to be excited about reading the upcoming selection; it's not simply a wordplay or a thinking activity.

Finally, we want to emphasize that what students need to get interested in and actively involved with are the ideas that will help them as they read. It is extremely important that motivating activities direct students' attention to the themes, topics, and concepts in the upcoming reading. With motivating activities, we are not just trying to get students interested and excited, we are trying to get them interested and excited about the upcoming selection.

Relating the Reading to Students' Lives

Relating the reading to students' lives is an extremely powerful approach for getting students to commit themselves to a text and to claim ownership of it. If we can see how something relates to our lives, then we are making a personal connection. We suddenly have a vested interest. Let us say you have a class of second graders and you run across an engaging story about a boy and his new puppy. One of your students, Charlie, just got a puppy for his birthday, and you realize this would be a great book for Charlie. To prepare him to read the story, you might get him to talk about his puppy, what he feeds it, where it sleeps, who takes care of it, and how he feels about it. Getting Charlie to think about his own experiences with a puppy will help him to better appreciate the events that take place in the story and the actions and emotions of the main character.

You can also relate the topics of expository material to students' lives. Say, for instance, your eighth- or ninth-grade students are going to read about electricity in a science text that day. As a prompt to get them thinking about the ways they use electricity in their own lives, you might write on the board, "Write about the different ways you used electricity so far today." Or, "Imagine your electricity went out this morning. Describe what your morning was like without it." Writing about a topic students will encounter in their reading is an effective way to build or evoke background knowledge.

Relating the reading to students' lives includes any kinds of activities that help students understand how what they read has meaning for the world they live in.

Relating the Reading to Students' Lives
Sample Activity: *Common Threads*

In *Common Threads,* the teacher helps to bridge the gap between the characters in a story and the students' experiences by having them think about experi-

ences in their own lives that are similar to the ones faced by the story's protagonist.

Selection: *The True Confessions of Charlotte Doyle* by Avi. This historical novel
is a gripping account of intrigue and murder on the high seas told by a 13-year-
old girl who finds herself the lone passenger on a sailing ship bound from England to America in 1832. Because of the unusual situation in which Charlotte
finds herself and the demands it places on her physically, mentally, and emotionally, she goes through a virtual metamorphosis. Charlotte begins her tale as
a prim and proper schoolgirl and ends up a seasoned sailor who runs away to
crew on a sailing ship.

Students: Sixth graders of mixed abilities.

Reading Purpose: To read and enjoy an exciting, well-written piece of historical fiction.

Goal of the Activity: To bridge the gap between readers' lives and the story's
main character and setting by helping them to make meaningful connections to
their lives and to introduce the basic elements of plot: problem, solution, and
change.

Rationale: The setting and situation described in this novel are very different
from what young readers will have personally encountered. However, although
the magnitude and nature of Charlotte's problems may be far removed from
today's 10- to 13-year-old readers, what lies at the heart of her story remains
the same: People adapt to difficult situations by drawing on inner resources and
modifying their behavior and attitude as circumstances demand. Focusing on
these universal themes and having students discover examples from their own
experiences can bridge the gap between young readers and the main character
and promote a deeper understanding of the text. The activity also helps students to focus on some of the primary elements of fiction: a character with a
problem, actions taken to solve the problem, and the character's change or re-
action.

Procedure: Begin by asking students to think about a difficult, strange, or unusual situation in which they have found themselves. For example, maybe they
were babysitting and one of the children locked himself in the bathroom, or perhaps they moved to a new school and didn't know anyone, or maybe they had
to take care of a sick sibling. Encourage students to talk about their difficult
situations, what they did about them, and whether the experiences changed
them in any way.

Tell the students that the reason you're having them think about these ideas
is that the main character in a book they will be reading faces an extremely difficult and unusual situation. They will learn just what that situation is when they
read the book, but first you want them to think about their own experiences
with unusual and difficult situations. Doing this will help them to understand and
enjoy the novel more.

Write these headings on the board: *Problem, Solution, How Changed?*

Next, hand out sheets of paper and have students fold them into thirds and write each of the headings in a column.

Before asking students to write their responses in each of the columns, model the activity by giving an experience from your own life and recording your responses on the board. Elaborate orally on these responses as you write them. Tell students that you are writing quickly and not worrying about spelling or using complete sentences and that they can do the same with their responses. What you want to get down is just the gist of the idea.

Problem	*Solution*	*How Changed?*
Was asked to give a speech at a banquet.	*Worried at first and didn't want to do it, then wrote the speech and practiced giving it.*	*Found I didn't mind talking in front of an audience, felt proud I had done something that I thought was hard for me.*

After this, have students write their own problems, solutions, and changes. After they have had a chance to record their own responses, let students share them with the rest of the class. You may want to record some on the board or a chart.

Problem	*Solution*	*How Changed?*
Got separated from parents in downtown San Francisco.	*Started roaming the streets, cried, eventually found my parents.*	*More careful to stay with parents when in a strange place, no longer afraid of policemen.*
Came to live in a country where I didn't know anybody and didn't know the language. I hated it.	*Went to school, listened to teacher and students, tried to be friendly.*	*Not so afraid anymore, can speak new language, have many friends. Now I like it.*

After ample discussion, hold up a copy of *The True Confessions of Charlotte Doyle* and read the title and author. Explain that Charlotte Doyle is the main character in the story, and have students predict from the cover illustration—which shows Charlotte on the deck of a 19th century sailing vessel—where the setting for the story might be. Tell students that the story takes place on a sailing ship in 1832, and ask them to predict what difficult situations 13-year-old Charlotte might confront. Explain that Charlotte will indeed face a number of problems throughout the novel. These will become obvious to them as they read. When they finish reading, you will talk about those difficulties, Charlotte's responses to them, and in what ways she changed.

Adapting the Activity: Common Threads can be used as a prereading activity for any novel, story, or biography in which the main character is faced with numerous problems to solve or obstacles to overcome. Literature abounds with these kinds of situations—realistic and historical fiction, biographies, and fantasies all contain numerous stories of heroes who triumph over difficulties. Examples include *First Apple* by Ching Yeung Russell, *Hatchet* by Gary Paulsen, *The Boxer* by Kathleen Karr, *Rachel Chance* by Jean Thesman, *Behind the Mask: The Life of Queen Elizabeth I* by Jane Resh Thomas, *China's Bravest Girl: The Legend of Hua Mu Lan* by Charlie Chin, and *Maniac Magee* by Jerry Spinelli. Also, instead of doing this as a whole group activity, you might have students work in groups of four to six.

Reflection: Most students are usually eager to talk about themselves, but some will have a tendency to ramble and will need to be encouraged to stick to the main topics of problem, solution, and change. Also, an activity such as this one begins as a prereading activity but is continued through the other two phases of reading. While they read, students might record problems, solutions, and changes in the main character. After they have finished the novel, they can discuss with each other what they discovered about problems, solutions, and change.

As with motivating students, in relating a selection to students' lives it is important to remember that the focus needs to be on the aspects of students' lives that are relevant to the targeted selection. As a colleague once pointed out, introducing a science selection about the ocean by asking whether students have ever been to the ocean and then presiding over a discussion of vacations at the seashore will be of minimal benefit to students in understanding the concepts in the chapter.

Building or Activating Background Knowledge

No text contains all the information necessary for a reader to understand it. All texts leave out a tremendous amount of information and rely on readers to fill in that information from their background knowledge. Thus, understanding any text requires a huge store of knowledge. All students come to school with a vast repertoire of concepts that teachers can tap into, but some students have different knowledge from others, and some have more knowledge than others. Some students have rich stores of knowledge relevant to what they read in school from reading widely themselves, being read to, traveling a good deal, living in various locations, taking trips to museums, going on nature outings, and belonging to groups such as the Boy Scouts, Campfire Girls, and the YMCA.

Other students, those from other countries and other cultures, have had equally rich experiences, but these may not be relevant to much of what the students read in school; they may not be the experiences assumed by the authors of many mainstream American school texts. Still other students have not had the benefits of this sort of rich experience. Because background knowledge is one of the most important factors influencing students' ability to comprehend and learn from a text (Bransford, Brown, & Cocking, 2000; Rand Study Group, 2002), one of your most important tasks is to be certain that all students have the background knowledge to read the texts you are using. This means carefully considering the text and the knowledge it assumes, carefully considering your students and the knowledge they have, and being sure that those who do not have that knowledge get it.

Sometimes this means that you are going to have to build students' background knowledge. If, for example, your seventh graders are going to read an article on poverty in Appalachia and the article assumes that readers already know quite a bit about Appalachia—where it is located, how populated the area is, what sorts of people live there—you are going to have to teach that information before they read the article.

At other times, students actually have the relevant information to read an upcoming selection, but they don't realize that they have it or they don't think in a way that summons it up. In these cases, you need to assist them in activating their prior knowledge. Activating prior knowledge means providing students with prereading experiences that prompt them to bring to consciousness information they already know. Sometimes students might write about what they know; other times they may talk about it. If this information is shared in a class discussion, it will then be available for both the students who produced it and the others in the class. Having this information readily available will help students to make connections with similar ideas when they meet them in the text.

Building Background Knowledge
Sample Activity: *Places, Events, and Times*

In *Places, Events, and Times,* you provide background information on the setting, events, and time frame of a selection.

Selection: *Number the Stars* by Lois Lowry. Ten-year-old AnnMarie and her family help their neighbors, the Rosens, flee to Sweden in order to escape Nazi persecution.

Students: Fifth and sixth graders of mixed abilities.

Reading Purpose: To understand, enjoy, and appreciate a well-written historical novel.

Goal of the Activity: To provide students with information on the geographic and historical setting of the novel so they can better understand and appreciate the situation faced by the main characters.

Rationale: The location and situation faced by the characters in *Number the Stars* may be unfamiliar to many students. Providing them with information regarding the setting, historical events, and time frame of this particular period in history will help them to better conceptualize the people, places, and events in the story. Having this information before they read will give students a solid foundation on which to build meaning as they read.

Procedure: Begin by writing *1943 Copenhagen, Denmark,* on the board. Then write *Germany.* Tell students that something very tragic was happening in Germany in 1943. If students are familiar with the Nazis, Adolf Hitler, and the Holocaust, let them discuss what they know. If not, briefly explain the situation to them. Tell them that during this time German troops began to "relocate" all the Jews of Denmark—to take them to concentration camps. Locate Germany, Denmark, and Copenhagen on a map.

Tell students that the story they will be reading, *Number the Stars* by Lois Lowry, takes place in Copenhagen, Denmark, in this period in history. Explain that the main character AnnMarie isn't Jewish, but her best friend Ellen is. You also may want to give some background information on the Jews and Judaism. Explain that it was because of where and when the Jewish people in the novel lived that they had to face situations calling for personal sacrifice, daring, and courage.

Adapting the Activity: Giving information on places, events, and time frames before students read a selection is appropriate any time these elements play key roles in a story or expository piece and are therefore important to students understanding and appreciating the ideas presented. Many selections, fiction as well as non-fiction, revolve around important historical events and figures. A few of the selections with which you might choose to use the Places, Events, and Time activity are *Shh! We're Writing the Constitution* by Jean Fritz, *Smoke and Ashes: The Story of the Holocaust* by Barbara Rogasky, *Jackie Robinson: He Was the First* by David Adler, *The Great American Gold Rush* by Rhoda Blumberg, and *George Midgett's War* by Sally Edwards.

Reflection: As you probably noticed, this activity is simple and straightforward. Nevertheless, the information will be quite helpful to some students and crucial to others in their understanding and appreciation of many historical-based texts. Sometimes, students have little or no knowledge about the places, events, and time frames in the selections they are asked to read. At other times, students may have misconceptions about these elements. Even those students who do have fairly well-developed, accurate views can benefit from further information or new insights. Accurate information on places and events can bolster students' reading experiences with historical-based texts, connect their reading to geography and history themes, and provide them with valuable information about the world in which they live.

Activating Background Knowledge
Sample Activity: *Think About It!*

Think About It! uses cooperative learning groups as a forum for students sharing knowledge about a topic in order to stimulate interest and activate prior knowledge.

Selections: *The Ultimate Field Trip 3: Wading into Marine Biology* by Susan Goodman, *Exploring the Deep Dark Sea* by Gail Gibbons, *The Oceans Atlas* by Anita Ganeri, *Down, Down, Down in the Ocean* by Sandra Markle, and other books that explore the wonders of the ocean.

Students: Fourth graders of average to high ability.

Reading Purpose: To add to old knowledge and gain new information about the ocean's features, ocean life, and protecting the ocean.

Goal of the Activity: To pique students' interest in learning more about the ocean prior to a four-week unit on "Exploring the Ocean," to activate their prior knowledge, and to give specific information about the topics of these texts.

Rationale: Sharing what they know about a topic can serve to stimulate interest, activate prior knowledge, and focus students' attention on the material that will be covered in the selections they read.

Procedure: Write the unit topic and subtopics on the chalkboard.

EXPLORING THE OCEAN

Ocean Features   *Ocean Life*   *Protecting the Ocean*

After a motivational activity the previous day involving a marine biologist who brought in slides and ocean artifacts, tell students that they will have an opportunity to learn more about the ocean in the next few weeks. They are going to read several books that talk about the features of the ocean, ocean life, and protecting the ocean. Point out that they know something about the ocean from what they learned from the guest marine biologist and from what they've read or from trips to the ocean. Explain that you'd like them to share that knowledge with each other.

Divide the class into groups of about six students each and appoint a facilitator and recorder for each group. Before the groups meet, talk about what they are to discuss—what they *know* about each of the three topics.

Explain that the facilitator will call on people to tell what they know about each of the topics, and the recorder will write down the information that students share. Briefly review the topics with students, and discuss some of the things they will want to think about for each. For example, you might write these prompts on the board:

Ocean Features: Think about what you would see if you could drain all the water from the ocean.

Ocean Life: Think about all the different kinds of living things that live in the ocean.

Protecting the Ocean: Think about the things that can be harmful to the ocean.

After discussing the prompts, give students about 10 minutes to discuss the three topics. At the end of the discussion time, let the recorder for each group read the responses for each topic. Also, spend a little time evaluating the activity: what worked, what didn't, and how they can improve on the activity.

Adapting the Activity: *Think About It!* can be used to activate knowledge for any selection with a topic or theme that is somewhat familiar to students. For example, you could use *Think About It!* before your ethnically diverse fifth graders read Russell Freedman's *Immigrant Kids,* before your California fourth graders read *Earthquakes* by Seymour Simon, before curious and scientifically inclined third graders read *Forest in the Clouds* by Sneed B. Collard III, or before your ethnically diverse seventh, eighth, or ninth graders read *American Islam: Growing Up Muslim in America* by Richard Wormser.

Reflection: After reading through the sample, you may wonder why we included it under Activating Prior Knowledge rather than Providing Text-Specific Knowledge. Obviously, the activity serves both of these functions, and it serves to build knowledge. It could also be considered a motivational activity, because any sort of social interaction is highly motivating for most students, particularly gregarious 10-year-olds. As we have noted, the various types of SRE activities do sometimes overlap, and that is just fine.

Providing Text-Specific Knowledge

In the previous activity, we assumed that the students had some background knowledge relevant to the topic of the upcoming selection, and our task was to activate it. In providing text-specific knowledge, we assume that students need some of the specific information that is in an upcoming text in order to deal with it adequately. For instance, if eighth graders are going to read a chapter on electricity in a science text, they will probably have some general understanding of electricity but won't know the precise topics covered or how they are organized. In this situation, you might tell them what those topics are and how the author has organized and structured the text. Or perhaps sixth-grade students are going to read the time-travel books *The York Trilogy* by Phyllis Reynolds Naylor. In order to fully understand and enjoy these stories, students will profit from knowing something about time-travel as it is portrayed in these particular stories. Giving them a few details about the sort of time-travel that takes place in the stories can be easily accomplished in a brief prereading discussion.

One way to build text-specific knowledge is to give students a preview of the material they are going to read (Chen & Graves, 1998; Graves, Prenn, & Cooke, 1985). A preview of a reading selection is similar to previews you see of movies and TV shows and can be used with both expository and narrative texts. A preview of an article, textbook chapter, or informational book could include the topics, events, people or places covered, and unusual or difficult vocabulary. In a preview of a novel or short story, you might introduce the setting, characters, and something about the plot.

Building text-specific knowledge can be achieved in a variety of different ways. Here we describe one way of doing so.

Providing Text-Specific Knowledge
Sample Activity: *In a Nutshell*

In a Nutshell uses an outline and deductive and inferential questioning to familiarize students with the content of the text.

Selection: "Waves," *Science in Your World.* This chapter from a science text discusses the physical phenomenon of waves as rhythmic disturbances that transfer energy—mechanical waves involve matter, and electromagnetic waves involve electric and magnetic fields. Some of the topics covered are how waves transfer energy, the properties of waves, and electromagnetic waves, which include radio waves, infrared waves, light, ultraviolet waves, X-rays, and gamma rays.

Students: Seventh graders of mixed abilities in a suburban setting; one English language learner.

Reading Purpose: To gain new understanding about the properties and functions of waves—both mechanical waves and electromagnetic waves.

Goal of the Activity: To give students information on the topics and structure of the text so that they will have a schema in place that includes both the concepts presented in the chapter and the organization of the chapter.

Rationale: Giving students an outline of the material they are going to read provides them with a conceptual framework for understanding and remembering what they read. Also, having them explain what information the outline reveals stimulates inferential and deductive reasoning, a kind of thinking that will serve them well in life as well as with the many other texts they read.

Procedure: Before the lesson, on either a transparency or the chalkboard, write the chapter title and subtitles.

WAVES

How Do Waves Transfer Energy?
Electromagnetic Waves
　　Radio Waves
　　Higher Frequency Waves
　　　Infrared Waves
　　　Light
　　　Ultraviolet Waves
　　　X rays and Gamma Rays
Lasers

Tell students that today you are going to take a look at the topics and subtopics from the chapter on waves before reading it. Tell them that noticing how a chapter is organized can help them to understand the ideas the author is presenting.

Draw students' attention to the outline, and challenge them to pick out the three major topics. Call on a volunteer to read them (*How Do Waves Transfer Energy?, Electromagnetic Waves, and Lasers*). Ask students to explain how they determined that these were the main topics. (They are not indented. Some have subtopics written below them.)

Next, ask students to identify which of the main topics have subtopics. (*Electromagnetic Waves* has the subtopics *Radio Waves* and *Higher Frequency Waves. Higher Frequency Waves* has the subtopics *Infrared Waves, Light, Ultraviolet Waves,* and *X rays and Gamma Rays*) If students are unable to come up with the correct responses, be sure to praise their efforts anyway, then show them the correct responses and how you arrived at them. (Main topics are flush left. Subtopics are indented under the main topic. Sometimes subtopics have subtopics of their own, which are also indented. Subtopics are details that explain more about a topic. For example, a main topic might be compared to a house, subtopics to the rooms in a house, and further subtopics to the objects in the room.)

After this, explain to students that now that they have identified the topics and subtopics in the chapter on waves, they are going to see how much information the author has given on the topic in just these few words. Tell them that they may be surprised at just how much they already know. Starting with the first main topic, guide students to the following conclusions.

Q. What do we know about waves from the statement "How Do Waves Transfer Energy?

A. Waves transfer energy.

Q. What do we know about waves from the topic "Electromagnetic Waves"?

A. Some waves are electromagnetic.

Q. What do we know about waves from the subtopic "Radio Waves"?
A. Some waves are called radio waves.

Q. What do we know about waves from the subtopic "Higher Frequency Waves"?
A. Waves have different frequencies, some higher and some lower. Radio waves probably have a low frequency since they are not listed under the subtopic "Higher frequency Waves."

Q. What do we know about waves from the subtopics "Infrared Waves," "Light," "Ultraviolet Waves," and "X rays and Gamma Rays"?
A. Infrared waves, light, ultraviolet waves, x rays, and gamma waves are all high frequency rays because they are listed as subtopics under "Higher Frequency Waves." Infrared waves probably have the lowest frequency of these waves because they are listed first in the sequence, and gamma rays probably have the highest frequency because they are listed last. (This sequence from lowest to highest can be deduced from the fact that radio waves are listed as a separate topic before the higher frequency waves, and therefore waves listed earlier probably have lower frequencies than the others.)

Q. What do we know about lasers from the topic "Lasers"?
A. Lasers have something to do with waves because they are listed as a topic in the chapter on waves.

Keep the questioning lively. Encourage students to keep thinking and to make inferences from the information given. Praise their participation, and tell students that their efforts now will payoff in their understanding and learning from the chapter on waves.

Adapting the Activity: This activity can be used prior to reading any material that can be outlined easily or in which the author has organized the material into topics and subtopics: textbook chapters, informational trade books, and articles. For instance, chapter 1 of *Garbage! The Trashiest Book You'll Ever Read* by Suzanne Lord would work well for this activity. The titles and subtitles for this chapter are as follows:

Garbage: The Never-Ending Story

What Do We Mean by Garbage?
How Long Has Garbage Been Around?
A Short History of Garbage
What Kinds of Garbage Are There?
    Natural Garbage
    Personal Garbage
    Industrial Garbage
    Hazardous Garbage
    Space Garbage

There is, however, one thing to be on the lookout for in selecting material. Check to see that the heading and subheadings accurately reflect the material the text contains. In some cases, headings turn out not to be good guides to the content of selections.

Reflection: As you probably noticed, there are some difficult concepts presented in this outline. Sometimes the materials your students will be reading offer real challenges. When this is the case, you want students to know that material is sometimes challenging but not impossible. If they approach learning with the attitude that they can successfully understand new ideas and information if they will put forth some extra effort, they will usually find that their efforts are rewarded. When you introduce students to difficult vocabulary and concepts, encourage them not to feel defeated if they don't immediately understand all the concepts. Explain that they will be learning fuller meanings of these terms as they read, that now they are just getting a head start in understanding the material. Also, some students may tend to be complacent and let their classmates do all the talking and all the thinking. Encourage the more reluctant participants, the drifters and dreamers, to participate in the activity. Saying something like "There are some good thinkers in this class we haven't heard from yet. Not everyone may get the chance to speak their answers, but everyone can think their answers. If you're thinking along with us, then you're doing your part."

In showing students the structure and content of the Waves chapter in In a Nutshell, we used a standard outline. Alternately, we could have presented the information as a graphic organizer, a frequently recommended visual display for which Richard and Jo Anne Vacca (1993) provide a convenient description. A possible graphic organizer for the Waves chapter is shown below in Figure 4-1.

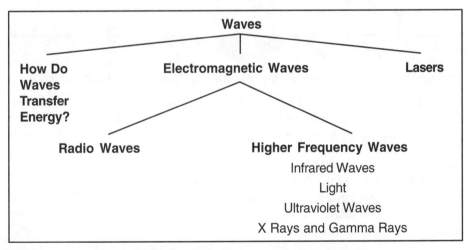

Figure 4-1. Graphic Organizer for "Waves" Chapter

There are at least two reasons you might want to sometimes use a graphic organizer rather than a standard outline. One is that the graphic organizer may be more informative. In the case of the Waves example, the graphic organizer very clearly shows that the topic *Higher Frequency Waves* receives a good deal of attention.

Another reason you might want to occasionally use a graphic organizer instead of an outline is simply to provide some diversity. Sometimes, varying the way you present information can spark interest in both you and your students.

Preteaching Vocabulary

As we stressed in chapter 3, one very important part of the background knowledge that readers possess has to do with their word knowledge. In chapter 2, we defined vocabulary instruction as instruction on words that are new labels for concepts that students already have—for example, teaching *gregarious* to ninth-grade students who already know what *friendly* means. That is the sort of learning task we deal with here.

Activities for preteaching vocabulary focus on helping students to pronounce and define words as they are used in the upcoming selection. The purpose of such activities is to provide students with this information before they read so that when they meet these words in the text they don't have to focus on deciphering individual word meaning but can focus their attention on the ideas the author is presenting. For example, before fourth graders read the "August" entries in Pam Conrad's *Pedro's Journal,* you might plan vocabulary activities that enable students to pronounce and learn a basic meaning for the words *mandarin, rosary, rudder, rigging,* and *trek.*

There are any number of vocabulary activities in which you can engage students prior to their reading a selection. We include two samples here.

Preteaching Vocabulary Sample Activity 1: *Paired Questions*

In *Paired Questions,* targeted words are presented in pairs of questions, one that can be answered affirmatively, and the other negatively. This activity is based on vocabulary instruction suggested by Kameenue, Carnine, & Freschi (1982).

Selection: *Mystery of the Tooth Gremlin* by Bonnie Graves. As 7-year-old Jesse struggles to recover his stolen first tooth *and* to read the requisite books for the class field trip, he discovers the importance of reading and the value of friendship.

Students: Second and third graders of mixed abilities.

Reading Purpose: To understand and enjoy a light-hearted mystery in chapter-book format.

Goal of the Activity: To increase students' understanding and enjoyment of a story by preventing them from stumbling over challenging words and to increase their knowledge and appreciation of word meanings.

Rationale: *Mystery of the Tooth Gremlin* is not a particularly challenging selection for the average second or third grader, but there are a few words that may pose difficulty—words that are in students' oral vocabularies but not their reading vocabularies, or words for which they have an available concept but not a label. Having students pronounce, read, and think about some of the words used in an upcoming story makes the reading task easier and more enjoyable. Also, an activity such as this one, which requires students to apply their knowledge of words to novel situations, encourages critical thinking and appreciation of words.

Procedure: After reading through this short (54-page) chapter book, select half a dozen or so words that might be stumbling blocks for some of your students. Develop paired questions using, for example, these words: gremlin, shrug, detective, imagine, pearl, and admire. One question should yield an affirmative answer, the other a negative answer. Write the paired sentences on the chalkboard:

> *Could a gremlin play a trick on you?*
> *Could you take a bath in a gremlin?*
>
> *Can you shrug a rug?*
> *Can you shrug your shoulders?*
>
> *Can a detective solve a crime?*
> *Can you plant a detective and watch it grow?*
>
> *Can you throw an imagine across the room?*
> *Can you imagine what a tree looks like?*
>
> *Can you wear a pearl?*
> *Can you park your bike in a pearl?*
>
> *Could your teacher admire your good work?*
> *Could your pencil admire dots on your paper?*

Read the sentences to students or have volunteers read them. Have students think about these questions, answer them for themselves, and then discuss the answers together. As a whole group or in small groups, students can compose paired sentences of their own that can be answered "yes" or "no" for each. Write these sentences on the board. For example, for *gremlin*, students might suggest:

> *Could you write a story about a gremlin?*
> *Would you wear a gremlin on your head?*

Adapting the Activity: This activity is readily adaptable to any selection—narrative or expository—that contains words that are in your students' oral vocabularies but perhaps not in their reading vocabularies, or words for which they have an available concept but not a label. For instance, you might introduce *independent, survive, sovereign, scoffed,* and *legislature* in paired sentences before your fifth graders read the first few pages of Jean Fritz's *Shh! We're Writing the Constitution.*

Reflection: We have found that students really enjoy vocabulary activities, especially when they are fun and offer some challenges, too. *Paired Questions* gives students a chance to be a bit silly and have some fun with words while also giving them new insights into word meaning and an appreciation of words themselves. Experimenting with words in this way also helps students to realize that words are not just printed marks on a page, but compact capsules of meaning that can be interesting and fun to use.

Preteaching Vocabulary Sample Activity 2: *Word Clues*

Word Clues introduces potentially difficult vocabulary using context-rich sentences in teacher-created worksheets.

Selection: "Thomas Nast: Political Cartoonist Extraordinaire" by Lynn Evans. Bavarian-born Thomas Nast is responsible for creating some of our most notable and enduring political symbols: the Republican elephant, the Democratic donkey, and Uncle Sam. As a young student, Nast did poorly in all subjects except art, and at 15 he began work as a draftsman for *Frank Leslie's Illustrated Paper.* In 1859, he began his 27-year partnership with *Harper's Weekly,* and together they became a powerful force against political corruption. Fiercely Republican in his views, Nast is credited with the election of many Republican candidates, that is, until 1884, when Nast and *Harper's* supported a Democrat for the first time, presidential candidate Grover Cleveland. In 1886, Nast and *Harper's* ended their association, and the political influence of both declined.

Students: Seventh to ninth graders of average to low ability.

Reading Purpose: To understand and recall some of the important highlights of a historical figure's life and work.

Goal of the Activity: To introduce potentially difficult vocabulary and to give students practice in using context clues to unlock word meaning.

Rationale: This piece, as will be the case with many expository selections, contains vocabulary that will prove difficult for some students. To give students practice in using context clues to unlock word meaning as well as learn the meanings of some key words, a worksheet activity that requires them to focus on context clues can be helpful.

Procedure: Before the lesson, select 5 to 10 words you suspect some of your students may have trouble reading and that are important to understanding the selection. From the Thomas Nast selection, we have chosen these words:

- *draftsman*—This is a relatively easy word to decode, but because students may not be familiar with this occupation and because it is central to understanding the article, we have included it.

- *emigrated*—This polysyllabic word is less easily decodable. Most students will probably have some idea of its meaning when it is seen in context.

- *reform, endorsed, symbol*—These are probably fairly easy to decode. However, understanding their meaning is critical to appreciating the substance and thrust of Nast's career.

- *corruption, critical*—These words may prove difficult at both the decoding and meaning levels, although most students will have a basic notion of the concept they represent.

For each of the words you select, present the word in a context-rich sentence or paragraph that provides clues as to the word's meaning. After this sentence or sentences, create two items that will give students practice in using context clues to unlock the word's meaning. Two examples are given in Table 4-2.

Table 4-2. *Word Clues* Worksheet (Two sample items)

---

1. Target word: *draftsman*

   Mr. Jones called on his best *draftsman* to sketch plans for the new ice arena.

   - Based on the sentence above, a draftsman would probably use pencils and rulers in his or her job.

        true   false

   - Draftsman probably means someone who
        a. runs
        b. draws
        c. teaches
        d. rides

2. Target word: *emigrated*

   Thomas Nast *emigrated* to the United States in 1840 when he was just 6 years old. He and his mother and sister settled in New York City.

   - Based on the sentences above, Thomas Nast probably left his home country and came to live in the United States.

        true   false

   - Emigrated probably means
        a. took clothes and food to poor people
        b. left one country to settle in another
        c. ran a very difficult uphill race
        d. borrowed enough money to buy a house

Before giving students the worksheet, write all the target words and the first item from the worksheet on the board. Explain that these are some of the words they will be encountering in their reading selection. Read the words out loud. Tell students you will give them a worksheet that will help them unlock the meaning of these words and that knowing them will make the article more interesting and understandable. Also tell students that the items on the worksheet will look something like what you have printed on the board. Read the target word and the sentence. Ask what words or phrases provide clues as to the word's meaning. After a brief discussion, complete the true-false and multiple-choice items, explaining the thought processes you go through in deciding which is the correct choice and being sure that students clearly understand the meaning of each word.

Ask if there are any questions, then distribute the worksheets. After students have completed the worksheet, briefly discuss their answers.

Adapting the Activity: In place of individual worksheets, present the material to the whole class using a transparency and overhead projector. Also, instead of you creating the worksheet items, you might choose to get students involved in creating Word Clues themselves. After students have become familiar with the activity, choose less difficult words and let students create their own worksheet items that help unlock word meanings; then let them try out their items on each other.

Reflection: On the one hand, because this type of activity takes quite a bit of teacher preparation time, you will probably want to use it primarily with those students who need the practice in using context clues. On the other hand, because using context clues to unlock word meanings is such a useful skill and many students would profit from becoming more adept with context clues, you may choose to use it fairly frequently. As we noted, students can learn to create instructional items like these themselves. Moreover, letting them do so gives them practice with specific words, practice with context clues, and a chance to write for a real audience—other students. Sometimes you may want to take advantage of these benefits by having your students write vocabulary items of this sort for students in lower grades or by asking teachers with upper grade classes if their students would be interested in developing word clue vocabulary items for your class.

Preteaching Concepts

As we noted in chapter 2, what distinguishes preteaching vocabulary from preteaching concepts is that vocabulary instruction teaches new labels for known concepts, while concept instruction focuses on words that represent new and potentially difficult ideas. *Reef,* for example, is a word that would probably represent a new concept for many second graders, *recession* would probably represent a new concept for fifth graders, and *oligarchy* would probably represent a new concept for eighth graders. As with teaching vocabulary, teaching concepts is also very important.

In addition to thinking about teaching new concepts, it is also important to think of ways to further extend and refine some of the concepts students already know. Knowing a concept is not an on-off matter. Students first develop a relatively simple and unsophisticated understanding of a concept and then gradually refine and extend their knowledge of that concept.

Ideally, your students will be reading material that is composed largely of vocabulary they can handle comfortably yet that also offers some opportunities to learn new words and deepens their knowledge of familiar words and concepts. For example, most of the words and concepts in *The Life and Death of Adolf Hitler* by James Cross Giblin are within the reach of competent eighth or ninth graders. Yet these same readers might need help with such concepts as *Nazi, Gestapo, dictator,* and *resistance.* The vocabulary of Beverly Cleary's *Ramona* books is probably in the comfort zone of competent fourth graders, yet it also offers opportunities to deepen students' knowledge of concepts such as *responsibility, indignant,* and *reassurance.*

In deciding when to preteach concepts, you need to decide just when it's most important to do so. If your eighth graders are going to read *The Life and Death of Adolf Hitler,* they are going to need some prior knowledge of the Nazi occupation and the Resistance and some familiarity with the Gestapo and dictatorships in order to fully understand and appreciate the events in Hitler's life and the motivations and emotions of Hitler, his followers, his victims, and those who resisted him. In this situation, you will need to supply the necessary information in some way. Or, perhaps your fourth graders could benefit from expanding their knowledge of the concept of responsibility. Has responsibility become an issue in your classroom because of some students? In this situation, presenting the word before students read, brainstorming its probable meanings, and then having students notice how the word is used in *Ramona Forever* will help them to understand the concept more fully.

Building students' knowledge and understanding of concepts is often a worthwhile prereading activity. The way you go about presenting concepts before students read will depend on how familiar they are with the concepts and how well they need to know them in order to achieve their reading goals. Additional information on preteaching concepts and the differences between various word-learning tasks is given in Graves (2000). Here we give two detailed examples of activities for preteaching concepts.

Preteaching Concepts Sample Activity 1: *Living Words*

Living Words uses charades and word clustering to activate students' prior knowledge of concepts as well as add to their existing understanding of those concepts.

Selection: *Harriet Tubman: Call to Freedom* by Judy Carlson. This biography chronicles the extraordinary life of Harriet Tubman, a Black woman of invincible spirit and determination who worked unceasingly to bring freedom and justice to Black people. Harriet was born in Maryland in 1820 or 1821 and died in Auburn, New York, in 1913. For almost a century Harriet fought for the ideals she believed in: human dignity, justice, and equality. Strong in body and spirit and empowered by an unshakable faith in God, Harriet led hundreds of slaves to freedom through the Underground Railroad, was an eloquent antislavery spokeswoman, worked in the Union Army as a nurse and a scout, established schools and homes for the poor, and supported the right of Blacks and women to vote.

Students: Sixth graders of low to average ability.

Reading Purpose: To understand and relate to the incidents of Tubman's life and the injustices she fought and triumphed over.

Goal of the Activity: To get students actively thinking about three concepts central to the Tubman biography—*freedom, slavery,* and *justice*—and to build on their existing knowledge of these concepts.

Rationale: To fully understand and appreciate what motivated Tubman to risk life and limb for her own freedom and that of other Black slaves, students need a good understanding of freedom, slavery, and justice. Activating and building on their knowledge of these concepts will help them to make stronger and more lasting connections with the text when they read it. An activity such as charades requires students to think critically and creatively about words in order to dramatize them in a way that will enable others to understand their meaning. The second part of the activity, word clustering, requires students to think about what they know and organize that thinking. Both activities will help students to better understand Tubman's motivations and actions when they read the biography and prepare them to add to their understanding of freedom, slavery, and justice.

Procedure: Before the lesson, write the words *freedom* and *slavery* on two separate slips of paper to give to the students for charades. On another sheet of paper, jot down as many words and phrases you can think of that describe or relate to freedom, slavery, and justice. This is to help you prepare for the word-clustering part of the activity.

To begin, tell students that they are going to play a short game of charades and that the words you have chosen for the game are very important in a book they will be reading. If they don't know how to play, explain that in charades one person tries to convey the meaning of a word or phrase by acting out its meaning while the other members of the group call out their guesses. If the group guesses correctly within the allotted time (2 minutes), it gets a point. Give a sample word such as *beautiful* and let a few students demonstrate how they would act out the word. Next, divide the class into two groups and choose someone to be the first "charader." Show that person a slip of paper with the word *freedom* written on it. Give him about 30 seconds to think about what he will do, then have him act out the word while the group tries to guess it. If someone can guess it in 2 minutes, that group gets the point. If not, give the same word to the first charader in the second group and let her act out the word. If group 2 cannot guess the word, let another person in group 1 act out the word. (Of course, the first charader cannot guess.) Keep charading until the word *freedom* is guessed. Write that word on the chalkboard. Next, show the slip of paper with the word *slavery* on it. Proceed in the same manner as with the word *freedom*.

After the words *freedom* and *slavery* have been guessed and you have written them on the chalkboard, add the word *justice* to the board. Point to the word *freedom* and ask students to give words or phrases that they think of when they hear the word. Write their responses on the chalkboard in clusters, as shown in Table 4-3. Then fill in any gaps in the students' knowledge with the words and phrases you jotted down prior to the lesson. Next, explain how these words and phrases relate to or describe freedom, slavery, and justice.

Table 4-3. Word Clusters

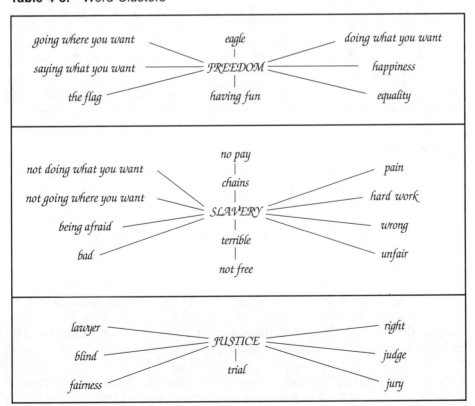

After the students have given their responses and you have included yours, review the concepts. Tell the students that freedom, slavery, and justice are ideas that are central in the biography of Harriet Tubman. Explain that Harriet, who was born in 1820 or 1821, was a slave in Bucktown, Maryland, until she ran away to Philadelphia when she was a young woman. Harriet returned to the South many times to help other Black slaves escape to the northern states and Canada. (Point out these locations to your students on a map.) In fact, Harriet spent her entire life serving the poor and enslaved. Harriet abhorred the idea of slavery and used every ounce of her intellect and energy to make freedom and justice not just words but a reality for Black people.

Adapting the Activity: *Living Words* is an activity that can be used any time you want your students to have a good grasp of concepts that are central to appreciating and understanding the selection that they are going to read. For example, before third or fourth graders read *Sarah, Plain and Tall*, you might have them act out and do a word clustering for *mother, father, wife, husband,* and *children,* as these roles and relationships play an important part in the novel, and expanding their understanding of them will add to your students' appreciation of the story.

Reflection: The concepts of freedom and slavery may prove difficult for some students to act out by themselves. Sometimes it's helpful to let small groups of students, rather than individuals, dramatize these concepts for other groups of students to guess. In this situation, the students would be allowed a few minutes to prepare their charade. You will also want to make it clear to students that the reason they are thinking about these concepts is that they are important to the biography they are about to read. Knowing what they mean will help them to better understand and enjoy the biography.

Preteaching Concepts Sample Activity 2: *Is It, or Isn't It?*

With *Is It, or Isn't It?* students use their prior knowledge to expand, elaborate, and refine a concept by identifying and creating examples and nonexamples of that concept.

Selection: "Rainy Season" by Nikki Grimes, from *Is It Far to Zanzibar?*

Students: Fourth graders of mixed abilities.

Reading Purpose: To visualize, understand, and enjoy a humorous poem.

Goal of the Activity: To help students enjoy the humor in "Rainy Season" and to introduce the concept of exaggeration as a literary device.

Rationale: Expanding and enriching students' understanding of exaggeration is a worthwhile activity in order to appreciate the humor in this poem.

Procedure: Say to your students, "I was so sleepy when I woke up this morning, it took half an hour to open my eyes. Then my cat meowed so loud, I'm sure he woke my sister in California. When I finally got out of bed, I tripped over a pile of dirty clothes 5 feet tall that my husband left on the floor!" You'll probably get a few odd looks and a couple of snickers from your students. Good— they're listening. Talk about what you said and why some people laughed. (It sounded silly: A pile of laundry wouldn't be 5 feet high; cats don't meow that loudly.) If the word *exaggeration* doesn't come up, write it on the chalkboard. Explain to the students that you are exaggerating what really happened that morning; you made everything "bigger" than it really was. Authors sometimes do that to make a point or to add humor to their writing. Next, show students how to change factual statements into exaggerations. First, ask them to give some factual statements, and write these on the chalkboard. For example:

> *Drew invited lots of people to his party.*

> *Jill loves the water.*

> *Mrs. Roney wears big earrings.*

Then show how to make these statements into exaggerations by taking the truth in these statements and stretching it. For example:

> *Drew invited the whole world to his party.*

> *Jill's in the water so much she's grown gills.*

> *Mrs. Roney wears earrings the size of wagon wheels.*

After giving these examples of exaggeration, write a few nonexamples of exaggeration on the chalkboard and have the students suggest how you might turn these statements into exaggeration.

> *Tania has a huge bug collection.—Tania has a bug collection the size of a house.*

> *The baby cried.—The baby cried buckets of tears.*

> *Damien likes ice cream cones.—Damien would walk 100 miles across a hot desert for an ice cream cone.*

Tell students that Nikki Grimes, the author of a book of poetry called *Is It Far to Zanzibar?* uses exaggeration in many of her poems. The poem "Rainy Season" is a good example. When students read the poem, they will discover how she uses exaggeration. You may also want to tell students that the literary term for exaggeration is *hyperbole.*

Adapting the Activity: This activity can be modified to use before reading almost any selection with an important central concept—either a literary device such as exaggeration or irony or a concept such as friendship or honesty. For example, before reading Bruce Brooks's *Everywhere*, Nina Ring Aamundson's *Two Short, One Long*, or Margaret Wild's *The Very Best of Friends,* students could create examples and nonexamples of the concept *friendship*. Giving examples and nonexamples of *tragedy* could help to increase students' perceptions and understanding of the novel *Cousins* by Virginia Hamilton or *Bridge to Terabithia* by Katherine Paterson. Before reading an informational article on drug abuse, eighth-grade students might list examples and nonexamples of drugs. Sometimes the concepts you choose to have students work with will appear in the piece itself, and sometimes they won't. For example, the word *exaggeration* doesn't appear in "Rainy Season," and such words as *discrimination, freedom,* and *justice* may not be used in a story that illustrates those ideas.

Reflection: Having students engage in this kind of activity, giving examples and nonexamples of a concept, not only provides an opportunity to expand their understanding of that concept but also gives them the chance to practice using their analytical and critical thinking skills. First, they must think about the attributes of a concept (analyze it), then come up with some examples that clearly represent or illustrate that particular concept and others that clearly do not. In addition, as Dorothy Frayer (Frayer, Fredrick, & Klausmeier, 1969) has shown in her excellent model for teaching concepts (also described in Graves, Juel, & Graves, 2001), truly understanding what something *is* entails understanding what it is *not*. Thus, giving students opportunities to consider both examples and nonexamples of concepts will sharpen their understanding of key concepts and begin to give them a sense of what it means to know a concept well.

Prequestioning

Posing questions before students read a selection gives them something to look for as they read. Thus, questions both direct attention and prompt students to be active, inquisitive learners. For example, one student might pick up the novel *Miracles on Maple Hill* by Virginia Sorenson, read the title, and ask, "I wonder what kind of miracles could happen on Maple Hill. What's Maple Hill, anyway? A hill? A town? What?" Of course, others students may pick up the same novel and begin reading without posing any sorts of questions. Initially, teachers need to prompt these students with questions, partly to help them deal with the upcoming selection and partly to model the process of asking questions. The long-term goal, of course, is to get students in the habit of asking questions.

In chapter 6, we discuss in detail the various kinds and levels of questioning you might involve students in after they read a selection: questions that prompt students to demonstrate an understanding of what they have read; questions that ask students to apply, analyze, synthesize, or evaluate information or ideas; and questions that encourage creative, interpretive, or metacognitive thinking. Questions posed *before* students read a selection can also prompt them to think on these various levels. In the sample activity that follows, questions asked before students read a selection encourage them to think analytically, critically, and creatively.

Prequestioning Sample Activity: *What Do You Want to Know?*

In *What Do You Want to Know?* students generate their own questions about a story and then write their personal responses to a teacher-generated question on a reader response chart.

Selection: *Journey* by Patricia MacLachlan. *Journey* is a compact, well-crafted novel about an 11-year-old boy whose anger and grief over his mother's abandonment is eventually replaced by acceptance and trust. When Journey's mother leaves him and his sister Cat with their grandparents, he is deeply hurt by her abandonment and struggles to understand her motivation. With the help of his grandfather's photography, as well Journey's own detective work with a box of torn photographs, Journey is able to piece together his past. These photographs help him to understand the present and give him hope for the future.

Students: Fifth and sixth graders of average to high ability.

Reading Purpose: To read and enjoy a sensitive, well-crafted piece of literature and to make personal connections with the thoughts and emotions of the main character.

Goal of the Activity: To focus students' attention by having them generate their own questions about the text and to also consider a specific question for the reader response chart that will help them to connect with the thoughts and emotions of the main character.

Rationale: Having students generate their own questions about a story establishes a strong, well-motivated purpose for reading. Moreover, encouraging students to give their personal responses to a teacher-posed question about a piece of literature can serve a number of other purposes. One is to help students feel secure in their response to a particular work and not be dependent on someone else's response. Another is to encourage respect for the unique responses of others. A third is to help students recognize the common elements in people's responses to the same piece of literature.

Procedure: Before students read the novel, bring in a camera and some pictures of yourself and your family. Show the camera and photos to your students and explain that a camera and photographs play a significant role in Patricia MacLachlan's novel *Journey*. Mention also that you will be using both a camera and photographs for a classroom literature project.

Explain that two of the main characters in *Journey* have unusual names. The protagonist, an 11-year-old boy, is in fact named Journey, and his older sister's name is Cat. They live on a farm with their grandmother and grandfather. Ask students to speculate on why a camera and family photographs might be important to the characters in the story. After students have discussed their ideas, tell them that when they go home that day you want them to look through their family photos and bring in a favorite picture of themselves to school. Tell them that you also will be taking their picture at school. Explain that the photos they bring in and the pictures you take will be used for a special project. At this time, display the reader response chart illustrated in Figure 4-2.

What Do YOU Think?

Title: | Journey | Author: | Patricia   MacLachian |

Question: | How did photographs help Journey? |

Erik	Jessica	Julie	Derek	Sarah
Emily	Josh	Rueben	Jenny	Matt
Molly	Sean	Britta	Jessica	Dawn
Brian	Roberto	Jake	Nassim	Gretchen

Figure 4-2.   What Do You Think? Reader Response Chart

Tell students that the chart will give them an opportunity to share their responses to *Journey* and to other stories and poems they read. The chart will also let them see how other people respond. The question they are going to consider is "How did photographs help Journey?"

Next, read the following two quotes found at the beginning of the novel:

> It is our inward journey that leads us through time—forward or back, seldom in a straight line, most often spiraling.
>
>   —Eudora Welty, *One Writer's Beginnings*

> Photography is a tool for dealing with things everybody knows about but isn't attending to.
>
>   —Emmet Gowin, *On Photography* by Susan Sontag

After you read the quotes, read the one-page introduction that precedes the first chapter. This describes the scene in the barn in which the mother leaves Cat and Journey. She tells Journey that she will be back, but after she has gone Journey's grandfather tells him that his mother won't return. Journey then hits his grandfather.

Have students generate questions from this scenario that they hope will be answered in the story. Write their questions on the board. Some of these might include: Why was Journey's mother leaving? Why did Journey hit his grandfather? How did Cat feel? What is grandfather going to do?

Adapting the Activity: Having students generate their own questions prior to reading is an activity that can be used before reading any kind of selection, narrative or expository. The reader response chart can also be used to publish student responses to any kind of reading material. Questions can focus on feelings such as "What part of the story made you feel saddest and why?" and "How do you think the character felt when . . .?" or speculation such as "Why do you think the author . . . ?" and "If there were another chapter in the book, what do you think the main character would do?" or interpretation such as "What do you think is the story's main theme?" The questions, whatever they are, should function to get students to think and respond.

Reflection: As you may have noticed, this activity accomplishes a number of prereading functions that lead up to the question-generating activity and the reader response chart. First, you do a bit of motivating with props (photos and a camera), then you provide text-specific knowledge with a short preview of the book and ask students to predict how a camera and photographs might be important in the story. Next, you relate the reading to the students' lives by asking them to bring photos of their own family to school to share. By introducing the reader response chart, you are also preparing the foundation for during-reading and postreading activities. As we noted at the beginning of the chapter, when you plan and implement scaffolded reading activities, this kind of overlapping will very often occur, and it should.

Predicting

Consider again the novel *Miracles on Maple Hill,* which we mentioned in discussing prequestioning. Let us say that the student who selected this novel from your library shelf reads the title and looks at the cover illustration. "Hmm," he thinks to himself, "*Miracles on Maple Hill.* I bet the miracles have something to do with maple syrup." That student, of course, is making a prediction about the story. When he reads, he will be looking to see if he is correct, if the miracles do indeed have something to do with maple syrup.

Predicting activities encourage students to speculate about the text based on various prompts: illustrations, titles or subtitles, key words from the text, character names or descriptions, or short excerpts from the text. After students make their predictions, one of their reading purposes will be to see if their predictions are accurate.

Encouraging students to make predictions about an upcoming selection serves at least two purposes. Not only does it focus their attention and give them a purpose for reading, it also models a useful reading strategy, one they can employ on their own with a variety of texts. Of course, the goal is to encourage reasoned predictions based on the information available, not wild guessing. Thus, predicting should often be accompanied by a thoughtful discussion of what prompted the predictions and how certain or speculative the predictions are.

Predicting Sample Activity: *I Predict*

I Predict uses visual cues from illustrations to stimulate students' curiosity and assist them in making predictions about a text's content and in setting purposes for reading.

Selection: *Starfish* by Edith Thacher Hurd. *Starfish* is a science concept book suitable for children in kindergarten through second grade. It tells about where starfish can be found and how they move, eat, and grow.

Students: First graders of mixed abilities.

Reading Purpose: To gain appreciation for the unique qualities of the starfish.

Goal of the Activity: To pique students' interest and to encourage them to make predictions about the book so they will have some definite purposes for reading.

Rationale: Predicting content is a natural and very appropriate prereading strategy for many informational selections. This science picture book is no exception. Students' inherent curiosity about animals can easily be channeled toward the selection's content by asking appropriate questions and leading students to make their own predictions. These predictions then become the purposes for students' reading.

Procedure: Before students read the book, hold up the picture on the cover showing a starfish on a rock or a piece of coral surrounded by other sea creatures and plants. Cover up the title of the book and ask students to predict what the book is about (starfish). Uncover the title, *Starfish*, and say the word.

Next, ask students what they might expect to learn in a book about starfish and what they predict this book will be about. Write students' responses on the board under the heading *What We Might Find Out About Starfish*. Possible responses include: *what they eat, where they live, what they do, how big they are*.

After several predictions have been made, ask students what it is they would most like to know about starfish. Give them a few minutes to think about this, and then review the predictions you have written on the board. Then tell students you are going to read the book aloud to find out how accurate their predictions were. Say that after you are done reading, you will talk about what they found, to see if their predictions about what they would learn were accurate.

Adapting the Activity: Using the cover illustration from a book or other visual aids to stimulate students' curiosity about a reading selection in order to make predictions about that selection is a technique that can be used effectively for almost any type of reading material. If appropriate illustrations don't accompany the selection itself, you can provide other types of materials: magazine illustrations, slides, photos, and concrete objects. For example, before fourth-grade students read Paul Goble's *Her Seven Brothers*, the Native American tale of a quill-working girl and her seven brothers who make bags, furniture, and clothing with beautiful embroidery of dyed porcupine quills, you might want to bring in porcupine quills or perhaps even an actual example of something embroidered with porcupine quills. The students might then predict why porcupine quills might be important to the story or why anyone would want to beautify objects with porcupine quills. Fifth-grade students might look at the jacket cover of *The Great Gilly Hopkins* by Katherine Paterson (which pictures Gilly with a huge bubblegum bubble about to burst and covering her face) and predict what kind of a person Gilly is.

Reflection: Ideally, predicting activities such as this one will prompt students to make similar kinds of predictions when reading on their own. You can encourage such predicting by saying things such as "Making predictions before reading and while you read can make reading more fun, because predicting is kind of like playing a guessing game. Maybe you're reading a story in which the author shows a character running a lot. When it comes to a point in the plot when a race is about to take place, you make a prediction based on what you know. 'I bet that character will win the race because she's had so much practice.' After she does win, you can congratulate yourself: 'Nice job. I was right!'"

Direction Setting

Direction setting is a third alternative to use as a focusing activity. Direction setting typically comes at the end of your prereading activities and functions as the final word of direction and encouragement you give to readers. Direction setting activities tell students what it is they are to attend to while they read. Sometimes you'll use oral instructions: "Read the story to find out if your predictions are correct." At other times, you'll want to write on the board, create a chart, or use a handout so students can reflect on them or refer back to them.

As the following two activities illustrate, direction-setting activities often follow other prereading activities and are typically brief and to the point.

Direction Setting Sample Activity 1:
Looking for Old, Looking for New

Looking for Old, Looking for New is designed to follow the *Think About It!* activity (pp. 76) and focuses students' attention on finding examples of topics they discussed in their groups and new information presented in the reading selections.

Selection: *Exploring the Deep Dark Sea* by Gail Gibbons, *The Ultimate Field Trip 3: Wading Into Marine Biology* by Susan Goodman, *The Oceans Atlas* by Anita Ganeri, and other books that explore the wonders of the ocean.

Students: Fourth graders of average to high ability.

Reading Purpose: To add to old knowledge and gain new information about the ocean's features, ocean life, and protecting the ocean.

Goal of the Activity: To increase comprehension by having students connect what they have learned in the *Think About It!* prereading activity to what is presented in the texts.

Rationale: After having engaged in the *Think About It!* activity, students are aware of the topics discussed in these trade books. However, they will still benefit from an additional reminder of what to attend to as they read. Giving students specific directions as to what they should look for *just before* they begin reading is another way to reestablish a purpose for reading and focus their attention on salient aspects of the text. Doing so will help to improve both understanding and recall.

Procedure: After you have completed the *Think About It!* activity, give each student a sheet of lined paper and tell them to fold it in half, making two columns. At the top of the left column have them write *Old Information*. At the top of the right column have them write *New Information*. Tell students as they read their first ocean book (the choice is theirs to make which book they read first) that they are to look for those features they discussed in their groups and for new ideas that they didn't discuss. Encourage students to jot down information in the appropriate column as they read—previously discussed ideas in one column and new information in the other. Tell them they will have a chance to discuss their findings when they finish reading the book.

   Proceed in a similar manner with the remaining two ocean books, discussing what students discovered in their reading and evaluating the importance of the features and issues they discussed beforehand and those found in the selection.

Adapting the Activity: *Looking for Old and Looking for New* can be used as a direction-setting activity any time the prereading activity includes having students discuss or write about what they know about the topics of a selection before reading it. As we mentioned in the *Think About It!* activity, you could also use *Looking for Old and Looking for New* when your ethnically diverse fifth graders read Russell Freedman's *Immigrant Kids,* your California fourth graders read *Earthquakes* by Seymour Simon, your curious and scientifically inclined third graders read *Forest in the Clouds* by Sneed B. Collard III, or your ethnically diverse seventh, eighth, or ninth graders read *American Islam: Growing Up Muslim in America* by Richard Wormser.

Reflection: This activity provides a good opportunity for students to work on critical thinking skills. When you discuss what students have recorded, they should be encouraged to look carefully and thoughtfully at the information they have chosen to record, identify what is more and less important in what they have recorded, and discuss why some information is more important than other information.

Direction Setting Sample Activity 2: *Looking for Answers*

Looking for Answers follows the *What Do You Want to Know?* activity (p. 93) and serves to focus students' attention on finding answers to the questions they generated prior to reading the story and toward considering the question posed for the reader response chart.

Selection: *Journey* by Patricia MacLachlan. (See description on page 93.)

Students: Fifth and sixth graders of average to high ability.

Reading Purpose: To read and enjoy a sensitive, well-crafted piece of literature and to make personal connections with the thoughts and emotions of the main character.

Goal of the Activity: To improve understanding and enjoyment of the story by focusing on finding answers to student-generated questions and to focus student thinking along the lines of the story's theme.

Rationale: Reviewing the questions that students posed prior to reading a selection, reminding them to think about these questions as they read, then after they have read, discussing whether or not their questions were answered helps students make meaningful connections with the text and improve their comprehension and recall of text ideas.

Procedure: After you have finished with the *What Do You Want to Know?* activity, tell students to read the first chapter of *Journey* to find out the answers to their questions (which you have written on the board). Ask them to jot down answers as they come across them in the text. After students have finished the first chapter, give them the chance to discuss whether their questions were answered and if they were answered in the way they expected them to be. This discussion might take place in the large group, in small groups, or in pairs.

At the end of the discussion on the first chapter, but before students begin to read the remainder of the novel, remind them that as they read the novel they should be thinking about the question "How did photographs help Journey?" so that when they finish they can write a short response for the reader response chart. Tell them to pause after each chapter and reflect on that question, writing down any ideas they have, either in journals or on a sheet of paper you provide for that purpose.

Adapting the Activity: *Looking for Answers* can be used any time that questions—either student generated or teacher generated—have been posed prior to reading a selection. Sometimes you may want to give general directions, such as having students pause at the end of a section or chapter to think about or write down their answers. At other times you may want to give more specific guidance by giving page numbers or even specific paragraphs that contain the information that students are seeking. The more difficult or obscure the text and the less open to interpretation the questions, the more helpful specific directions will be.

Reflection: You will probably have noticed that although this activity is quite simple and straightforward, it overlaps not only with another prereading activity but also with during-reading (silent reading) and postreading (discussion after reading the first chapter) activities. While all pre-, during-, and postreading activities are tied to each other in one way or another, it is particularly difficult to consider direction-setting activities without also considering what precedes and follows. Also, as we mentioned at the beginning of this section, direction-setting activities are often quite brief. One purpose they serve is to remind students of what they have done previously, whether it is to find out how the questions they posed are answered, whether or not their predictions are accurate, or how a selection's topic or theme relates to their lives. If they have asked the questions "Why was Journey's mother leaving?", "Why did Journey hit his grandfather?", "How did Cat feel?", and "What is Grandfather going to do?", then a direction setting activity will encourage them to look for answers to these questions in the text.

Suggesting Strategies

Over the past two decades, a number of reading comprehension strategies have been identified as valuable for understanding, remembering, and enjoying text (National Reading Panel, 2000; Pearson, Roehler, Dole, & Duffy, 1992; Pressley, 2000; Snow, 2001). Some of these include using prior knowledge, asking and answering questions, determining what is important, imaging, summarizing, dealing with graphic information, and monitoring comprehension. As we noted in chapter 2, teaching students to use reading strategies is an important part of reading instruction, but it is not a topic we discuss in this book. However, suggesting that students use strategies they have already been taught is discussed here.

A prereading activity you will sometimes want to use consists of reviewing one or more strategies that students have already learned and suggesting that they employ these strategies while reading a specific selection. Such activities encourage students to engage in previously taught strategies as they read, something for which a number of students need prompting. Thus far we have alluded to several strategies in our prereading activities: using prior knowledge, making inferences, determining what is important, using context clues to unlock word meaning, asking and answering questions, and making predictions.

Repeatedly reminding students of strategies they have learned and pointing out selections in which they are particularly appropriate is crucial if students are to actively use them and make them a part of their reading repertoire. For instance, you might suggest that students use imaging as they read, consciously creating pictures in their heads of the people and events in the story or, if there are illustrations in the text, to look carefully at those. If they are reading material that is going to be important for them to remember, you might have them summarize each paragraph or subtopic. You might also have them look for the most important point in each section of an article or textbook chapter.

Suggesting strategies is by no means meant to take the place of strategy instruction. Teaching students about strategies, what they are and when and where to use them, and providing practice in their use requires in-depth, long-term instruction, the sort discussed in Graves et al. (2001). However, once students have learned strategies, they should be encouraged to apply them when appropriate. The last sample activity in the chapter encourages students to use strategies they have been taught previously.

Suggesting Strategies Sample Activity: *A Quick Look*

With *A Quick Look,* students skim a selection in order to build a conceptual framework before reading it.

Selection: "Communities," chapter 5 in the informational trade book *The Wigwam and the Longhouse* by Charlotte and David Yue. This chapter provides a substantial amount of information about the Woodland Indians' communities, focusing on the types of settlements they had, the organization of their families, the food they ate and how it was obtained and prepared, their clothing, recreation, art, technology, festivals, work, and warfare.

Students: Fifth graders of average ability.

Reading Purpose: To understand and remember important aspects of the community life of the Woodland Indians.

Goal of the Activity: To encourage students to use skimming as a prereading strategy for understanding and remembering information.

Rationale: In many informational texts, the large number of names, dates, and facts can overwhelm readers. Establishing a framework for these facts and figures before tackling the text itself can aid students in making sense of the material as well as remembering it. One strategy for building this framework is to skim through the material before reading to try to determine the general thrust of the selection and some of the major topics it includes.

Procedure: Before students read the chapter, remind them that it is sometimes helpful to skim a chapter before reading it. In skimming they should look for clues such as headings, boldface type, pictures, graphs, and other information that stands out or looks important. Remind them that they are trying to find out what sort of information is being presented before they actually read the chapter. Explain that doing this will help them to better understand and remember the material.

Have students turn to the chapter in their books. Ask for a volunteer to read the chapter title, and write the title "Communities" on the board. Tell students that chapter titles help to point our attention in the right direction, and ask them what the title alone tells them about what they might learn in this chapter. Then write their responses on one side of the board and explain that you will compare these with what they actually find in the chapter.

Tell students to take a few minutes now to skim the entire chapter, and explain that after they have finished they will have the chance to discuss their findings. They might also want to jot down some notes.

After students have skimmed the chapter, call on a volunteer to find and read the first heading (Settlements). Write that heading on the board. Then, ask other students to read the remaining headings and add those to the board.

Communities

Settlements
Families and Kinships
Food
Clothing
Art and Technology
Recreation
Festivals and Work
Warfare

Ask students what else besides headings suggests the chapter's content. Some of their responses should be *drawings, illustrations,* and *bold print.* Ask them to briefly explain what these items told them about the chapter's content. (The drawing on page 51 shows how a typical settlement was set up; the illustrations on page 70 identify and name the various types of games the Woodland Indians had.)

Review the expectations students had given from the title alone (those written on one side of the board), and supplement or modify these with the new information students gleaned from skimming the chapter. Then, have students read the chapter, fitting specific information from the chapter into the framework they have created for understanding it.

Adapting the Activity: Skimming a selection before reading it is particularly useful when the text is divided into sections with titles and subtitles or has illustrations, graphs, sidebars, or other types of supplementary material that highlight important information. This means that skimming is appropriate for many of the expository material students read in school: articles, textbook chapters, biographies, informational books. "Your Body Systems and Health," from *Health: Focus on You* by Linda Meeks and Philip Heit is an example of an excellent chapter for skimming because it outlines with its subheadings, accompanying photos, and diagrams each of the body's nine systems. With just a brief skimming of the chapter, ninth-grade students will have a framework in place with which to learn about the nine body systems: skeletal, muscular, integumentary, nervous, endocrine, digestive, circulatory, respiratory, and urinary.

Reflection: Here we make three points. First, you may have noticed some similarity between this surveying activity and *In a Nutshell*. Both include an outline of the major topics of a selection. However, in *In a Nutshell* the teacher produces the outline, whereas in *A Quick Look* students use the strategy of surveying to create their own outline. Second, surveying is an excellent and very widely applicable activity. In fact, when students are reading expository material, if they are reading it to learn something and not just to be entertained, and if they want to be efficient in their learning, then surveying is definitely a must. Trying to glean information from a text without first getting an idea of what information it contains and how the text is organized is nearly futile. Third, even though the activity we present here is a fairly lengthy one that might take 30–40 minutes of class time, we still view the role you are playing here as that of suggesting a strategy rather than initially teaching it. Teaching students who do not know how to survey to become skilled at surveying requires much more protracted and rich instruction than that described here.

Prereading Activities: A Final Word

As we said at the outset, prereading activities serve to motivate and prepare students to read. Sometimes just one brief prereading activity will be sufficient to ensure a successful reading experience for your particular group of students with the specific selection they will be reading. At other times you may want to provide your students with several prereading activities. As always with SREs, what you plan will be determined by the selection itself, the overall purpose for reading the selection (information or enjoyment), and your students' strengths and needs. Prereading activities must also be coordinated with the activities students will be doing during and after reading.

The more students want to read, the better they understand the purposes for which they are reading, and the more background information they bring to a text, the more they will both contribute to and take from what they read. Every reading experience will be easier, more enjoyable, more productive, and more memorable if students are motivated and prepared.

References

Bransford, J. D., Brown, A. L., & Cocking, R. R. (2000). *How people learn: Brain, mind, experience, and school.* Washington, DC: National Academy Press. Expanded edition. Excellent summary of cognitive research on learning.

Chen, Hsiu-Chieh, & Graves, M. F. (1998). Previewing challenging reading selections for students for whom English is a second language. *Journal of Adolescent and Adult Literacy, 41,* 370–371. Experimental study showing the value of previewing for English language learners.

Frayer, D. A., Fredrick, W. C., & Klausmeier, H. J. (1969). *A schema for testing the level of concept mastery* (Working Paper No. 16). Madison, WI: Research and Development Center for Cognitive Learning. The original source of the Frayer model for teaching concepts.

Graves, M. F. (2000). A vocabulary program to complement and bolster a middle-grade comprehension program. In B. M. Taylor, M. F. Graves, & P. van den Broek (Eds.), *Reading for meaning: Fostering comprehension in the middle grades* (pp. 116–135). New York: Teachers College Press. Description of a comprehensive vocabulary program.

Graves, M. F., Juel, C., & Graves, B. B. (2001). *Teaching reading in the 21st century* (2nd ed.). Boston: Allyn & Bacon. Comprehensive elementary reading methods text book.

Graves, M. F. , Prenn, M. C., & Cooke, C. L. (1985). The coming attraction: Previewing short stories to increase comprehension. *Journal of Reading, 28,* 549–598. A clear description of how to write previews and a summary of much of the research on previewing.

Kameenui, E. J., Carnine, D. W., & Freschi, R. (1982). Effects of text construction and instructional procedures for teaching word meanings on comprehension and recall. *Reading Research Quarterly, 17,* 367–388.

National Reading Panel. (2000). *Teaching children to read.* Bethesda, MD: National Institute of Child Health and Human Development. Authoritive review of the research on beginning reading.

Pearson, P. D., Roehler, L. R., Dole, J. A., & Duffy, G. G. (1992). Developing expertise in reading comprehension. In S. J. Samuels & A. E. Farstrup (Eds.), *What research has to say about reading instruction* (2nd ed, pp. 145–199). Newark, DE.: International Reading Association. Presents an up-to-date view of reading comprehension instruction, with particular emphasis on teaching comprehension strategies.

Pressley, M. (2000). What should reading comprehension instruction be the instruction of? In M. Kamil, P. Mosenthal, P. D. Pearson, & R. Barr (Eds.), *Handbook of reading research,* (vol. 3, pp. 545–561). Mahwah, NJ: Erlbaum. Consideration of a variety of component parts that constitute a comprehensive instructional program aimed at developing reading comprehension.

RAND Reading Study Group (2002). *Reading for understanding: Toward an R&D program in reading comprehension.* Santa Monica, CA: Rand Education. Also available on-line at http://www.rand.org/multi/ achievementforall/reading/. A widely respected summary of what we know about reading comprehension.

Vacca, R. T., & Vacca, J. A. L. (1993). *Content area reading* (4th ed.). New York: HarperCollins. Provides a clear and concise description of structured overviews with quite a few examples.

Children's Literature

Aamundsen, N. R. (1990). *Two short, one long.* Boston: Houghton Mifflin. 102 pages.

Adler, D. A. (1989). *Jackie Robinson: He was the first.* New York: Holiday House. 48 pages.

Anaconda. G. (1999). *Charo: The Mexican cowboy.* San Diego: Harcourt Brace. 32 pages.

Avi. (1990). *The true confessions of Charlotte Doyle.* New York: Orchard. 215 pages.

Baker, L. (1990). *Life in the rainforests.* New York: Scholastic. 31 pages.

Blumberg, R. (1989). *The great American gold rush.* New York: Bradbury. 135 pages.

Brooks, B. (1990). *Everywhere.* New York: HarperCollins. 70 pages.

Conrad, P. (1991). *Pedro's Journal.* Honesdale, PA: Boyds Mills Press. 80 pages.

Carlson, J. (1989). *Harriet Tubman: Call to freedom.* New York: Fawcett Columbine. 116 pages.

Chin, C. (1993). *China's bravest girl: The legend of Hua Mu Lan.* San Francisco: Children's Press. 32 pages.

Cleary, B. (1984). *Ramona forever.* New York: Morrow. 182 pages.

Clements, A. (1996). *Frindle.* New York: Simon & Schuster. 105 pages.

Collard, S. B. III. (2000). *Forest in the clouds.* Watertown, MA: Charlesbridge. 32 pages.

Edwards, S. (1985). *George Midgett's war.* New York: Scribner. 138 pages.

Evans, L. (1988 November). "Thomas Nast: Political Cartoonist Extraordinare," *Cobblestone,* 9, 11.

Freedman, R. (1980). *Immigrant kids.* New York: Dutton. 72 pages.

Fritz, J. (1987). *Shh! We're writing the Constitution.* New York: Putnam. 64 pages.

Ganeri. A. (1994). *The oceans atlas.* New York: DK. 64 pages.

Gibbons, G. (1999). *Exploring the deep dark sea.* Boston: Little, Brown. 32 pages.

Giblin, J. C. (2002). *The life and death of Adolf Hitler.* New York: Clarion. 256 pages.

Goble, P. (1988). *Her seven brothers.* New York: Bradbury. 32 pages.

Goodman, S. (1999). *The ultimate field trip 3: Wading into marine biology.* New York: Simon & Schuster. 48 pages.

Graves, B. B. (1997). *Mystery of the tooth gremlin.* New York: Hyperion. 54 pages.

Grimes, N. (2000). "Rainy season." In *Is it far to Zanzibar?* New York: Lothrop, Lee & Shepard. 32 pages.

Hamilton, V. (1990). *Cousins.* New York: Philomel. 125 pages.

Hirschfelder, A. (1986). *Happily may I walk: American Indian and Alaska natives today.* New York: Scribner. 152 pages.

Houston, J. (1977). *Frozen fire.* New York: McElderry. 149 pages.

Hurd, E. T. (2000). *Starfish.* New York: HarperCollins. 33 pages.

Karr, K. (2000). *The boxer.* New York: Farrar. 176 pages.

Lord, S. (1993). *Garbage! The trashiest book you'll ever read.* New York: Scholastic. 102 pages.

Lowry, L. (1989). *Number the stars.* Boston: Houghton Mifflin. 137 pages.

MacLachan, P. (1985). Sarah, plain and tall. New York: Harper & Row. 64 pages.

MacLachlan, P. (1991). *Journey.* New York: Delacorte. 83 pages.

Markle, S. (1999). *Down, down, down in the ocean.* New York: Walker. 32 pages.

Meeks, L., & Heit, P. (1990). "Your body systems and heath." In *Health: Focus on you.* Columbus, OH: Merrill.

Naylor, P. R. (1980–81) *The York Trilogy.* New York: Macmillan.

Paulsen, G. (1987). *Hatchet.* New York: Bradbury. 195 pages.

Rogasky, B. (1988). *Smoke and ashes: The story of the Holocaust.* New York: Holiday House. 187 pages.

Russell, C. Y. (1994). *First apple.* Honesdale, PA: Boyds Mills. 128 pages.

Simon, S. (1991). *Earthquakes.* New York: Morrow. 32 pages.

Sorensen, V. (1956) *Miracles on Maple Hill.* New York: Harcourt. 180 pages.

Spinelli, J. (1990). *Maniac Magee.* Boston: Little, Brown. 184 pages.

Thesman, J. (1990). *Rachel Chance.* Boston: Houghton Mifflin. 175 pages.

Thomas, J. R. (1998). *Behind the mask: The life of Queen Elizabeth I.* New York: Clarion. 224 pages.

Wild, M. (1990). *The very best of friends.* San Diego: Harcourt Brace Jovanovich. 32 pages.

Wormser, R. (2002). *American Islam: Growing up Muslim in America.* New York: Walker. 130 pages.

Yue, C., & Yue, D. (2000). *The wigwam and the longhouse.* Boston: Houghton Mifflin. 118 pages.

Chapter

5

During-Reading
Activities

During-reading activities, the second set of optional activities in a Scaffolded Reading Experience (SRE), assist students as they are reading. After you have motivated and prepared students to read with prereading activities, the next step is to actually read. Here students will meet and interact with the text. They will begin to extract and construct meaning from the text by reading or, occasionally, by being read to by another. During-reading activities include what students do themselves as well as what you do to assist them in their reading. In chapter 2, we described the five following categories of during-reading activities:

1. Silent reading

2. Reading to students

3. Guided reading

4. Oral reading by students

5. Modifying the text

These categories, of course, reflect only one of many ways to organize and think about during-reading activities. Also, these sorts of activities can sometimes be used as pre- or postreading experiences. For example, reading to students can work as a prereading activity, and oral reading by students can be a postreading activity. As always, we list different types of activities to suggest possibilities, not limit them.

During-reading activities involve students with the text in a way that best suits the students, the text, and their purposes for reading it. Some questions you might ask before designing during-reading activities are as follows: How might the reading task best be accomplished? What might I do to actively involve students with the text? What can I do to help make this material come alive for students as they read? What would make this material more accessible to students? What might students do as they read that will make the text more understandable, memorable, or enjoyable?

Table 5-1 outlines the during-reading activities described in this chapter.

Table 5-1.   During-Reading Activities

Silent Reading	
Reading to Students	*Let's Hear It! (p. 112)*
Guided Reading	*Problem, Solution, Change (p. 115)* *Dear Diary (p. 118)* *Group and Label (p. 121)* *Who, What, When? (p. 124)* *Fill the Grocery Cart, Stack the Cupboard (p. 126)*
Oral Reading by Students	*The Echo (p. 131)* *Radio Show (p. 133)* *Flag It (p. 134)*
Modifying the Text	*Focusing (p. 138)*

Silent Reading

Silent reading will be the most frequent during-reading activity. Reading, obviously, is the primary activity of the scaffold—the raison d'etre—and most often students will be doing this reading silently by themselves. The other activities in the scaffold are designed to support students' reading: to prepare them for it, to guide them through it, and to take them beyond it.

Reading to Students

Although most of the time students will be reading a selection silently, sometimes, it is appropriate for students to have the material read to them. This is particularly true for children who are just beginning to read, but it is also true for experienced readers. If the material cries out to be heard, for whatever reason—because the language is beautiful and inspiring, because students need a good send-off for a lengthy or challenging selection, because the concepts are new and require interpretation—then hearing the words may help students to grasp the material so that when and if they do read it on their own, it will hold more meaning, pleasure, and interest for them.

Reading aloud to your students not only makes certain texts accessible to them, it also provides a model for expressive reading. By reading aloud, you can show your enthusiasm for information, ideas, and language. As storyteller and author Bill Martin Jr. (1992) has said, "A blessed thing happened to me as a child. I had a teacher who read to me."

Because this book deals specifically with reading (as opposed to listening), the sample activity for Reading to Students is done in conjunction with students doing some reading on their own. However, we do not want to miss this opportunity to recommend a powerful approach to reading to kindergarten and primary grade children and to emphasize the importance of reading to children as one critical component of a complete reading program.

The approach we want to recommend is called Text Talk. It was developed by Isabel Beck and Margaret McKeown (Beck & McKeown, 2001; McKeown & Beck, in press) as a way of maximizing the benefits of reading aloud to kindergarten and primary grade children. As Beck and McKeown and others (e.g., Whitehurst et al., 1994) have pointed out, read-aloud experiences are sometimes not as effective in building children's language skills as they could be. Text Talk focuses on using réad alouds to promote comprehension and the development of vocabulary and other language skills. Very briefly, the procedure consists of using texts that are a bit challenging, asking open-ended questions on important aspects of the selection, probing students for further responses when initial responses are brief and incomplete, and teaching widely used yet sophisticated vocabulary. The Beck and McKeown's articles provide much more detail on the approach.

Of course, Text Talk is just one approach to reading aloud, and various approaches can help to achieve a variety of goals. As Jim Trelease (2001) has pointed out so powerfully in *The Read-Aloud Handbook*:

> A large part of the educational research and practice of the last twenty years confirms conclusively that the best way to raise a reader is to read to that child—in the home and in the classroom. This simple, uncomplicated fifteen-minute-a-day exercise is not only one of the greatest intellectual gifts you can give a child; it is also the cheapest way to ensure the longevity of a culture.

We most emphatically agree. Reading to children builds their vocabularies, their knowledge of the world, their knowledge of books and many of the conventions employed in books, and—probably most important—their interest in reading. Moreover, as Camille Blachowicz and Donna Ogle (2001) observe, reading aloud to children "can be one of the most enjoyable times of the day for both a teacher and a class."

Reading aloud to students is one way to demonstrate the beauty and power of language, and for students who struggle with reading on their own or have had little exposure to books, it may be the most significant way. The activity that follows demonstrates both of these functions.

Reading to Students Sample Activity: *Let's Hear It!*

In *Let's Hear It!,* a prose selection that invites student participation is read aloud to students.

Selection: *Sounds All Around* by Wendy Pfeffer. This informational trade book explains how sounds are made and the many purposes they serve.

Students: Second graders of mixed abilities.

Reading Purposes: To understand and enjoy a delightful informational book about sounds and to learn new science vocabulary and concepts.

Goal of the Activity: To pique students' interest in reading about science concepts by demonstrating how ideas can be communicated and learned in an enjoyable and playful way.

Rationale: Reading science books aloud can help students to learn science vocabulary and concepts. By encouraging students' active participation, abstract science concepts can be made more concrete and meaningful.

Procedure: Assemble some sound props on a table—items such as a drum, a rubber band, a harmonica, or other things that will produce a sound. Say to students, "All of these things can make something. Can you guess what it is?" Have students guess what each of these items can make. Next, beat the drum, pull the rubber band tight and pluck it, and blow on the harmonica. If students haven't already guessed prior to your demonstration that all of these objects can make sound, they will now! Talk about sound. How was it made with each object? Was it the same sound or different? Which was the loudest sound? Which was the softest? Why?

Tell students that you are going to read a book aloud to them by Wendy Pfeffer called *Sounds All Around* and that they are going to help make the sounds in the book. After you read the book aloud, they will get to read it on their own and experiment with making sounds.

The first page begins, "Snap your fingers. Clap your hands. Whistle!" After you read these sentences, invite students to make the sounds (*snap, clap,* and *whistle*). As you read through the rest of the book, call on individual students to make the sounds the author writes about—for example, "happy sounds, sad sounds, scary sounds, and mad sounds."

There are also things students can do as you read through the text, things the author suggests. For example, "Feel your throat as you sing, talk, or hum." Or, "Now, be quiet. Feel your throat." Each time students try these activities, ask them to explain what they felt, then read the text that explains the phenomenon. For example, "Your fingertips tingle because your vocal chords shake to make a sound. They shake back and forth very fast. This is called *vibrating.* That makes the air around them vibrate. These vibrations move through the air in waves called *sound waves.*"

Read through the rest of the book, having students produce sounds or do other experiments suggested by the text, taking as much time as you think appropriate.

Adapting the Activity: Not all science trade books will invite the kind of active participation that *Sounds All Around* does, but many will. Other ways to actively involve children with the text is to ask students to repeat certain key lines after you read them or to answer questions in unison. For example, when reading *Spectacular Spiders* by Linda Glaser, you can have children answer the question "How many legs does a spider have?" After reading the phrase "Spider has eight skinny legs with very fine hairs," children can shout out "eight." Then read the phrase again to reinforce their answer. Beware of asking too many questions, however. For a 32-page picture book, about three or four is a good number of questions. Also, when read aloud, picture books about science topics can make difficult or new concepts accessible with engaging prose, colorful illustrations, and photographs. These and other good read-aloud science books for children in grades K–3—such as, *Hello, Fish!: Visiting the Coral Reef* by Sylvia Earle with photographs by Wolcott Henry, *Down, Down, Down in the Ocean* by Sandra Markle, and *Baby Whale's Journey* by Jonathan London—are recommended by Terrence E. Young and Coleen Salley (2000) in "Read-Aloud Science Books."

Older students profit from having books read aloud to them as well, both fiction and nonfiction. Sometimes, reading just the first chapter is enough to motivate students to read the book on their own or to introduce a book that some students might have difficulty getting into by themselves. Because first chapters in novels must accomplish many tasks—establishing the setting and tone of a book, introducing the characters, and beginning the plot—they can frequently be more challenging than the rest of the book. Thus they are a natural place to give students a helping hand. Books for which you might read the first chapter for your students include *Canyons* by Gary Paulsen, *Maniac Magee* by Jerry Spinelli, and *Journey* by Patricia MacLachlan. Each of these books may prove somewhat more challenging than usual for some students. Reading poetry aloud to students is also very appropriate, to prepare them to read poems silently and as an introduction and preparation for performing poetry.

Reflection: *Let's Hear It!* is a straightforward but very useful activity. Your oral reading and soliciting of students' participation and response not only makes the ideas in text meaningful and memorable, it also serves as an enticement for reading in general, as it demonstrates to students what written words are meant to do: inform, entertain, enlighten, and inspire. It's also fun for you and your students.

Guided Reading

Much of the time, particularly with narratives, students will read the material from beginning to end without stopping to record or reflect on what they are reading. The interactions that take place are often personal ones between the reader and the text. As Louise Rosenblatt (1978) has explained, the primary concern with narratives is likely to be with what happens to students as they read rather than what they remember afterwards. Responses to what they have read might be shared after they have read, or perhaps not at all. Sometimes, however, it is appropriate to guide students' reading, to help them focus on, understand, and learn from certain aspects of the text. Guided reading means just that—guiding the thought processes that accompany reading. Guided reading activities can make the reading experience more positive for students, assist students in achieving the deep and lasting understanding critical in today's world (National Research Council, 1999; Perkins, 1992; Snow, 2001), lead students to make connections between ideas in the text, and help them to use their existing experience and knowledge to understand what is presented in the text.

Although guided reading activities are by no means always needed with narratives, they can be very useful. You might think that students would understand and enjoy a story more if they focused their attention on certain aspects of character, setting, plot, or theme. Maybe you want them to be aware of colorful or unusual language, or perhaps you would like them to make personal responses to what they read, make predictions, or consider how they or the characters are feeling. These are all good reasons for designing guided reading activities.

Though useful with narratives, guided reading activities are most frequently used to help students understand and remember the information presented in expository materials. Some general kinds of guided reading activities for expository texts might include the following:

- Having students focus on various organizational patterns of text, such as sequencing, cause and effect, or comparison-contrast

- Encouraging critical thinking by having students note examples of fact and opinion, make inferences, draw conclusions, or predict outcomes

- Leading students to manipulate the text in ways that will help them to better understand and retain key concepts, such as recording main ideas and their supporting details, outlining, summarizing, semantic mapping, or creating time lines

- Having students monitor their understanding of what they read

As with any SRE activities, the value and effectiveness of guided reading will depend on your students, the material they are reading, and the purposes for reading it. Guided reading should get students thinking about and manipulating the ideas and concepts in the material in a way that will help them to understand, enjoy, and remember it better. All five of the sample activities that follow are designed to do just that.

Guided Reading Sample Activity 1: *Problem, Solution, Change*

In *Problem, Solution, Change,* students record in journals what they feel to be any problems the main character faces, solutions to those problems, and changes that took place in the main character because of the problem and solution.

Selection: *The True Confessions of Charlotte Doyle* by Avi. (See description on page 71.)

Students: Sixth to seventh graders of mixed abilities.

Reading Purpose: To read and enjoy an exciting adventure story by focusing on the basic plot elements of problem, solution, and change.

Goal of the Activity: To focus students' attention on the elements of plot as they develop and unfold throughout the novel and to encourage students to make connections between ideas in the text and their knowledge of the world.

Rationale: Having students think about the problems a main character faces, how he or she solves that problem, and what sorts of changes take place within the character because of the problem and resolution can help students to discover one of the most salient features of fiction: characters comfront problems, find ways to solve them, and are changed in the process. Because of the number and magnitude of the dilemmas young Charlotte faces, *The True Confessions of Charlotte Doyle* is an outstanding vehicle for this process.

Procedure: (Ideally, this activity would follow the *Common Threads* prereading activity on page 70 in which students have recorded problems, solutions, and changes in their own lives.) Begin by reading the prologue to the novel aloud.

These three pages are entitled "An Important Warning" and begin, "Not every thirteen-year-old girl is accused of murder, brought to trial and found guilty." The narrator warns the reader that "if strong ideas and action offend you, read no more. For my part I intend to tell the truth as *I* lived it." In this prologue, the reader learns that Charlotte began her story as a proper young lady about to embark on a voyage from England to America. However, the reader is also forewarned that the events that transpired on Charlotte's journey change her drastically and that keeping a journal enabled her to relate "in perfect detail everything that transpired during that fateful voyage across the Atlantic Ocean in the summer of 1832."

If you have done the *Common Threads* prereading activity, remind students of some of their responses and then have them predict what sorts of problems a 13-year-old girl might encounter on a voyage such as Charlotte took, how she might go about solving those problems, and how she might be changed because of them.

Explain that part of the pleasure and purpose of reading literature is to experience adventures and make discoveries through the actions and thoughts of the main characters in a story. In most fiction they read, students will find a character who is faced with a problem. *The True Confessions of Charlotte Doyle* is no exception. This is an adventure-packed novel in which Charlotte is faced with numerous and very difficult problems that she must solve on her own. In the process of dealing with each of these dilemmas she is changed just a bit, until by the end of the novel she is a very different person.

Remind students that Charlotte kept a journal of her experiences, and tell them that they will be keeping a journal as they read the novel. Their journal will focus on Charlotte's problems, solutions, and changes. Explain that keeping their own journal will help them to keep track of these events, and that in doing so they will be able to extend and enrich their own knowledge and explore new ideas along with the main character, Charlotte.

Next, provide students with several sheets of lined paper to serve as their journal. Have them fold the paper in thirds to form three columns. This will allow students to record their ideas regarding Charlotte's problems, solutions, and changes. Bind the pages that will make up each student's journal together in some manner. A simple staple will do, or you might want students to create a front and back cover from construction paper, which they can embellish later.

Before students begin reading the novel and recording Charlotte's problems, solutions, and changes, you might want to read the first chapter aloud and then demonstrate how to make the journal entries. After reading the chapter aloud, have students suggest problems, solutions, and changes. Write these suggestions on the board.

Remind students that there are no right or wrong responses. Anything that they think constitutes a problem, solution, or change should be recorded. Also, sometimes a problem may not have an immediate solution, or any change in Charlotte may not be recognizable at the moment. They may need to read further in the novel to discover solutions and changes, and they may also identify some problems that aren't resolved in the novel.

When students are clear as to what they will be doing, have them begin reading the novel and recording problems, solutions, and changes in their journals.

Tell them that when they finish they will have an opportunity to share what they discover about Charlotte and her adventures.

Adapting the Activity: This type of activity is appropriate for almost any novel in which the main character is faced with numerous problems to solve or obstacles to overcome. Just a few examples are *Cousins* by Virginia Hamilton, *The Wanderer* by Sharon Creech, *Hatchet* and *Soldier's Heart* by Gary Paulsen, *Dixie Storms* by Barbara Hall, *A Hand full of Stars* by Rafik Schami, *The Folk Keeper* by Franny Billingsley, *Number the Stars*, by Lois Lowry, and *Rachel Chance* by Jean Thesman. As a matter of fact, it is probably harder to find novels or short stories that do *not* lend themselves to such an analysis than to find those that do.

Reflection: Although most students will probably have little trouble identifying the problems that come up in the novel, some may find it difficult to identify Charlotte's solutions, and even more will have a hard time finding the changes that took place in Charlotte. It's a good idea to encourage students not to become bogged down looking for precise answers. They should realize that not everyone will see Charlotte's problems, solutions, and changes in the same way and that some solutions may not come until the end of the novel, and some not at all. The idea of the activity is for them to see that problems cry out for solutions and that change is a big part of the problem-solving process. Because fiction mirrors life, it provides an interesting and convenient way to take a look at this process.

It is worth noting the general function this guided reading activity has served, because it is a very useful function and one that guided reading activities can serve fairly frequently. What we have done is to focus students' attention on an aspect of the text that helps them to understand and appreciate this text and that will aid them in appreciating a number of texts they read in the future. We have given them a minilesson similar to those Nancie Atwell (1998) recommends. This certainly has not been a full-blown lesson in which we have attempted to give students a definite strategy for identifying problems, solutions, and changes that often occur in narratives; you may at some time want to provide a more substantial strategy lesson on this topic, which we consider at some length in Graves, Juel, and Graves (2001). At the very least, the minilesson will give students a start in learning to look for such patterns in literature.

Also, this response activity is only one of many types that might be implemented for this selection. Another procedure, a two-column response journal described by Hilda Ollmann (1992), could be used for this novel as well as for many other stories, poems, or expository pieces. When following this procedure, students write quotes from the text in one column and their personal responses to the quotes in another. For example, an entry for chapter 1 in *The True Confessions of Charlotte Doyle* might look like this:

In the text	*In my head*
p. 15. *"'But . . . that would be all men, Mr. Grummage! And . . . I am a girl. It would be wrong!' I cried, in absolute confidence that I was echoing the beliefs of my beloved parents."*	*I know I would feel horrified too if I were in Charlotte's place. To be the only girl with all those men. I'm sure I would have not gone on that ship!*

Response journals of this type are one way to actively involve readers with text and to encourage analytical, evaluative, and creative thinking.

Guided Reading Sample Activity 2: *Dear Diary*

In *Dear Diary* students compose diary entries from the point of view of the pro-tagonist.

Selection: *Harriet Tubman: Call To Freedom* by Judy Carlson. (See description on page 88.)

Students: Fifth graders of mixed abilities and from a variety of ethnic back-grounds.

Reading Purpose: To learn more about the plight of Blacks in America during the mid-1800s and to appreciate and be inspired by the courage, resourceful-ness, and commitment of Harriet Tubman.

Goal of Activity: To help students become involved with the text at a personal and emotional level by identifying with the subject of the biography and to en-courage use of the comprehension skills of summarizing and determining what is important.

Rationale: Writing diary entries that reflect historical events as well as the thoughts and emotions of the protagonist not only requires that the reader sum-marize important events, it also challenges the reader to experience these events through the senses of another person. Such role-playing will encourage empathy and promote comprehension and recall.

Procedure: Read the first chapter of the biography aloud to the students. Then ask them to tell what they learned about Harriet Tubman from this chapter and to give a word or phrase that describes her. Write their suggestions on the chalkboard. Some of their comments might include the following: *a slave, brave, spiritual* or *religious, strong, determined.*

   Explain that the author chose to begin the biography by describing an incident that took place when Harriet Tubman was in her 20s. The next chapter begins with Harriet at age 6, and the chapters that follow proceed in chronological or-der. The last chapter ends with Harriet's death at 93. Tell the students that ev-ery chapter includes much action and vivid details and that these actions and details reveal the extraordinary person that Harriet Tubman was. Then introduce writing diary entries with something like this: "Harriet was illiterate, but she had thoughts and strong opinions that she expressed in both words and actions. Let's pretend that Harriet could read and also express herself in writing. What would she write, and to whom? Harriet had strong feelings about cruelty and injustice. She wanted to see wrongs righted. She wanted to move people to action. She wanted her voice to be heard, but of course at that time it was too dangerous to speak out. Let's say that Harriet decided to pour out her thoughts and feelings in a diary." If students are unfamiliar with diary entries, read a few examples, perhaps from Anne Frank's *The Diary of a Young Girl*. You might also want to allude to Alice Walker's story *The Color Purple*, in which the protagonist works through her pain by writing letters to God. Older students might be familiar with the novel or with the movie.

Ask the students if, after hearing the first chapter, the following letter is one that Harriet might write to Dear Diary.

> *Dear Diary,*
>
> *I have just completed a successful journey on the Underground Railroad. The trip wasn't easy, and I can tell you there were many times I thought I'd be caught or thrown off. But I made it with the help of a lot of kind folks and am now in Philadelphia—a free woman at last.*
>
> *I am going to continue to fight for liberty for my people as long as my strength lasts. I think all people deserve to live in freedom. Don't you think so, too?*
>
> *Your friend,*
>
> *Harriet*

Discuss the letter with the students. Focus on what Harriet chose to write about and why.

As a class, compose another Dear Diary letter for the chapter and write it on the chalkboard. Have students think about what else Harriet may choose to write in her diary and why.

Before students begin reading the biography on their own, tell them that as they read through the book you want them to write a letter from Harriet Tubman to her diary after each chapter. The letter should reflect the incidents and concerns Harriet experiences in that chapter. They should try to put themselves in Harriet's shoes, to try and write as she would write. The students will have 10 diary entries by the end of the book.

To give you an idea of what students might write, we have included some sample letters:

From Chapter 2, "Growing Up a Slave"

> *Dear Diary,*
>
> *Why are people so mean? I just can't understand it. I am just 6 years old and try to work hard for my masters, but they beat me anyway. I see them whip the other slaves, too, and for no reason. No one has the right to*

treat another human being so cruelly, do they? I think that slavery is wrong and that everyone should be free. What do you think?

Your friend,

Harriet

From Chapter 3, "Nat Turner's Rebellion"

Dear Diary,

Things are bad. A man named Nat Turner tried to free my people, but he got caught and they shot him. Now our masters won't let us meet for church on Sundays or read the Bible, even, and yesterday the traders came and took my two sisters. I'm afraid I'll never see them again, and every night I have a horrible nightmare that the traders are going to come and take me. I am so afraid. What should I do?

Your Friend,

Harriet

From Chapter 4, "The Turning Point"

Dear Diary,

I'm 13, but I feel so old. I thought things couldn't get worse, but they did. An overseer hit me in the head with a two pound weight and I nearly died. And all the time I was sick, Master tried to sell me. I prayed hard for the Lord to change his heart and make him a Christian. But then when I heard some of us was going to be sold to the chain gang, I changed my prayer. I told the Lord that if he wasn't going to change that man's heart, he should kill him so he won't do no more mischief. Then Master up and died! I felt it was me who had killed him. And since my head was hurt, I have these sleeping spells and dreams that I think are telling me the future. Do you think I killed my master and that dreams can predict the future?

Your Friend,

Harriet

Adapting the Activity: One additional activity that students could undertake here is to compile their letters and publish them in a booklet entitled something like *The Diary of Harriet Tubman*. Diary entries might be composed as a group activity, too. Students can get together after reading each chapter and decide what they will put in a letter and then compose one letter for the group.

This activity—writing diary entries from the point of view of the protagonist— can be done with any kind of material in which the main character is confronted with obstacles to overcome or problems to solve. For example, while reading *The Glory Girl* by Betsy Byars, sixth-grade students could write diary letters from the point of view of the main character, Anna, as she struggles to find her own identity as the only nonsinger in a family of gospel singers. Another good book for this activity for third or fourth graders is Jerry Spinelli's *Fourth Grade Rats.* The protagonist, Suds, goes through some interesting inward struggles as he tries to please his friend Joey and make the transition from third-grade "angel" to fourth-grade "rat." Writing diary entries from Lily's point of view in Patricia Reilly Giff's *Lily's Crossing* would be a fun and worthwhile activity for fifth graders, especially while studying the World War II years. Diary entries for Gilly or for Lyddie from Katherine Paterson's *The Great Gilly Hopkins*, would also make interesting writing and reading for sixth, seventh, or eighth graders. A variation on this theme would be to have students write "Dear Abby" type letters instead of "Dear Diary" ones. In these letters, students would ask for advice as well as tell about the events, thoughts, and feelings they experience through the story characters.

Reflection: In addition to actively involving students in the life and thoughts of the protagonist, this activity provides an ideal opportunity to review the elements and formatting of an informal letter. To extend the activity, students might write letters to newspaper columnists in which they ask for advice or sound off on an issue in Letters to the Editor. Letters could be reviewed and discussed by a panel of student "experts" who then write responses to the letters. Letters and responses could be read aloud to the entire class or in small groups. Also, students might write letters to the characters in a novel. For instance, seventh- through ninth-grade students might write to young Sade, who becomes a refugee after her mother is assassinated in Nigeria, in Beverly Naidoo's compelling novel *The Other Side of Truth,* or to the author herself to discuss aspects of the story as they unfold. They might also write a letter to a friend or classmate telling about the events that take place in each chapter or their reactions to characters or events.

Guided Reading Sample Activity 3: *Group and Label*

In this semantic mapping activity (Heimlich & Pittelman, 1986; Pearson & Johnson, 1978), students, working in pairs or groups, read a selection and sort the information in it into various categories.

Selection: *What Is a Reptile?* by Robert Snedden. In this 32-page informational book complemented with full-color photos, diagrams, a glossary, and an index, the author begins in chapter 1 by explaining what a reptile is. In chapter 2 he lists the four main groups of reptiles, and in the remaining nine chapters he describes the characteristics, behavior, and life of a variety of reptiles.

Students: Fourth-graders of average to high ability.

Reading Purpose: To learn about, appreciate, and build a schema for reptiles and the characteristics that make them distinct from any other class of animals.

Goal of the Activity: To help students understand and remember the four main groups of reptiles and their most salient characteristics by identifying and categorizing these and writing them on a chart.

Rationale: Because this book contains a great deal of information worth remembering about this intriguing class of animals, having students organize this information in a way that will show how it is related will help them to understand the concepts and remember them. The semantic mapping activity introduced in this activity can be used with other reading students do as well.

Procedure: Give each student two sheets of paper and tell them you are going to conduct an experiment. Next, tell them to put their heads on their desks and close their eyes while you place several items on the table (a flower, a dish, a button, a fork, a chalk eraser, a hat, a ball, a small mirror, a comb, a pencil, a toothbrush).

Have students gather around the table and look at the objects, giving them 20 seconds to do so. Tell them to return to their seats while you scoop the items into a paper bag. Then tell students to write down on one of their sheets of paper as many items as they can remember, advising them not to worry about spelling at this time. Give them a minute to record their answers, then collect the papers.

Tell students to once again close their eyes. Take several different items from another bag, but this time arrange them on the table in three groups. Group 1: a small paint brush, a tin of paints, a pack of colored chalk, crayons; group 2: a measuring cup, a cookbook, a spatula, a wooden spoon; group 3: a piece of lined paper, a pencil, an eraser, a dictionary.

While students still have their eyes closed, tell them that you have arranged the items into three groups: drawing and painting items, cooking items, and writing items. Tell them that they will have only half the time they did before to look at the items but that they are still to try and remember as many items as they can.

Have students return to the table. Point to each group of items and say, "Drawing and painting items, cooking items, and writing items." This time, give students 10 seconds to look at the items before you put them away. Then give them a minute to write down as many as they can remember on their second sheet of paper. Collect the papers and tally the number of correct guesses for each set on the chalkboard.

Barring some bizarre result, students will remember considerably more of the grouped items than the ungrouped ones. Encourage them to deduce why they remembered more of the grouped items. Explain to students that it is almost always easier to understand and remember information if you group it into sets of things that have common characteristics. For example, if they were reading a book about games to find something suitable to play at their birthday party, as they read they might group the games in their mind into these sorts of categories:

- Games for 4 or more people
- Games that use the equipment I have

- Games that my mom would let us play in the house
- Games you have to play outside
- Games that sound the most fun to me

After they finish reading, they might add a final category: Games I want to play at my birthday party.

Show them the book *What is a Reptile?* by Robert Snedden and explain that it is a great book with which to practice the grouping technique because it has lots of intriguing information about reptiles, that they will want to remember. Tell them the information will be easier to remember if they group like things together.

Give students copies of the chart shown in Table 5-2 and explain the categories to them.

Table 5-2. Four Groups of Reptiles

Turtles and Tortoises characteristics	Snakes and Lizards characteristics	Crocodiles and alligators characteristics	Tuataras characteristics
_____	_____	_____	_____
_____	_____	_____	_____
_____	_____	_____	_____
_____	_____	_____	_____
_____	_____	_____	_____

After explaining how to complete the chart, have students work in pairs or groups, taking turns reading the text aloud and completing the chart by writing at least five characteristics for each of the four groups of reptiles. After students have finished reading and completing their charts, bring the whole class together again. Have students, as a group, complete the same chart, which you have on a transparency.

Adapting the Activity: This activity can be used any time a text lends itself to grouping information. For example, this technique would work well with Joanna Cole's *The Magic School Bus* series. In these books, Cole provides a great deal of information on a variety of subjects (the human body, the solar system, inside the earth, at the waterworks) in a narrative style. Even though these books are packed with information, children love them because they are humorous and have plots and characters with whom youngsters can identify. Using semantic maps can help students to organize the information to better understand and retain it. Other books appropriate for this activity are *Tide Pools* by Carmen Bredson, *Frogs, Toads, Lizards, and Salamanders* by Nancy Winslow Parker and Joan Richards Wright, and *Outside and Inside Birds* and *Inside and Outside You* by Sandra Markle.

Reflection: Obviously, semantic maps that are designed to serve as reading guides will vary from selection to selection, because they will reflect the information contained in each one. Also, while semantic mapping is often useful as a during-reading activity, it is also a worthwhile prereading or postreading activity. As a prereading activity, semantic mapping can be used to activate prior knowledge; as a postreading activity it can be used to recall and organize information contained in the reading material. For example, before seventh-grade social studies students read books about pioneers—such as *Pioneer Children of Appalachia, Spanish Pioneers of the Southwest,* and *Pioneer Settlers of New France,* by Joan Anderson—you might develop a semantic map for the concept *pioneers.* Write *pioneer* on the board along with categories such as *People Who Were Pioneers, Pioneer Activities, Reasons for Being Pioneers,* and *Characteristics of Pioneers,* and have students suggest words and phrases for each category. After students have read a specific book about pioneers, you could do this same activity. *Pioneer* would still be the target word, but the categories you select and students' responses to those categories will reflect the information that was presented in the text. This postreading activity works well for any number of selections whose topics or themes might range from frogs to friendship.

Considered more generally, the matter of grouping items is frequently worth considering as you plan instruction. As George Miller (1956) pointed out, we can generally remember only five to nine ungrouped items—seven-digit phone numbers are a good example. If, however, we group items into meaningful categories, each category functions more or less like a single item, and the total number of items we can remember is greatly increased. Miller's finding has been one of the most important and influential discoveries of modern psychology and has generated a host of studies that confirm and extend his work (Bransford, Brown, & Cocking, 2000). Thus, for example, if we head off to the supermarket with 20 ungrouped items to buy and don't have a list, we are likely to be in trouble. If, on the other hand, we take those 20 items and group them as three vegetables, two fruits, two dairy products, and so forth, we stand a good chance of remembering all of them. It's exactly the same with students learning from a text. In order to remember information, they need to group it in meaningful categories.

Guided Reading Activity 4: *Who, What, When?*

In *Who, What, When?* students record on a time line the important names, events, and dates from a chapter in a trade book that chronicles the life of an important historic figure, Elizabeth Cady Stanton.

Selection: *You Want Women to Vote, Lizzie Stanton?* by Jean Fritz. Jean Fritz tells the inspiring and fascinating story of the life of Lizzie Stanton and her struggle to have, and make available to others as well, the same rights as men, including the right to vote.

Students: Fifth graders of average ability.

Reading Purpose: To gain new knowledge of the history of the women's rights movement and insights into the contributions of one of the key players in women's right to vote, Elizabeth Cady Stanton.

Goal of the Activity: To help students conceptualize important events in Lizzie Stanton's life that led up to the 19th Amendment (giving women the right to vote) by recording these events in chronological order.

Rationale: This text is filled with dates, persons, and events in Lizzie Stanton's life that led to women being granted the right to vote in the United States. Having students record these facts on a time line will help to fix names and events in their minds.

Procedure: Before students begin reading, provide them with a time line as shown in Table 5-3.

At the end of whatever prereading activities you do, explain that *You Want Women to Vote, Lizzie Stanton?* contains many dates, persons, and events that led to granting women the right to vote. Each of these in some way serves as a benchmark, both in the life of Lizzie Stanton and in the fulfillment of her goal for women's rights. In order to help students visualize the path to the 19th Amendment, they will record these facts on a time line.

Show students a sample of the time line they will each receive. This could be drawn on the board, a transparency, or a strip of butcher paper. Table 5-3 shows what the time line might look like.

Table 5-3. Time Line

1815 Lizzie born	1840	1847	1848	1851	1854	1860	1863	1866
1869	1872	1875	1878	1880	1887	1888	1902	1920 19th Amendment passed

Tell students that the time line has several significant dates on it. Ask students to guess what might have happened on some of those dates. Then explain that as they read the book about Lizzie Stanton, they are to write down what actually happened on those dates. Before students begin reading the book on their own, have them skim the first chapter for any of the dates on the time line. (The only date in this chapter is 1815, Stanton's birth). Have students predict what this first chapter will probably be about, then read the rest of the book, using the time line to record significant events.

Because some students might be tempted to skim the chapter for names and dates and not do a thorough reading, tell them that after they have read the chapter and recorded the persons, dates, and events on their time line, they should reread the chapter to make sure they have understood how these persons and events are related and how they are likely to influence what happens in subsequent chapters. As their time lines will reveal, it took a lot of time, work, and commitment on the part of Lizzie and many others to make the Nineteenth Amendment a reality—more than a century, as a matter of fact, from the time of Lizzie's birth in 1815 to the passage of the 19th Amendment in 1920. Tell students that this process is not unlike one they go through: working hard to make things happen that are important to them.

Adapting the Activity: Time lines can be used whenever the reading selection includes a number of persons, dates, and events that can be understood and recalled better if visually presented in chronological order. For example, time lines might be used with students in grades 6 through 8 with any one of the books from the *How Did We Find Out About?* series by Isaac Asimov and other informational selections such as *Bill of Rights* by Milton Meltzer, *The High Voyage: The Final Crossing of Christopher Columbus* by Olga Litowinsky, *Across America on an Emigrant Train* by Jim Murphy, *To See the Heart: The Life of Sitting Bull* by Judith St. George, and *The Century That Was: Reflections on the Last 100 Years* by Jim Giblin. Because Harriet Tubman and Lizzie Stanton lived during the same period (Harriet was born in 1820 and died in 1913) and both fought for the rights of others, students might enjoy and benefit greatly from doing time lines for both *You Want Women to Vote, Lizzie Stanton?* by Jean Fritz and *Harriet Tubman: Call to Freedom* by Judy Carlson and comparing these.

Because fictional narratives also have a chronological structure, time lines can be useful with them, particularly if they have an unusual chronological structure that might be confusing. However, most students will be able to follow the chronology of most narratives without using a time line.

Reflection: Many history trade books and texts are fairly dense text, and to read them successfully students may need various kinds of during-reading help. A time line is only one possibility. After reading the text yourself, you will discover the ideas and information that you want your students to focus on, manipulate, and retain. These will determine the makeup of your reading guide.

Rather than have students note sequence, as the time line does, you may decide that your students' purposes are better served by having them focus on cause and effect: This event happened because of that, and as a result this happened. Your reading guide will then reflect this goal. Reading guides are scaffolds designed to help students reach reading goals. They are also, as we have pointed out, opportunities for minilessons, and one topic very appropriate for mini-lessons is organizational patterns. Thus, when the text students are going to read exemplifies a particular pattern—simple listing, sequence, cause and effect, compare and contrast, and the like—you have a teachable moment for a minilesson on that pattern.

Guided Reading Activity 5:
Fill the Grocery Cart, Stock the Cupboard

In *Fill the Grocery Cart, Stock the Cupboard,* while reading each chapter of the text students record (either with words or pictures) in their "grocery cart" the food items mentioned in the text that zoo animals are fed. At the end of each chapter, students "unload" their grocery carts by putting their items, which they draw and label, in a "zoo food" cupboard.

Selection: *Lunch at the Zoo* by Joyce Altman. This engaging expository trade book tells what, how, and why zoo animals are fed, stressing the importance of good nutrition as well as feeding animals in a way that is as natural and palatable for them as possible. A chart at the end of the book gives the names of a number of zoo animals, listing the food they eat in the wild and the food they are fed at the zoo.

Students: Third graders of high ability.

Reading Purpose: To gain knowledge of the diet of a variety of zoo animals, how they are fed, and why they are fed these foods, and to gain an appreciation of the care that zoo personnel take in ensuring that zoo animals are cared for and well fed.

Goal of the Activity: To help students gain an appreciation of the variety of foods it takes to keep zoo animals healthy and happy and of the zookeepers who are in charge of making sure animals get the food and nutrition they need to lead healthy lives. It will also give students practice in ferreting out details embedded in a text that relate to a specific topic or theme.

Rationale: This text contains a great deal of information about the diets of various zoo animals and the reasons for these diets. Having students focus on these foods as they read will help them to gain an understanding and appreciation of the variety of the diets for zoo animals and what an unusual array of food items might appear in a zoo larder.

Procedure: Before students begin reading, engage them in as many prereading activities as you think are necessary to prepare them for a successful reading of the text. One of those activities might be relating the reading to students' lives. Here you might encourage them to talk about the sorts of things they eat for breakfast, lunch, and dinner. If students have helped with grocery shopping, have them think about the things that they or their parents put in the grocery cart for breakfast, lunch, and dinner meals. Ask questions like "What if there were a supermarket for zoo animals? What kinds of things do you think zoo keepers might put in their carts for the animals they take care of?" Let students talk about the possibilities.

Show them the book *Lunch at the Zoo* and briefly discuss what it is about. Tell them they will get a chance to read this book and find out many interesting things about what zoo animals eat and how they are fed. Tell them that you are going to give them grocery carts to use as they read, one grocery cart for each chapter (an 8 1/2 x 11 sheet of paper with the outline of a grocery cart on it). In each of the four chapters, as students read about different kinds of food the animals are fed at the zoo, students are to "put food in their grocery cart," by either drawing the food item or writing a word or phrase that represents it, as

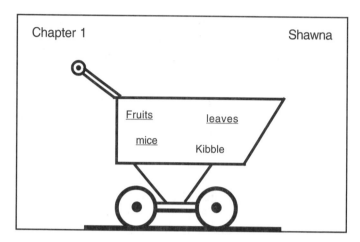

Figure 5-1.   Grocery Cart

shown in Figure 5-1.

Next ask, "What do your mom and dad do with the food when you get it home from the grocery store?" (Put it in the refrigerator or cupboard.) When you get to the end of the chapter, what do you think you might do with the food you've "put in your grocery cart"?

Show students a cupboard you have made out of poster board or butcher paper, as shown in Figure 5-2.

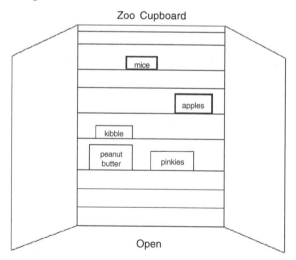

Figure 5-2.   Zoo Cupboard

Explain to students that when they finish with each chapter, they will get to help stock the zoo cupboard with the items from their grocery carts. They will do this by drawing each food item found in their grocery carts on a 3 x 5 card, labeling it, and putting it on a shelf in the cupboard (attach with glue, tape, pin, or thumbtack, depending on where the cupboard is displayed and what it's made of). Supply students with items necessary for this activity: four sheets of paper with a grocery cart outline (one for each chapter), 3 x 5 cards, crayons or markers, pencil, and glue or tape.

Adapting the Activity: The *Fill the Grocery Cart, Stock the Cupboard* activity can be adapted in a variety of different ways for situations in which you want students to remember particular details of any given topic. For a continuation of the *Fill the Cart, Stock the Cupboard* (with a slight variation), after reading *Lunch at the Zoo* students might read a book on human food and nutrition—such as *Good Enough to Eat: A Kid's Guide to Food and Nutrition* by Lizzy Rockwell, *The Food Pyramid* by Joan Kalbacken, or *Food Rules!: The Stuff You Munch, Its Crunch, Its Punch, and Why You Sometimes Lose Your Lunch* by Bill Haduch—and do the *Fill the Cart, Stock the Cupboard* activity, comparing the food for animals with the food for humans with an eye to discover the nutrients needed to sustain life in all animals, humans included. Other variations of this activity include having students record salient information inside the outline of an object that relates to the reading selection. For example, while reading *Brooklyn Bridge* by Lynn Curlee, fourth-grade students might put the items it takes to build a bridge in the outline of a toolbox. Students reading about pioneers of the American west could put selected items in a covered wagon, and students reading a book about New World explorers on a sailing ship could record significant events in the outline of a sailing ship.

Reflection: In an activity such as this one, it will be students' inclination to skim the text to find the items they are searching for rather than reading all the text. This is fine if they are practicing a skimming strategy. However, to encourage a more thorough reading of the text, one possibility is to have students work in partners or small groups, with students taking turns being the reader (the person who reads the text aloud) and the "shopper" (the one who puts the food items in the grocery cart). Group members can be responsible for drawing the food items on 3 x 5 cards to place in the "zoo cupboard"—one or two items per person, depending on the number of items mentioned in the chapter. Also recommended for this activity is teacher modeling, showing students how you would go about reading the text as you search for specific information, explaining your thought processes as you read. Another recommendation for this activity is to read a few pages of the first chapter aloud to the group and have students raise their hands when they hear something mentioned about "zoo food" or whatever specific details for which students are to be watching. You would then show how you would put that item in the grocery cart by either drawing a picture of the item or writing the word or words for it in the grocery cart.

Oral Reading by Students

Having students read aloud can achieve some of the same purposes that reading *to* students accomplishes: students experimenting with and enjoying the sound of language as well as focusing on meaning. If done in a supportive, nonthreatening way, students' read-aloud activities can also enhance their interest and enjoyment of reading, improve fluency, increase vocabulary, and add to their storehouse of knowledge and concepts.

Two popular read-aloud activities are choral reading and readers' theater. In choral reading—using contrasts such as high and low voices, different voice combinations and contrasts, sound effects, movements, gestures, and increasing or decreasing tempo—students combine their voices to convey and construct the meaning of a text. Choral reading can accomplish several purposes. It gives students the opportunity to hear printed language, and because choral reading requires repeated readings, the chances to add words to their reading vocabularies and become increasingly fluent in reading also increase. Choral reading has traditionally been used with poetry, but some narratives lend themselves to this activity as well. Primary grade students might enjoy doing a choral presentation of Michael Rosen's *We're Going on a Bear Hunt*— a repetitive tale with wonderful rhythmic lines, imagery, and alliteration— and third or fourth graders studying Japan might enjoy making a choral presentation out of David Wisniewski's picture book, *The Warrior and the Wiseman*, a Japanese folk tale. Middle grade students might enjoy reciting (to quote Jim Trelease, 2001) the "wondrously funny" poem "The Cremation of Sam McGee," in Robert W. Service's book by the same name, and selected poems from Shel Silverstein's *Where the Sidewalk Ends*.

Readers' Theater, in which students take turns or assume roles in reading portions of text aloud, can be used effectively with poetry, and narratives and has even been done successfully with expository materials (Young & Vardell, 1993). In readers' theater, students present drama, prose, or poetry by "reading the text out loud using their voices, reading fast or slow, loudly or softly, emphasizing certain words or phrases to reading rate, intonation, and emphasis on the meaning-bearing cadences of language to make print come alive" (Hoyt, 1992). Read-aloud expert Judy Freeman (in press) suggests that middle grade students might enjoy transforming the poems in Sharon Creech's novel *Love that Dog: A Novel*, into a readers' theater performance. Fifth- or sixth-grade students studying U.S. history could turn Julius Lester's *To Be a Slave* into a powerful readers' theater presentation. In this book, Lester chronicles the tragedy of slavery through many eloquent and provocative voices: the slaves themselves and the comments from various newspaper editors of the times. With readers' theater, students can make this piece of history come to life.

Choral reading and readers' theater provide an entertaining, cooperative, nonthreatening atmosphere in which students can build meaning from text and learn more about language: its purpose, beauty, and power. They are outlets for oral interpretation and are opportunities to perform, to gain confidence in speaking and reading.

In addition to performance activities such as choral reading and readers' theater, reading text aloud can be used in conjunction with what Linda Hoyt (1992) has described as "oral interactions": dialogue that is stimulated in response to the ideas and information students discover as they read various texts. As students read through material silently, they mark certain passages as "hot spots": ideas they liked, didn't understand, or disagreed with, or passages that answered a question posed by themselves, another student, or the teacher. In pairs or groups, students then share their "hot spots" by reading the passages aloud and talking about them.

Choral reading, readers' theater, and oral interactions are only three of many oral reading activities you can use in your classroom. Here we describe how you might implement each of them.

Oral Reading Sample Activity 1: *The Echo*

In *The Echo,* the teacher reads a poem, one line at a time, with students repeating selected phrases in unison.

Selection: "The Earth and the People," from *Magic Words* by Edward Field. This evocative poem is inspired by creation stories from the Netsilik Inuit Indians.

Students: Third and fourth graders, several of whom are students whose first language is not English.

Reading Purpose: To enjoy the beauty, rhythm, and language of poetry, as well as to learn about and appreciate the culture, stories, and traditions of the Inuit.

Goal of the Activity: To provide an enjoyable, low-stress situation in which students can expand their reading vocabularies, improve fluency and diction, gain language proficiency, and gain confidence in reading aloud.

Rationale: Because much of the meaning and effect of poetry relies on auditory devices such as repetition of sounds, cadence, and rhythm, it must be heard to be truly appreciated. Because some of the vocabulary in this selection may prove challenging for some 9- and 10-year-old readers, especially English language learners, the poems in this collection are ideal for choral presentation, especially an activity as supportive as The Echo. Children will enjoy hearing and reciting poetry that captures so evocatively another time and place. Choral reading also provides a safe environment for less able readers to practice their reading skills and for English language learners to grow in their understanding of English words and phrases.

Procedure: Briefly discuss with students what "magic words" means. Then tell them that you would like to share a poem with them entitled "The Earth and the People" by Edward Field from a collection of poems called *Magic Words,* which were inspired by Inuit creation stories. Give students a little background information on the Inuits and creation stories. (Field himself gives a fascinating account of his inspiration and basis for these poems in the book.) Tell students you are going to read the poem aloud and that you want them to think about what makes this poem a "creation" poem.

Next, display the poem on a chart or overhead projector with the echo lines or phrases highlighted. Read the poem slowly and have students read along with you, having them repeat highlighted lines in unison.

Read the poem aloud a few more times, having students again repeat the same selected lines in unison.

When students seem to be comfortable with the poem, divide the class into two groups. Have one group stand on one side of the room and read the nonhighlighted lines with you, and have the other group stand on the opposite side and echo the selected lines. Let students practice reading the poem this way, then have the students switch parts. However, continue only if students express interest. The purpose of the activity is not to achieve a polished performance but for the students to read and have fun. Be sure to applaud your students' efforts.

Although you do not want to do much of this if students aren't very interested, if students do show interest in the poem you might want to have them prepare it to perform for another class.

Adapting the Activity: *The Echo* may be done with any number of poems and even some prose material. *Spectacular Spiders* by Linda Glaser, for example, lends itself to echo choral reading for first or second graders, with the students echoing the last phrase in each line. *Joyful Noise: Poems for Two Voices* by Paul Fleischman is also nicely suited for an echo reading activity for third or fourth graders.

For choral reading in general, some good choices for primary students are *The New Kid on the Block* by Jack Prelutsky, *Animal Trunk: Silly Poems to Read Aloud* by Charles Chigna, *Hail to Mail* by Samuel Marshak, *Country Crossing* by Jim Aylesworth, and *You Read to Me, I'll Read to You: Very Short Stories to Read Together* by Michael Emberly. For middle graders some choices are *Where the Sidewalk Ends* by Shel Silverstein and *If I Were in Charge of the World and Other Worries* by Judith Viorst. Victoria Forrester's *A Latch Against the Wind* is a good choice for eighth or ninth graders.

Reflection: Having students echo selected lines or phrases of a poem is only one way to implement a choral reading experience. Some selections lend themselves to solos, ensembles, or whole-group work. Because the language in "The Earth and the People" is somewhat sophisticated, it lends itself particularly well to an echo reading.

Be cautious of trying to have students recite lengthy passages, which may result in mottled production or expressionless singsong. Successful and enjoyable experiences are often those in which students have only simple, single phrases to recite, such as "The very first people" from "The Earth and the People."

We want to emphasize that choral reading can be effective with bilingual students. Choral reading gives students repeated exposure to English words, it leads them toward automaticity in recognizing English words, it gives them practice with English structures and intonation patterns, it gives nonnative speakers an opportunity to participate and succeed in the same activity that native speakers are engaged in doing, and it does all of this in a nonthreatening environment.

Oral Reading by Students Sample Activity 2: *Radio Show*

Selection: *The Whipping Boy* by Sid Fleischman. When the obnoxious Prince Brat decides to run away from the palace, he takes his whipping boy, Jemmy, with him. In a series of adventures in which the two lads meet up with all manner of low life outside the castle and end up trading identities, the two come to know themselves and each other better, and in the end they become friends.

Reading Purpose: To understand and enjoy the setting, language, and characterization in an award-winning piece of historical fiction.

Students: Fourth or fifth graders of average to high ability.

Goal of the Activity: To help students interpret and appreciate a piece of literature by using oral language to help make print come alive. To foster an understanding of life in England in a past era and to appreciate the enduring value of friendship.

Rationale: As the story suggests, life is more fun when it is shared. So too with literature. Performing this tale not only gives students a chance to practice and hone their interpretive reading skills, it also exposes them to the effective use of language and the insights we can gain about ourselves through literature.

Procedure: Students in this class have performed works in the readers' theater a number of times prior to this activity. They also have made a collection of story tapes they call "radio show" tapes for students to listen to in their spare time. The best of these have been duplicated and given to the media center so that other students in the school can listen to them.

Read the first few chapters aloud to students, delivering the dialogue of the two main characters, Jemmy and Prince Brat, with the pizzazz you would like to inspire in students for their own oral readings. After you have finished reading, discuss with students whether they think this would be a good story to perform as a readers' theater activity and to add to their collection of "radio show" tapes. If they show interest, divide the class into groups of three or four students and assign each group two or three chapters from the novel. (There are 20 short chapters in this 90-page book.)

After students have prepared their chapters, begin with the first chapter and make a tape recording of their readings, complete with sound effects or other embellishments they have invented.

Adapting the Activity: Terrell Young and Sylvia Vardell (1993) have reported readers' theater success with nonfiction materials across the curriculum: in math, using David M. Schwartz's *How Much Is a Million?* and in science using Joanna Cole's *The Magic School Bus Lost in the Solar System* and Billy Goodman's *A Kid's Guide to How to Save the Planet.* For the latter selection, a seventh-grade teacher turned the text into a readers' Theater script by creating a radio call-in show hosted by Earthman Jack and other DJs. Other possible nonfiction texts for creating readers' theater texts are Tomie dePaola's *The Popcorn Book* with second or third graders, Russell Freedman's *Buffalo Hunt* with third through fifth graders, and Ina Chang's *A Separate Battle: Women and the Civil War* with seventh or eighth graders. Shelbey Anne Wolf (1993) has used readers' theater successfully with Arlene Mosel's *Tikki Tikki Tembo* with English language learners.

Reflection: Students usually enjoy performing, and because a part can be made as brief as necessary for a particular student to succeed with it, every student can experience success in reading a part. However, if some students are reluctant to participate as readers, they can be assigned to create sound effects, introduce the readers, or be in charge of production (operating and caring for equipment). In time and with encouragement, it is likely that the reluctant readers will risk taking a reading part, but until then they will learn about language by listening to others and gain confidence in their abilities by contributing to the group project.

Oral Reading by Students Sample Activity 3: *Flag It*

In *Flag It* students use self-stick notes to mark passages in the text. *Flag It* combines teacher oral reading, guided silent reading, and student oral reading to stimulate discussion on certain aspects of a text. This activity is based on one suggested by Linda Hoyt (1992).

Selection: *No Copycats Allowed!* by Bonnie Graves. In *No Copycats Allowed!* second grader Gabrielle is starting a new school, and she's desperate to make friends. So desperate, in fact, that she's willing to part with her beloved name, Gabrielle, changing it to Gabby, Gabbie, and Gabi. In fact, Gabrielle's willing to do just about anything to be like the girls at her new school—Libby, Addie, and Debi—to win their friendship, with unexpectedly disastrous results.

Students: Third-graders of average ability.

Reading Purpose: To enjoy a light-hearted story with the secondary purpose of considering how the author uses copycat behavior in the main character, Gabrielle, to develop the theme of learning to be yourself.

Goal of the Activity: To help students better understand the characters and events in the story and to appreciate literature's capacity to portray universal themes; to give students an opportunity to practice oral reading and provide a forum for sharing ideas and listening to the ideas of others.

Rationale: *No Copycats Allowed!* is a story with both external and internal conflict. Having students look for examples of outward action that reflects what a character is experiencing inwardly, intellectually and emotionally, can help them understand what motivates people to make the choices they do. Also, reading aloud gives students a chance to hear well-written material and practice their oral reading skills. Discussion gives students the opportunity to think more carefully about their responses, to practice defending and justifying a viewpoint, and to hear and learn from others' interpretations.

Procedure: Begin by discussing the cover illustration, which shows Gabrielle sitting alone at her desk, arms crossed, with a worried expression on her face, while behind her three girls are smiling at each other, obviously enjoying each other's company. Ask students to explain what is happening in the picture, how the girl in the foreground feels, and why she might feel that way. What is she doing that shows the way she feels?

Explain that Gabrielle is new at Morningside school and doesn't know anybody. Encourage students to talk about how Gabrielle might feel and how they would feel similar in a situation and how they would act. Explain that both Gabrielle's brother, Dillon, and her father give her advice on how to behave in her new school. Read the first chapter aloud, but before you do, ask students to listen for the advice Dillon gives her. Then read the second chapter, but this time have students listen for the advice Gabrielle's father gives her. (Dillon says she should "be like everyone else"; her father, Mr. Gilbert, encourages her to just "be herself.") Have children discuss whose advice they think is the best and to speculate on which Gabrielle will follow.

Tell students that they are going to be trying a new activity called *Flag It* as they read the rest of *No Copycats Allowed!* on their own. In this activity, they will use self-stick notes to keep track of the incidences in the story in which Gabrielle follows Dillon's advice by copying someone else. (The self-stick notes for Dillon's advice have a cat drawn on them to stand for a copycat.) After they have finished reading the chapter book, they will get the chance to read these portions aloud and discuss how they show copycat behavior and how Gabrielle is feeling in each of these situations.

Demonstrate how students will do this activity by reading the third chapter aloud, pausing at those places that you think illustrate copycat behavior, showing students how and where you would place the self-stick note. For example, you put a flag on page 17 where Gabrielle says, "I want to be a writer, too" after Libby tells her that's what she's going to be when she grows up, and you put another on page 17 where Gabrielle starts skipping when Libby does. You also put one on page 19 where Gabrielle decides to change her name to Gabby to match the spelling of Libby's name, and on page 20 where she asks her teacher for a new name tag and writes her name the new way.

After you have modeled this procedure and students understand what they are to do, give them pads of self-stick notes and have them read the book silently on their own, flagging those passages that illustrate Gabrielle's copycat behavior.

When students have finished reading, have them get together in pairs or small groups to read their passages aloud and discuss how they illustrate being a copycat and what motivates Gabrielle to copy the other girls. Before you have students meet in pairs or groups, we recommend that you lead a demonstration of the oral reading and discussion procedures that students are to use. This might consist of calling on volunteers to read their flagged passages for chapter 4 and explain why they think the passage illustrates copycat behavior. Doing this will allow you to clear up any misunderstandings before students work on their own. While students are meeting in their groups, you might sit in on a group as a participant or circulate among the groups to give support and encouragement.

The activity might conclude with a whole group discussion. Students can read their passages aloud and tell why they think they show copycat behavior. In addition, some sort of evaluative discussion is in order, with students answering such questions as the following:

- Was this a worthwhile activity? Why or why not?
- Did group work go smoothly? Why or why not?
- If we use this activity again, what might we do differently?

Adapting the Activity: *Flag It* can be used with any number of narrative or expository materials in which you want students to focus on a certain aspect of the text. For example, you might have third or fourth graders flag those incidents in Jerry Spinelli's *Fourth Grade Rats* in which Suds exhibits ratlike characteristics. In the discussion, students can tell how Suds feels about his ratlike behavior in each of these incidences. *Flag It* might also be used with an informational book such as *Inside and Outside You* by Sandra Markle for fifth-grade students to flag the five most interesting things they learned about their insides. While eighth or ninth graders read the biography *Ida B. Wells: Mother of the Civil Rights Movement* by Dennis Brindell Fradin and Judith Bloom Fradin, they might flag the 10 most important events in Wells' life. Their individual responses, which are likely to reflect some interesting differences, will make for lively discussions.

Reflection: As you can see, *Flag It* is a guided reading activity with an oral reading component. An activity such as this is typically preceded by prereading components, which could include a number of different activities but should definitely include a discussion of the story's characters, setting, and problem. Also prerequisite to this activity is having students think about copycat-like behaviors, the trait they will be focusing on in this particular *Flag It* activity. To encourage this engagement, students could either write about or discuss incidences in their own lives that exemplify circumstances where they have felt compelled to copy the behavior of others rather than to be themselves.

We have presented this activity as if this were the students' first encounter with the book; however, you might introduce this activity after students have read through the story once for pure pleasure. This will depend on you and your students' preferences. Some students do better reading a story from beginning to end without having to stop and physically interact with it. Others would profit from stopping and considering matters from time to time.

Modifying the Text

As mentioned previously, the purpose of scaffolded reading activities is to ensure that students have success in reading—that they are able to engage in extracting and constructing meaning as they read and will gain new knowledge, new insights, and a sense of accomplishment from their reading. For some students, achieving success requires that you present a selection in a format that is a variation of the original. Sometimes, because of what is required by your school district or what is available, the material may be too challenging or too lengthy for some students. Unfortunately, this is very frequently the case with your less skilled readers (Allington, 2001). When a selection is too difficult for some of your students and you cannot find a substitute that meets your needs, modifying or shortening the text is a viable option. In both the short run and the long run, children will become much better readers if they read texts with which they can be successful.

Let us say, for instance, that you are an eighth grade social studies teacher and your school district requires that students learn the concepts presented in the state-adopted U.S. history text. Although the text is written at a grade 6–8 reading level, the reading ability of the students in your class ranges from grades 3–12. If the material in this text is going to be made accessible to the students reading well below eighth grade, something may need to be done to the material. This might mean tape recording some sections, assigning only certain portions of the text to read, or writing (or having older students write) simplified versions or summaries of the most important concepts. In a situation like this, you might also add a more sophisticated selection for your stronger readers.

As another example, suppose your second grade class contains a number of English language learners and the social studies curriculum includes selections on families and community workers. Most of the trade books and pamphlets included in the prepackaged unit supplied by your school demand English reading skills. In this situation, you might pair your English language learners with students from a sixth-grade class and have the older students help the second graders write books of their own, one on community workers and the other on families. The sixth graders could then write a simplified version of the community workers booklet based on the topics in the social studies selections. For the booklet on the family, the English language learners could dictate information about their own families, which the sixth graders would write down in a booklet for the second graders to read. Obviously, the English language learner students will not be reading the same words as the students who read the trade books and commercially prepared pamphlets, but the ideas will be similar and they will be reading.

Sometimes it isn't feasible or even advisable for students to read an entire selection. When lack of time or other constraints make reading an entire selection impractical, shortening the reading assignment is one workable option. In doing this, you have students read only selected portions of a chapter, the topics you think are most important for them to understand. Of course, students will miss some of the information presented in the chapter, but assuming that they cannot or will not read all of it, success in reading part of it is certainly preferable to failure in reading all of it. Moreover, as Walter Kintsch and Tuen van Dijk (1978) have shown, what readers typically remember after reading a text is its gist; by no means do they remember everything.

Another way to make difficult material accessible to your students is to tape-record a selection for students to listen to as they read along silently with the text. Either you or competent students can make the recordings, or you can purchase commercial tapes. Recordings can make material accessible to less able readers as well as provide a model for good oral reading.

Work by Isabel Beck and Margaret McKeown and their colleagues (Beck, McKeown, Hamilton, & Kucan, 1997, 1998) on questioning the author suggests another possibility for modifying text. Readers sometimes blame themselves for not understanding text when in fact the fault may lie with the writer. The writer may have assumed too much background knowledge on the part of his or her audience or has simply not presented ideas clearly or with sufficient elaboration to make them understandable. When you run across texts like these, you might have the students themselves rewrite the text so that it makes sense to them. "How would you write this paragraph," you might ask them, "to make it more understandable?"

Students should acknowledge the author's expertise and knowledge but not be intimidated by it or believe that printed text is beyond reproach. Grappling with the ideas—rewording, rearranging, and embellishing— may be the only way that meaning-building will take place. Students at all levels of reading ability can profit from rewriting text in order to understand it. Students might do this rewriting in groups or pairs, with their main questing being "How can we rewrite this—rephrase, reorganize, add, subtract—to make it more understandable?"

Doing something with the reading material to make it more accessible to students is yet another way to help ensure that students both understand and enjoy what they read. The example below represents one possibility.

Modifying the Text Sample Activity: *Focusing*

In *Focusing,* instead of assigning an entire chapter or selection, you choose certain portions of the material for students to read.

Selection: "Electricity," in *Science in Your World* by John Hacket & Richard Moyer. In this science text chapter, static electricity, current electricity, and circuits are discussed. Other topics covered are electricity in the home, electric motors, and measuring electric usage. A special section on pacemakers is also included.

Students: Seventh graders of low to average ability.

Reading Purpose: To expand student's knowledge of electricity—what it is and how it is used.

Goal of Activity: To focus on certain key concepts in the text and to make these ideas more accessible to students by creating a reading assignment of a length that they can handle successfully.

Rationale: In deciding what portions of this chapter on electricity the students would read, we took into account what students already knew about the topic, the difficulty of the material, and how much time we could spend covering the chapter. Because they had previously studied static and current electricity, we decided to briefly review these topics in a group discussion and then have students read the sections on circuits, electricity in the home, electric motors, and measuring electric usage on their own.

Procedure: Prior to the lesson, write the following outline on the chalkboard:

> *Electricity*
>
> *Static Electricity—Discuss*
> *Current Electricity—Discuss*
>   *Circuits—Read pages 82–84*
> *Electricity in Your Home—Read pages 86–89*
>   *Electric Motors—Read pages 90–91*
>   *Measuring Electric Usage—Read pages 92–93*
>   *Pacemakers—Read page 96; optional*

Draw students' attention to the outline on the board. Tell them that because you have already discussed static and current electricity, they are to read only the sections on circuits, electricity in the home, electric motors, and measuring electric usage. The section on pacemakers is optional reading. Explain that after they have finished reading, the class as a whole will discuss the required sections and volunteers can discuss the section on pacemakers.

Adapting the Activity: Shortening selections by assigning only certain portions of a piece works best for expository material that contains previously covered information, text that is too lengthy and too challenging to be read in its entirety by your students, or material that contains information your students don't need to deal with at the present time. If you wanted your fifth-grade students to get the information in Michael L. Cooper's book *Indian School: Teaching the White Man's Way,* for example, but you didn't think that your students could handle the book alone in the time they had, you could assign reading specific chapters to groups of students who would be responsible for writing a summary of their chapter and make these available for other students to read. Or, instead of every student reading each of the folktales included in Virginia Hamilton's collection of African American folk tales, *The People Could Fly,* groups of seventh-grade students could choose one of the tales to read and then present a dramatization of their chosen tale. In that way, although students read only one story, they are able to learn about and enjoy each of them.

Reflection: The purpose of students reading the chapter on electricity was to add to their knowledge of electricity. An activity such as this one reduces the amount of information that students have to deal with, thereby increasing the chances that they will successfully understand and retain the most crucial concepts they need to further understand electricity and related topics. Reducing the amount of text that students have to read is an extremely simple task, both conceptually and practically. However, it can be quite beneficial in terms of students successfully building meaning with those parts of the text they do read.

During-Reading Activities: A Final Word

How do you decide what sort of during-reading activities will benefit your students? First of all, as is the case with any of the three phases of an SRE, the kinds of activities your students engage in will depend on their needs, interests, and abilities; the material they are reading; and their purposes for reading. Are they reading for pleasure or information? What is it they need or want to get from the text? If they are reading primarily to enjoy a well-told tale, then preparing a study guide for them would definitely be a waste of time. However, if their purpose is to understand the salient features of the industrial revolution as they are described in a social studies text, they might be able to benefit from a reading guide designed to help them focus on cause and effect. As is the case with prereading, the purpose of during-reading activities is to provide a scaffold that will help to ensure that students achieve their reading goals. As is also the case with prereading as well as with postreading, there is also the matter of time to consider. There simply is not time for you to create all of the activities you might like to do, and therefore you must focus on creating those that will best help your students to succeed in the reading they do.

References

Allington, R. L. (2001). *What really matters for struggling readers.* New York, Longman. A number of evidence-based suggestions for designing programs for struggling readers.

Atwell, N. (1998). *In the middle: Writing, reading, and learning with adolescents* (2nd ed.). Portsmouth, NH: Boynton/Cook. In this very popular book, Atwell discusses her concepts of reading and writing workshops, minilessons, and a number of other modern pedagogical approaches to literacy instruction.

Beck, I. L., & McKeown, M. G. (2001). Text talk: Capturing the benefits of read-aloud experiences for young children. *Reading Teacher, 55,* 10–20. Suggests a read-aloud procedure that scaffolds children's efforts and keeps the focus on important text ideas.

Beck, I. L., McKeown, M. G., Hamilton, R. L., & Kucan, L. (1997). *Questioning the author: An approach to enhancing student engagement with text.* Newark, DE: International Reading Association. An entire monograph on the authors' approach.

Beck, I. L., McKeown, M. G., Hamilton, R. L., & Kucan, L. (1998, Spring/Summer). Getting the meaning: How to help students unpack difficult text. *American Educator, 22,* 66–71, 85. A brief description of the questioning-the-author approach.

Blachowicz, C., & Ogle, D. (2001). *Reading comprehension: Strategies for independent learners.* New York: Guilford Press. Contains a host of very practical ideas for creating readers who can read and learn on their own.

Bransford, J. D., Brown, A. L., & Cocking, R. R. (2000). *How people learn: Brain, mind, experience, and school.* Washington, DC: National Academy Press. A very well done summary of what we know about how people learn by some very able educational psychologists.

Freeman, J. (in press). More books kids will sit still for (3rd ed.). Englewood, CO: Libraries Unlimited. Annotated bibliography of great read-alouds by an expert on the subject.

Graves, M. F., Juel, C., & Graves, B. B. (2001). *Teaching reading in the 21st century* (2nd ed.). Boston: Allyn & Bacon. This comprehensive text contains a thorough discussion of how to teach comprehension strategies as well as information on how to teach most of the other components of a comprehensive elementary reading program.

Heimlich, J.E., & Pittelman, S.D. (1986). *Semantic mapping: Classroom applications.* Newark, DE: International Reading Association. A very practical guide to using semantic mapping for a variety of purposes.

Hoyt, L. (1992). Many ways of knowing: Using drama, oral interactions, and the visual arts to enhance reading comprehension. *Reading Teacher, 45,* 580–584. The brief article does just what the subtitle says it will.

Kintsch, W., & Van Dijk, T. (1978). Toward a model of text comprehension and production. *Psychological Review, 85,* 363–394. A technical and challenging yet very insightful discussion of how we understand and remember text.

Martin, B. Jr. (1992). Afterword. In B. E. Cullinan (Ed.), *Invitation to read: More children's literature in the classroom* (pp. 179–182). Newark, DE: International Reading Association. A heartfelt statement on the importance of reading aloud by a well-noted children's author and educator.

McCauley, J. K., & McCauley, D. S. (1992). Using choral reading to promote language learning for ESL students. *The Reading Teacher, 45,* 526–533. Clearly explains the value of choral reading for English language learners.

McKeown, M. G., & Beck, I. L. (In press). Taking advantage of read alouds to help children make sense of decontextualized language. In A. van Kleeck, S. A. Stahl, & E. B. Bauer (Eds.), *Storybook reading.* Mahwah, NJ: Erlbaum. A somewhat more technical description of the text-talk approach to scaffolding and focusing children's efforts during read-alouds.

Miller, G. A. (1956). The magical number seven, plus-or-minus two: Some limits on our capacity for processing information. *Psychological Review, 63,* 81–97. A true classic, significant for its contributions to both theory and practice.

National Research Council. (1999). *Improving student learning: A strategic plan for education research and utilization.* Washington, DC: National Academy Press. Carefully outlines four broad goals of a strategic plan to use research-based information to improve students' learning.

Ollmann, H. E. (1992). Two-column response to literature. *Journal of Reading, 56,* 53–59. Suggests a format for students to use in interpreting and responding to literature.

Pearson, P. D., & Johnson, D. D. (1978). *Teaching reading comprehension.* New York: Holt, Rinehart and Winston. Probably the first text to present a view of teaching reading consistent with cognitive psychology, this book contains one of the earliest treatments of semantic mapping.

Perkins, D. (1992). *Smart schools: From training memories to educating minds.* New York: Free Press. Perkins's first full-length statement documenting the need for teaching for understanding and some ways to do so.

Rosenblatt, L. (1978). *The reader, the text, the poem: The transactional theory of the literary work.* Carbondale, IL: Southern Illinois Press. One of several presentations of Rosenblatt's very influential response theory.

Snow, C. E. (2001). *Reading for understanding: Toward an R&D program in reading comprehension.* Santa Monica, CA: Rand Education. Also available online at http://www.rand.org/multi/achievementforall/reading/. A well-done and widely respected summary of what we know about reading comprehension and plan for further research.

Trelease, J. (2001). *The read-aloud handbook* (5th ed.). New York: Penguin. This bestseller contains a wealth of insights for both teachers and parents.

Whitehurst, G. J., Arnold, D. S., Epstein, J. N., Angell, A. L., Smith, M., & Fischel, J. E. (1994). A picture book reading intervention in day care and home for children from low income families. *Developmental Psychology, 30,* 679–680. Empirical study showing an effective approach for reading aloud to young children.

Wolf, S. A. (1993). What's in a name? Labels and literacy in readers' theater. *The Reading Teacher, 46,* 546–551. Discusses the potential of readers' theater for students labeled "at risk."

Young, T. A., & Vardell, S. (1993). Weaving readers' theater and nonfiction into the curriculum. *The Reading Teacher, 46,* 396–406. Suggests ways to use readers' theater with informational trade books.

Young, T. E., & Salley, C. (2000, March). Read-aloud science books. *BookLinks,* pp. 10–14. Recommends specific science books for reading aloud.

Children's Literature

Alexander, G. (1991). *The jungle book.* New York: Arcade. 32 pages.

Altman, J. (2001). *Lunch at the zoo.* New York: Holt. 88 pages.

Anderson, J. (1986). *Pioneer children of Appalachia.* New York: Lodestar. 32 pages.

Anderson, J. (1989). *Spanish pioneers of the Southwest.* New York: Lodestar. 32 pages.

Anderson, J. (1990). *Pioneer settlers of New France.* New York: Lodestar. 32 pages.

Asimov, I. (1990). *How did we find out about Neptune?* New York: Walker. 59 pages.

Avi. (1990). *The true confessions at Charlotte Doyle.* New York: Orchard. 215 pages.

Aylesworth, J. (1991). *Country crossing.* New York: Atheneum. Unpaged.

Billingsley, F. (1999). *The folk keeper.* New York, Atheneum. 162 pages.

Bredson, C. (1999). *Tide pools.* New York: Franklin Watts. 64 pages.

Byars, B. (1983). *The glory girl.* New York: Viking. 122 pages.

Carlson, J. (1989). *Harriet Tubman: Call to freedom.* New York: Fawcett Columbine. 116 pages.

Chang, I. (1991). *A separate battle: Women and the Civil War.* New York: Lodestar. 103 pages.

Chigna, C. (1998). *Animal trunk: Silly poems to read aloud.* New York: Abrams. Unpaged.

Cole, J. (1990). *The magic school bus lost in the solar system.* New York: Scholastic. 32 pages.

Cooper, M. L. (1999). *Indian school: Teaching the white man's way.* New York: Clarion. 103 pages.

Creech, S. (2000). *The wanderer.* New York: Joanna Cotler Books. 305 pages.

Creech, S. (2001). *Love that dog: A novel.* New York: HarperCollins. 112 pages.

Curlee, L. (2001). *Brooklyn Bridge.* New York: Simon and Schuster. 35 pages.

Davidson, M. (1986). *I have a dream: The story of Martin Luther King, Jr.* New York: Scholastic. 127 pages.

dePaola, T. (1978). *The popcorn book.* New York: Holiday House. Unpaged.

Earle, S. (1999). *Hello, fish!: Visiting the coral reef.* Washington, DC: National Geographic Society. 32 pages.

Emberly, M. (2001). *You read to me, I'll read to you: Very short stories to read together.* New York: Little, Brown/Megan Tingley. 32 pages.

Field, E. (1998). "The earth and the people." In *Magic words.* San Diego: Gulliver Books. Unpaged.

Fleischman, P. (1988). *A joyful noise: Poems for two voices.* New York: Harper & Roul. 44 pages.

Fleischman, S. (1986). *The whipping boy.* New York: Greenwillow. 90 pages.

Forrester, V. (1985). *A latch against the wind.* New York: Atheneum. 120 pages.

Fradin, D. B., & Fradin, J. B. (2000). *Ida B. Wells: Mother of the Civil Rights Movement.* New York: Clarion. 178 pages.

Frank, A. (1967). *The diary of a young girl.* New York: Doubleday. 308 pages.

Freedman, R. (1988). *Buffalo hunt.* New York: Holiday House. 52 pages.

Fritz, J. (1995). *You want women to vote, Lizzie Stanton?* New York: Putnam. 88 pages.

Hacket, J. K., & Moyer, R. H. (1991). *Science in Your World.* New York: Macmillan/McGraw-Hill.

Giblin, J. (Ed.). (2000). *The century that was: Reflections on the last 100 years.* 165 pages.

Giff, P. R. (1997). *Lily's Crossing.* New York: Delacorte. 180 pages.

Glaser, L. (1999). *Spectacular spiders.* Brookfield, CT: Millbrook Press. Unpaged.

Goodman, B. (1990). *A kid's guide to how to save the planet.* New York: Avon Books. 137 pages.

Graves, B. (1998). *No copycats allowed!* New York: Hyperion. 51 pages.

Haduch, B. (2001). *Food rules!: The stuff you munch, its crunch, its punch, and why you sometimes lose your lunch.* 106 pages.

Hall, B. (1990). *Dixie storms.* San Diego: Harcourt Brace Jovanovich. 197 pages.

Hamilton, V. (1985). *The people could fly: American black folktales.* New York: Knopf. 178 pages.

Hamilton, V. (1990). *Cousins.* New York: Philomel. 125 pages.

Kalbacken, J. (1998). *The food pyramid.* 47 pages.

Kennedy, R. (1985). *Amy's eyes.* New York: Harper & Row. 112 pages.

Lester, J. (1968). *To be a slave.* New York: Dutton. 160 pages.

Litowinsky, O. (1991). *The high voyage: The final crossing of Christopher Columbus.* New York: Delacorte. 150 pages.

London, J. (1999). *Baby whale's journey.* San Francisco: Chronicle. 40 pages.

Lowry, L. (1989). *Number the stars.* New York: Dell. 137 pages.

MacLachlan, P. (1991). *Journey.* New York: Delacorte. 83 pages.

Markle, S. (1991). *Inside and outside you.* New York: Bradbury. 39 pages.

Markle, S. (1994). *Outside and inside birds.* New York: Bradbury. 40 pages.

Markle, S. (1999). *Down, down, down in the ocean.* New York: Walker. 32 pages.

Marshak, S. (1990). *Hail to mail.* New York: Holt. Unpaged.

Meltzer, M. (1990). *Bill of rights.* New York: HarperCollins. 179 pages.

Mosel, A. (1968). *Tikki tikki tembo.* New York: Holt. 32 pages.

Murphy, J. (1993). *Across America on an emigrant train.* New York: Clarion. 150 pages.

Naidoo, B. (2001). *The other side of truth.* New York: HarperCollins. 272 pages.

Osofsky, A. (1996). *Free to dream: The making of a poet, Langston Hughes.* New York: Lothrop, Lee & Shephard. 112 pages.

Parker, N. W., & Wright, J. R. (1990). *Frogs, toads, lizards, and salamanders.* New York: Greenwillow. 48 pages.

Paterson, K. (1978). *The great Gilly Hopkins.* New York: Crowell. 148 pages.

Paterson, K. (1991). *Lyddie.* New York: Dutton. 182 pages.

Paulsen, G. (1987). *Hatchet.* New York: Bradbury. 195 pages.

Paulsen, G. (1990). *Canyons.* New York: Delacorte. 184 pages.

Paulsen, G. (1998). *Soldier's heart.* New York: Delacorte. 106 pages.

Pendergraft, P. (1987). *Miracle at Clement's Pond.* New York: Philomel. 199 pages.

Pfeffer, W. (1999). *Sounds all around.* New York: HarperCollins. 32 pages.

Prelutsky, J. (1984). *The new kid on the block.* New York: William Morrow. 159 pages.

Rockwell, L. (1999). *Good enough to eat: A kid's guide to food and nutrition.* Unpaged.

Rosen, M. (1989). *We're going on a bear hunt.* New York: McElderry Books. Unpaged.

Rylant, C. (1990). *A couple of kooks and other stories about love.* New York: Orchard. 104 pages.

Rylant, C. (1991). *Appalachia: The voices of sleeping birds.* San Diego: Harcourt Brace Jovanovich. Unpaged.

St. George, J. (1996). *To see the heart: The life of Sitting Bull.* New York: Putnam. 182 pages.

Sanfield, S. (1989). *The adventures of high John the conqueror.* New York: Orchard. 170 pages.

Schami, R. (1990) *A hand full of stars.* New York: Dutton. 195 pages.

Schwartz, D. M. (1985). *How much is a million?* New York: Lothrop, Lee & Shepard. Unpaged.

Service, R. W. (1987). *The cremation of Sam McGee.* New York: Greenwillow. 30 pages.

Silverstein, S. (1974). *Where the sidewalk ends.* New York: Harper & Row. 166 pages.

Snedden, R. (1995). *What is a reptile?* San Francisco: Sierra Club. 32 pages.

Spinelli, J. (1990). *Maniac Magee.* Boston: Little, Brown. 184 pages.

Spinelli, J. (1991). *Fourth grade rats.* New York: Scholastic. 84 pages.

Thesman, J. (1990). *Rachel Chance.* Boston: Houghton Mifflin. 175 pages.

Viorst, J. (1983). *If I were in charge of the world and other worries.* New York: Atheneum. 56 pages.

Walker, A. (1982). *The color purple.* San Diego: Harcourt Brace Jovanovich. 290 pages.

Wisniewski, D. (1989). *The warrior and the wiseman.* New York: Lothrop, Lee & Shepard. 32 pages.

Chapter

6

Postreading
Activities

Postreading activities, the last set of optional activities in the Scaffolded Reading Experience (SRE), assist students in making a reading experience meaningful by engaging them in a variety of activities that serve a variety of purposes. They might, for example, give students an opportunity to check what they have learned from the selection to find out whether they have gotten what they wanted and needed from it. They might give students an opportunity to cement their learning, working with the newly learned information in a way that makes it their own. They might give students a chance to consider how what they just read relates to other reading they have done or to their lives beyond the classroom, or they might accomplish a variety of other purposes. Because the purposes of reading are so diverse, the purposes of postreading activities are also diverse.

As Francis Bacon observed, "Some books are to be tasted, others to be swallowed, and some few to be chewed and digested." Not every reading experience has to be followed by some sort of activity. There will be times when students read, reflect, and respond in their own personal way. When students are just "tasting" a selection, their reflection and response may be extremely brief. Sometimes, however, it is appropriate to provide activities that encourage students to do something with the information and ideas in a selection after they have read it—to chew and digest. To determine the appropriateness and the type of activity called for, we turn once again to our model—do the students, selection, and purpose suggest or require postreading activities?

Postreading activities encourage students to *do* something with the material they have just read: to think—critically, logically, and creatively—about the information and ideas that emerge from their reading, and sometimes to transform their thinking into action. When doing recreational reading, we often perceive information from a text with very little effort or thought, and that is fine, for recreational reading. However, for much of the reading that we or our students do in school, it isn't fine. As we explained in chapter 3, particularly in our discussion of constructivism (Fosnot, 1996; Perkins, 1999; Phillips, 1995, 2000) and reader response theory (Beach, 1993; Galda & Guice, 1997; Marshall, 2000; Rosenblatt, 1938, 1978), reading is an active, constructive process. Until we do something with what we have read, until we take the effort to work with the meaning we have gleaned from the text and internalize it, we are a long way from getting the most we can from a text. In many cases, in order to really own a text, we follow a process like this:

$$\text{Read} \quad \longleftrightarrow \quad \text{Think and Elaborate} \quad \longleftrightarrow \quad \text{Respond}$$

As the model illustrates, in some cases we read, think and elaborate, and respond; and that response may foster further thought and elaboration, which may in turn foster further response and perhaps more reading. Response can take a variety of forms: speaking, writing, dramatics, creative arts, construction, or application and outreach activities. When engaging in postreading activities, students recall what they've read and demonstrate understanding, but they also do much more than this. They apply, analyze, synthesize, evaluate, and elaborate the information and ideas they glean from the text and connect the information and ideas to their prior knowledge—to other things they've read, to information and ideas they already have, and to the world in which they live. Postreading activities also provide opportunities for students to extend ideas, to explore new ways of thinking, doing, and seeing—to invent and create, to ponder the question "What if?"

In chapter 2 we described the following eight categories of postreading activities:

1. Questioning
2. Discussion
3. Writing
4. Drama
5. Artistic, graphic, and nonverbal activities
6. Application and outreach activities

7. Building connections
8. Reteaching

The activities in the first seven categories encourage students to think in the ways we just suggested: to recall, understand, apply, analyze, synthesize, evaluate, and elaborate information and ideas; to make logical connections between ideas; and to go beyond given information or ideas to explore new ways of thinking and of expressing themselves.

To these we add an eighth category, reteaching. Reteaching is the safety net in the reading scaffold. You don't want students to leave a reading selection without a sense of accomplishment, of a job well done. Sometimes, if that goal hasn't been achieved, it means retracing steps to find out what didn't work and why, and then perhaps trying a different approach. You and your students are jointly accountable for a successful reading experience.

Obviously, this list is not the only way that postreading activities might be described or categorized. As with pre- and during-reading categories, our postreading categories are options. Although not all reading selections are meant to be "digested," some sort of postreading experience is often appropriate. Not engaging in postreading activities is a bit like taking a trip and promptly forgetting about it. If you want to keep that vacation memory alive, you need to do something further with it, such as put together a scrapbook, or organize your slides, videos, and photographs and share these with friends. Postreading activities allow students to relive the reading adventure and to discover new insights to take from it, explore ways to act upon those discoveries, and build bridges to other experiences, whether those experiences take place in their lives or in other texts.

Table 6-1 outlines the postreading activities described in this chapter.

Table 6-1. Postreading Activities

Questioning	*What Do You Think?* (p. 154) *The Yellow Brick Road* (p. 157)
Discussion	*Three's a Charm!* (p. 163) *Both Sides* (p. 165)
Writing	*Compare and Contrast* (p. 169) *What If?* (p. 172)
Drama	*History Comes to Life* (p. 177)
Artistic, Graphic, and Nonverbal Activities	*Postcards* (p. 184)
Application and Outreach Activities	*Getting to Know You* (p. 188)
Building Connections	*Problems and Solutions* (p. 191)
Reteaching	*Play It Again, Sam* (p. 196)

Questioning

Questioning activities encourage students to think about and react—either orally or in writing—to the information and ideas in the material they have read. Questions can be of various sorts, but it is important that at least some of them give students the opportunity to engage in higher level thinking (Beck & McKeown, 2001; Pearson & Duke, 2002). Some questions will simply assess whether students remember what they have read; other questions should foster students understanding, applying, analyzing, evaluating, creating, and thinking metacognitively. Below are some questions illustrating various levels that might be appropriate for fifth-grade students after reading Jean Fritz's *Shh! We're Writing the Constitution*. These types of thinking are taken from Lorin Anderson and David Krathwohl's 2001 revision of Bloom's taxonomy.

- *Remembering:* How many delegates were supposed to attend the grand convention in 1787?
- *Understanding:* How did the delegates keep the proceedings a secret?
- *Applying:* What are some things you might do to keep a meeting secret?
- *Analyzing:* Why did the delegates decide to keep the proceedings a secret?
- *Evaluating:* Do you think it was a good idea to keep the meetings a secret? Why or why not?
- *Creating:* What if the delegates had decided there should be three presidents presiding over the nation instead of one? What might have happened?
- *Thinking metacognitively:* Did you understand the author's description of the three branches of government? If you didn't, what might you do to make this explanation more clear to you?

Questions that stimulate these various kinds and levels of thinking are appropriate for either expositive or narrative material. After students read narratives, questions that prompt them to focus on elements of theme, plot, setting, character traits, motives, and development are all appropriate. For example, in Jerry Spinelli's *Fourth Grade Rats*, in order to please his best friend the protagonist, Suds, tries hard to make the transition from being a third-grade "angel" to a fourth grade "rat." In doing so he acquires some pretty obnoxious behavior. Questions such as "At first, why didn't Suds want to become a rat?", "What happened to make him change his mind?" and "What did he finally decide about being a rat and why?" can help students to discover the story's theme.

Questions that involve feelings are also appropriate for narratives. Students can be guided to examine the feelings of the characters in the story and their own emotional reactions as well: "How do you think Suds felt when he started saying no to his mom? Why do you think he felt this way? How do you think Suds's mom felt when he said no to her? Why do you think she felt this way? How did you feel about Suds's behavior toward his mother?"

Questions that lead students to think about universal themes and feelings help them to make the connection between literature and real life. If students can see themselves and their situations in the story characters, they may come to understand and appreciate art as a vehicle for expressing our common humanity.

Questions for both narratives and expository texts can guide students toward becoming metacognitive readers. "Were there parts of the text you didn't understand? Why didn't you understand them? What might you do to better understand them? Should you reread parts of the text, take some notes, draw a map, do some background reading, ask a friend for assistance?" These kinds of questions encourage students to monitor their own understanding and focus their attention on considering and implementing fix-up strategies.

In responding to questions, students should generally be aware of their audience. For whom are they answering the questions? Themselves? Their teacher? Other students? The author? In the questions listed above for *Shh! We're Writing the Constitution*, the audience was the teacher. However, questions might also be constructed from the point of view of the author, as if he or she were asking questions of the readers. For example, for the novel *The Star Fisher* by Lawrence Yep, author-asked questions might include the following: "What do you like best about the character Emily? What is your favorite scene in the story and why do you like it? Did Emily say or do anything that helped or inspired you? If she did, what was it?" Students would answer these questions as if they were writing to Lawrence Yep himself. For the informational book *Touch, Taste, and Smell* by Steve Parker, author-asked questions might be "What did you find most interesting about how you perceive a smell? Why did you find this part interesting? When you came across a word you didn't understand, what did you do? How could I have helped you better understand what the word meant?"

Students can also ask and answer their own questions. For example, after reading a chapter on California missions in their social studies text, they might write five questions they still have about the issues or topics in the chapter. To answer the questions they might refer back to the text or look for the answers in other sources. Another possibility is to have students develop a set of questions for the books they read that other students will answer. These questions can be written on a sheet of paper and placed in the book. Whoever reads the book next would write answers to the questions and give them to the student author. Together the two students could discuss the questions and answers.

Another line of questioning has been suggested by Isabel Beck and Margaret McKeown and their colleagues (Beck, McKeown, Hamilton, & Kucan, 1997, 1998) which they have labeled "questioning the author." As we mentioned in chapter 5 when we talked about modifying text, students are often under the impression that if they do not understand what they read, the fault lies with them and not with the author. This may or may not be the case. Students need to realize that authors are not infallible; they are not always the lucid communicators they attempt to be. Asking questions such as "What was the author trying to tell you?", "How could the author have expressed the ideas in a clearer way?", and "What would you want to say instead?" can prompt students to actively participate in building meaning from text.

Although postreading questioning activities sometimes serve to assess students' reading comprehension and their ability to think at various levels, the primary purpose of the postreading questioning we have described is to allow and encourage students to delve more deeply into the texts they read. Questioning activities tap into students' innate curiosity about the world and provide opportunities for them to think about and respond to information and ideas on a variety of levels. Below are two examples of questioning activities.

Questioning Sample Activity 1: *What do YOU Think?*

In *What do YOU Think?* students write their personal responses to the question "How do you think photographs help Journey?" This is a question that is based on the story's main theme. These responses are then displayed on a reader response chart. This activity is a continuation of the prereading activity What do *You Want to Know?* found on pages 93–95.

Selection: *Journey* by Patricia MacLachlan. (See description on page 93.)

Students: Sixth and seventh graders of low to average average ability.

Reading Purpose: To enjoy a sensitive well-crafted piece of literature and to make connections between the ideas developed in the story and the reader's own life.

Goal of the Activity: To help students feel secure in their responses to a particular work and not be dependent on someone else's response, to encourage respect for the responses of others, and to help students recognize the common and diverse elements in different readers' responses to the same piece of literature.

Rationale: *Journey* is one of those well-crafted stories that deserve to be "chewed and digested." It also invites personal response because of the unique way it portrays universal themes. Through the actions of the characters in *Journey*, readers discover a novel way to deal with the common dilemmas of hurt and disappointment. By thinking about the question "How do you think photographs help Journey?" they must connect what they know about how problems are solved in general with Journey's problem and solution in particular. By noting how others respond to the same question, they will discover similarities and differences between responses.

Procedure: After students have finished reading the novel, have them share their ideas about what they thought were some very important artifacts in the story—items that were especially important to Journey. Cameras and photographs are likely to be high on the list. Ask students to explain how these were used in the story and explain why they thought these were significant items. (For example, Grandpa is always taking pictures, and Journey finds the box of torn photographs under the bed.) If you have done the *What Do You Want to Know?* prereading activity, explain that they now probably understand why you wanted them to bring their photos for the reader response chart. (If you haven't done the *What Do You Want to Know* prereading activity, ask students at this point to bring their photos to school to display on the reader response chart. Show them the chart and note that it will give them an opportunity to share their responses to *Journey* and to other stories and poems they read. The chart will also let them see how other people respond. The question you want them to consider for this novel is "How did photographs help Journey?" After their pictures have been assembled, continue with this activity.)

At this point, display the reader response chart, which is shown in Figure 6-1. Discuss how the photographs reveal the uniqueness of each individual in the

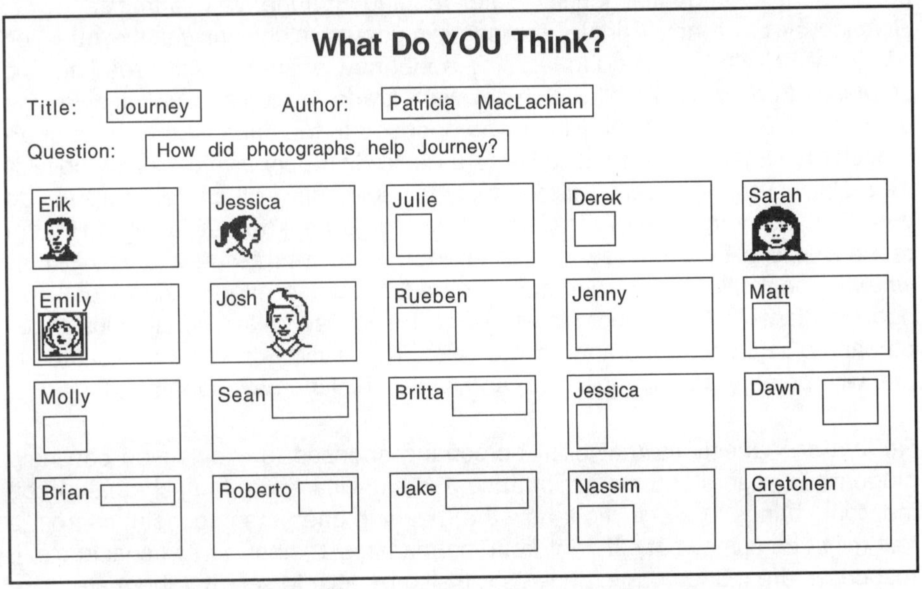

Figure 6-1. What Do You Think? Reader Response Chart

class. Explain that just as each person is a unique individual with special hairstyles, smiles, poses, clothes, skin color, and the like, their responses to a piece of literature will also be different. (Ask students why they think this might be so.) Explain further that just as each person's picture shows his or her unique qualities, it also reveals the similarities he or she shares with others. Have students discuss similarities (eyes, hair, teeth, clothes, etc.). Students' responses to stories will also have similarities. Explain that as time goes on and they read more stories and poems, it will be fun to use the chart to see just what those similarities and differences are.

Remind students of the question you wanted them to think about as they read *Journey*—"How do you think photographs helped Journey?"—that is posted on the chart.

You may want students to write their responses at this time or give them time to consider the question further. Before students write their responses, explain that these might be as short as a sentence or as long as a paragraph. They are to use as many words as it takes to express their opinions.

After students have written responses, post these on the reader-response chart next to their photographs. At some time after the responses have been posted on the chart, let each student read his or her response; then discuss the similarities and differences between them.

Adapting the Activity: Because photographs are central to the theme of this novel, *Journey* is an ideal springboard for introducing the reader response chart with student photos. However, this type of chart can be used with any number of expository works, novels, short stories, and poems; simply change the title, author, and question. For example, after reading Isaac Asimov's *How Did We Find Out About Our Genes?* sixth, seventh, or eighth graders might answer the question "Why do you think people want to know what effect heredity has on our personality and intelligence?" After reading *Strange New Animals, New to Science* by Lawrence Pringle, the same students might answer the question "Why are people interested in learning about new animals?" After reading *The Happiest Ending* by Yoshiko Uchida, sixth-grade students could answer the question "Why do you think Rinko was opposed to the Japanese custom of arranged marriages?" After reading Richard Peck's Newbery award-winning novel *A Year Down Yonder*, seventh-grade students could answer the question "Why do you think Grandma Dowdel told Mary Alice to go back to her family?" Reader responses can be recorded in a class journal as well as on a chart. Simply write the book title, author, and question on the top of a page (a scrapbook size book works well), have students write their responses on individual strips of paper, and glue these to the appropriate page. This activity can also be adapted to use with primary grade students to encourage thinking beyond the text.

Reflection: Questions that elicit personal responses to a selection can help students to understand the importance and significance of the schemata each individual brings to a selection: how the meaning one person constructs from a text might be somewhat different from the meaning another person constructs. If responses are made public, students will also be able to see that there are common responses. However, when constructing personal response questions, teachers need to be careful not to invade students' privacy. "How did you feel when . . ." questions might be appropriate if students are writing responses in personal journals, but they may not be in situations where there is an audience.

There are many other ways you might approach personal-response questions. In some instances these questions might be preceded by factual and inferential questions designed to ensure that students understand the selection before they give personal responses to it. For example: "Where did Journey find the box of torn photographs? Why do you think his mother tore them up? Why do you think she left the photographs for someone to find instead of throwing them away?" Students might discuss these questions in groups or answer them personally in a journal. After they have done so, they can answer the question "How do you think photographs helped Journey?" for the reader response chart or record their responses in the class journal.

Personal-response questions might be followed by application questions such as "How could you use your family photographs to understand something about your past?" A question of this sort might best be answered in a personal journal rather than on a chart or class journal. It applies personally to the student, who may want to refer to it at a later date in order to actually act upon it.

Questioning Sample Activity 2: *The Yellow Brick Road*

In *The Yellow Brick Road,* questions are developed that follow in sequential order the information that is central to understanding the selection. These questions create what Isabel Beck and Margaret McKeown (1981) call a story map—a set of questions which, when answered, constitute the essence of the story. In addition to the basic story map questions, story maps sometimes include extension questions, which ask students to go beyond the selection itself and relate it to their lives or other selections they have read, to make judgments about the text or its author, to deal with literary aspects of the selection, or to make some other type of connection between the text and the world outside the text.

Selection: *The Runaway Rice Cake,* written by Ying Chang Compestine and illustrated by Tungwai Chau. On the morning of the Chinese New Year's Eve, the whole Chang family—Momma, Pappa, and brothers Ming, Cong, and Da—pitch in to make the traditional New Year's Eve rice cake, the *nian-gao,* with the last of the family's rice flour. When the rice cake is steamed and Momma Chang lifts a knife to cut it, the *nian-gao* cries, "Ai yo! I don't think so!" and pops out of the pan. It runs outside, through the courtyard, with the Chang family in hot pursuit, past the animals, into the village market, onto the village docks, through the village, too fast to be caught by anyone. While racing up a steep side street, it collides with an old woman, and Momma Chang is able to capture it. When youngest brother Da learns that the old woman has not eaten in two days, he (to his two older brothers' dismay) offers her the family's one and only rice cake. Sympathetic to her plight as well, the rice cake says, "Grandmother needs me so! To her I will go." The starving, grateful old woman eats the entire *nian-gao* because it is so delicious. The Chang family returns home hungry and empty-handed, only to be greeted by neighbors who, having heard of their good deed, bring a variety of food offerings into the Chang house. When the Chang family invites the neighbors to share the food, they decline, as the food was meant for the Changs. Momma and Pappa tell the boys to eat first. Ming says he's not hungry, that Cong and Da can have his share. Cong says he's not hungry, either, and that Da can have his share. Da says he's sure there's enough food for everyone. When he lifts the cover from the bowl, the bowl grows larger and fills with dumplings. More bowls and baskets appear on the table filled with food to overflowing, enough for the Changs and all the neighbors to have a proper Chinese New Year's Eve feast and celebration, and thus everyone's unselfishness is rewarded.

Students: Third graders of mixed abilities.

Reading Purpose: To understand and enjoy a story in the folktale tradition and to learn some of the customs and events surrounding the Chinese New Year.

Goal of the Activity: To focus students' attention on the important events of the story in the order in which they take place.

Rationale: Like most traditional folktales, *The Runaway Rice Cake* includes a number of events that follow a predictable order. Having students answer questions about important story events in the sequence in which they occur can help promote comprehension of this particular story as well as help to develop a general schema for story sequence.

Procedure: Decide first what the starting point for the story is. Next, list briefly the major events that reveal the essence of the story in the order in which they occur. Write a question for each event. Below are the major events and matching questions for *The Runaway Rice Cake*.

> *Event 1:* The Chang family makes a *nian-gao* for their Chinese New Year celebration. (What did the Chang family make for their New Year's Eve celebration?)

> *Event 2:* When Momma Chang starts to cut the *nian-gao,* it comes alive and pops out of the pan. (What happened when Momma Chang started to cut the *nian-gao?*)

> *Event 3:* The *nian-gao* runs off, with the Chang family in hot pursuit, past the animals, into the village market, onto the village docks, through the village, too fast to be caught by anyone. (Why couldn't anyone catch the *nian-gao?*)

> *Event 4:* The *nian-gao* collides with an old woman, and Momma Chang is able to capture it. (How was the *nian-gao* finally captured?)

> *Event 5:* Because the starving old woman hasn't eaten in two days, Da insists that she should have some of their *nian-gao*. (Why did Da offer the family's *nian-gao* to the old woman?)

Event 6: The old woman eats the entire *nian-gao* because it is so delicious. (Why did the old woman eat the entire *nian-gao?*)

Event 7: Hearing of their good deed, when the Changs return home empty-handed, neighbors appear with food for them. (Why did the neighbors bring food for the Changs?)

Event 8: Pappa Chang invites the neighbors to join them for the New Year's celebration, but they refuse to eat any of the food that they brought for the Changs. (What wouldn't the neighbors do with the food they brought?)

Event 9: All the Chang family members offer their food to another family member, except for Da, who says there is enough for everyone. (What did all of the Chang family members, except for Da, offer to do with the food?)

Event 10: When Da says there is enough food for everyone, food magically appears, enough for all to enjoy an abundant New Year's Eve feast and celebration. (What happened when Da said there was enough food for everyone?)

After the basic story map is constructed, the extension questions can be written. Here are two Extension Questions that might be used with this story.

Extension 11: Name an instance from your own life or from something you have read about or seen on television in which people were rewarded for being unselfish.

Extension 12: The Runaway Rice Cake is a traditional folktale. Name some other traditional folk tales you're familiar with and note some of the things they have in common with *The Runaway Rice Cake.*

After constructing the questions, write a number for each on the "yellow brick" spaces as shown in Figure 6-2. Have students work in pairs of different abilities to write the answers to the questions on a separate sheet of paper, or put the questions on a transparency and have students answer them as a group activity.

Adapting the Activity: This activity can be used for any story in which the events proceed in chronological order. Simply identify the events of the story that reveal its basic meaning and write a question for each. Then write one or more extension questions. The *Yellow Brick Road* activity might be used with *How the Ox Star Fell From Heaven*, a simply and clearly told Hmong folktale by author-illustrator Lily Toy Hong; the Zimbabwean folktale *Mufaro's Beautiful Daughters*, written and illustrated by John Steptoe; Aesop's fable *Androcles and the Lion*, retold and illustrated by Janet Stevens; *No Dinner: The Story of the Old Woman and the Pumpkin,* a lively folktale from India by Jessica Souhami; and many other folktales, fables, and fairy tales.

Another way to use The *Yellow Brick Road* story map is to laminate the yellow brick road (without the questions on it) to a manila file folder to use as a game board for the folktales and fairy tales that students read. Write two questions for each event in the individual stories on separate index cards. Number

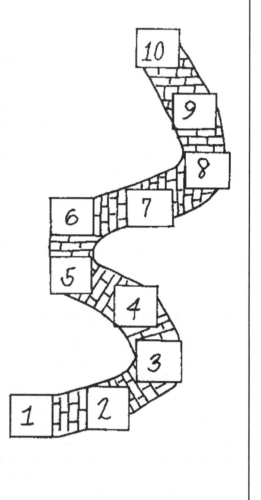

1. What did the Chang family make for their New Year's Eve celebration?

2. What happened when Momma Chang started to cut the *nian-gao*?

3. Why couldn't anyone catch the *nian-gao*?

4. How was the *nian-gao* finally captured?

5. Why did Da offer the family's *nian-gao* to the old woman?

6. Why did the old woman eat the entire *nian-gao*?

7. Why did the neighbors bring food for the Changs?

8. What wouldn't the neighbors do with the food they brought?

9. What did all of the Chang family members, except for Da, offer to do with the food?

10. What happened when Da said there was enough food for everyone?

11. Name an instance from your own life or from something you have read about or seen on television in which people were rewarded for being unselfish.

12. *The Runaway Rice Cake* is a traditional folktale. Name some other traditional folktales you're familiar with and note some of the things they have in common with *The Runaway Rice Cake*.

Figure 6-2. The Yellow Brick Road Story Map

one set of cards 1A, 2A, 3A, and so on, and the other set 1B, 2B, 3B, and put possible answers on the back of each card. Players take turns answering from either set A or B in chronological order. If a player answers to her partner's satisfaction, she can move up to the next space. The other player then has the chance to move forward by answering the other question correctly. The first person to reach the end is the winner. The story board game and folder can be used for many different selections; simply change the questions to coincide with the story. The answers for some questions—such as "Why did Da offer the family's *nian-gao* to the old woman?" "Why did the old woman eat the entire *nian-gao*?", and "Why did the neighbors bring food for the Changs?"—could be open for interpretation. Some rules will need to be established beforehand to determine acceptable answers.

Reflection: You may have noticed that most of the basic questions in our story map were literal ones dealing with specific events of the story. Beck and McKeown (1981) define a story map as a sequenced list of important events and ideas in a story, and they note that story maps include some inferential questions, as fully understanding a story requires at least some inferences. We certainly agree. Nevertheless, we have found that our story maps for simple stories, such as *The Runaway Rice Cake,* contain largely literal questions. For this reason, as our example showed, story map questions are not the only type of questions to ask on reading selections. Once students understand the essence of the story, then interpretive, analytical, and creative questions—extension questions—are appropriate and important to pursue. However, in Beck and McKeown's judgment and ours, these are best considered after the story map has been established in students' minds.

Although the story map was developed for narratives, similar guidelines can be followed when constructing questions for informational material by creating questions that coincide with the organizational approach taken by the author. For example, questions for texts that present lists of details and concrete examples can reflect that organization: "What are three words that describe the Vietnam Memorial?" Of course, you generally want to ask only questions that deal with important details and examples, even if, as too often is the case, the text presents unimportant details (Beck & McKeown, 1981). Other organizational patterns can also be paralleled with questions. Cause-and-effect questions can be developed for text that presents issues by using that format: "What were the effects of the Boston Tea party?" Similarly, compare-and-contrast questions can be created for selections that use the compare-and-contrast format: "In what three ways are lizards and snakes alike? In what three ways are they different?" Whatever organizational scheme the author has chosen to develop his or her topic can be used and underscored by posing questions that parallel that organization.

Also, students themselves can be taught how to develop questions for selections for other students to answer. As a during-reading activity, students can compose questions while they read a selection that a partner or group member will answer as a postreading activity. Before students develop questions, however, they will need instruction on how to develop questions and the various kinds of questions they might ask.

Questioning activities encourage students to think about what they have read and to probe more deeply. By asking the appropriate kinds of questions, you can channel students' thinking and improve their comprehension and recall, as well as foster critical and creative thinking.

Discussion

Almost every classroom reading experience will include some sort of discussion—exchanging ideas out loud. The key word here is *exchanging;* some like to use the term *dialogue* to describe the give-and-take nature of discussion. The intent of discussion is to freely explore ideas, to learn something new or gain a different perspective because of the information or insights that more than one person has to give. Discussion is an active exchange of ideas, ideally one in which everyone has the opportunity to participate equally. Discussion provides an opportunity to solidify, clarify, or modify knowledge. Discussion activities give students a forum in which to talk about the meaning they constructed from texts, listen to the insights of others, and weigh their responses in light of those of their classmates. Here they can think about, ponder, consider, analyze, evaluate, and make connections between the text and their own lives and among the text, their personal experiences, and the thoughts and experiences of other students.

Discussion groups can be teacher led or student led. They can involve the entire class, small groups, or pairs. Whatever format is used, here are a few guidelines for implementing discussions:

- Develop a clear purpose or purposes. What is the discussion to accomplish? Are students examining two or more sides of an issue? Are they looking to discover a book's theme? Are they trying to solve a problem, or master the content of a text? Discussion should not be rigidly structured, but without clear purpose or focus it runs the risk of deteriorating into meaningless chitchat.

- Discussion leaders (as well as participants) should be supportive, uncritical, and open-minded. Leaders should encourage response from all members of the group and be sparing with their own comments and suggestions.

- Discussion prompts might include or begin with literal level questioning but should go beyond this to stimulate critical and creative thinking as well. Discussions should incorporate a number of levels of thinking: recalling, applying, analyzing, synthesizing, evaluating, and interpreting.

- When differences of opinions arise concerning literal or recall questions, the text should be consulted in order to verify or refute.

- Encourage group members to evaluate discussions. Was the purpose achieved? Did everyone get a chance to participate equally? What were the strengths and weaknesses of the discussion? What might be done differently in the future?

Two sample discussion activities are described below.

Discussion Sample Activity 1: *Three's a Charm!*

In *Three's a Charm!,* three groups of students find specific examples of three important concepts in the text and report their findings to the class.

Selection: *I Have A Dream: The Story of Martin Luther King, Jr.*, by Margaret Davidson. This biography traces the emergence of Martin Luther King, Jr. as a powerful civil rights leader and pacifist from his youth in Atlanta, Georgia, through his assassination at age 39 in Memphis, Tennessee. the biography stresses King's compassion, intelligence, and eloquence, as well as his unquenchable spirit and commitment to justice, equality, and peace.

Students: Fifth to seventh grade students of middle to high ability.

Reading Purpose: To understand and appreciate the purpose and results of Martin Luther King Jr.'s efforts to promote civil rights.

Goal of the Activity: To stimulate students' use of recall and critical thinking skills and to provide an opportunity for students to work together in order to come to a consensus.

Rationale: This text is rich in examples of King's methods and strategies to peacefully bring about change in policies and attitudes toward Black Americans. To single out just three of these methods as particularly noteworthy requires that students recall the significant strategies and evaluate the effectiveness of each. In order to reach consensus on the three most effective tools, students must substantiate their choices with sound reasoning as well as exercise such skills as persuasiveness and diplomacy.

Procedure: Tell students that Martin Luther King, Jr. and others in the Civil Rights Movement used a number of different strategies to achieve their ends, but probably there were three that were used most often and most effectively. Explain that they will get the chance to talk about what three they think were most effective, listen to what others think, and come to a common agreement.

Divide the class into three groups and appoint a leader and three recorders for each. Explain that the groups are to meet and decide what they think were the three main tools of the Civil Rights Movement. (Boycotts, sit-ins, and protest marches were the principal three, but students may find others.) Instruct students to bring their copy of King's biography with them when their group meets. Each group should review the biography to identify the three methods and be ready to give specific examples of each from the text. Encourage students in each group to take turns telling about a strategy and locating examples of it in the text. (You may want to model this procedure before students meet in their groups.) Explain to students that after the groups have decided what they think were the three most effective strategies, the three recorders will write the specific examples of each of the three strategies from the text. Give the groups about 15 or 20 minutes of discussion time, while you circulate among the groups giving help, encouragement, and praise where needed. After the discussions are completed, let the three recorders for each group report their group's findings. Compare and contrast each group's answers. Was there a consistency among the three choices? If so, what was the reason for this consistency? Was there a discrepancy? If so, can group members defend their choices?

Also, as a class, evaluate how the discussion groups went, considering such matters as whether all group members contributed, if students listened to each other, if they supported and encouraged each other's contributions. As David Johnson and his colleagues Johnson, Johnson, & Holubec, (1994) noted, this sort of group processing is crucial to students learning to work in groups effectively.

Adapting the Activity: This activity can be used for almost any reading selection; simply choose concepts that coincide with that particular selection. For example, after reading *Trapped by the Ice!: Shackleton's Amazing Antarctic Adventure* by Michael McCurdy or *Spirit of Endurance: The True Story of the Shackleton Expedition to the Antarctic* by Jennifer Armstrong, the prompt for the *Three's a Charm!* activity could be "What were the three most important things that helped the 27 men in the Shackleton expedition survive their almost 2-year ordeal in the Antarctic?" After reading Beverly Cleary's *Strider*, which is written in a diary format, the prompt might be "What were the three most important days in Leigh Bott's year?" After reading Eve Bunting's *The Summer of Riley* about a boy who has just 21 days to save his dog after it has been taken from him, the prompt might be "What were the three hardest things William had to do to save Riley?" Of course, even though three is often considered a magic number, this activity might have other numbers of items. Anything from two to six often works well.

Reflection: Ideally, students will have been given the focusing question before they read so they can be looking for the three "big" or "most important" ideas, perhaps using bookmarks or jotting down notes in their journals. Again, as this activity so clearly illustrates, pre-, during-, and postreading activities are linked. Students' attention is focused before they read. While they read, they are looking for the "big ideas" as they construct meaning with the text. After they read, they check their responses against those of others, evaluate, and make decisions based on their ideas, the text, and their group members' ideas. The discussion that follows is always lively as well as illuminating because students tend to have strong ideas about what they perceive as "most important."

This activity serves as a useful background against which to consider two related questions: To what extent should we take the position that there are right answers, and to what extent should students be expected to come to a consensus when engaged in group activities? These are huge questions, ones which themselves may not have right answers. To the extent that they do have answers, those answers are deserving of a book rather than a brief comment such as we are including here. Nevertheless, we feel obligated to give brief personal responses to each of them.

With respect to there being right answers, we would note, as we did in chapter 3, that we agree with current cognitive-constructivist thinking, which stresses that much of the meaning a reader constructs from a text is constructed by the reader alone. However, this does not mean that the reader constructs *all* meaning; it does not mean that all texts are equally open to the reader's interpretation, and it does not mean that there are no wrong answers. Children are growing up in a world in which they need to consider the evidence and make important decisions. We need to guide them in becoming critical readers: readers who consider the text and other information and arrive at defensible interpretations.

With respect to a group's need to come to a consensus, we would stress that this is usually the most desirable outcome. Children, adults, and societies need to work toward consensus. However, we do not believe that students should be forced into a consensus. If, after their best efforts at agreement, students in a group still disagree on some matters, then all sides need to be heard, and the reality that such disagreements will occur should be acknowledged and accepted.

Discussion Sample Activity 2: *Both Sides*

Both Sides is a discussion web activity (Alvermann, 1991), in which students use a graphic aid to help them look at both sides of an issue before drawing conclusions. In this activity students meet in pairs and then as groups of four to reach a consensus about a question raised by their reading.

Selection: *Frozen Fire*, by James Houston. (See description on page 68.)

Students: Sixth graders of mixed abilities.

Reading Purpose: To understand and enjoy an exciting survival story.

Goal of the Activity: To help students understand how literature can be a medium for learning about the various ways people have of responding to similar situations and issues, and to provide all students with the opportunity to voice their opinions and work toward coming to a group consensus.

Rationale: *Frozen Fire* poses a number of questions worth pondering. One in particular arises from an incident in which Matthew discovers gold nuggets at a frozen waterfall. The boys have given up their search for Matthew's dad and are desperately trying to make their way back to Frobisar. Their food supply is nearly gone and death is imminent if they don't reach Frobisar soon. However, overjoyed at the fortune within his grasp, Matthew loads his pockets and backpack with the precious metal against Kayak's warning that the gold will only be a hindrance to their struggle to get home. Because most students this age are intrigued by the idea of instant fortune, the question "Should Matthew have taken the gold nuggets?" will make for a lively discussion.

Procedure: On the chalkboard, a transparency, or individual worksheets duplicate the chart in Figure 6-3.

Reasons

———		———
———		———
———		———
———		———
———		———
———		———

NO   Should Matthew have taken   **YES**
the gold nuggets?

Conclusions

Figure 6-3. Both Sides Chart

Pair students and explain that they are to discuss the pros and cons of Matthew's taking the gold nuggets. Encourage them to come up with good reasons for both sides of the issue, and to write these down on a sheet of paper. Stress that initially the goal is to get down all possible reasons for and against taking the gold, not to support one position for the other. Explain that they might want to refer to their books but need only write key words or phrases in the appropriate column. They should to try and give an equal number of reasons in each column. Figure 6-3A gives some sample responses.

Reasons

Didn't belong to him   Didn't belong to anybody
Were worthless in the Arctic   Would make him rich
Kayak told him not to   Would have made his dad happy

NO   Should Matthew have taken   **YES**
the gold nuggets?

Would slow Matthew down   Could buy things for Kayak's
                                  family

Could cost him his life   If took only a few, would have
                                  been a little richer

Conclusions

Figure 6-3A. Both Sides Chart with Sample Responses

After the partners have had a chance to jot down their reasons, pair one set of partners with another set. Ask the new groups of four students to compare their reasons why Matthew should or shouldn't have taken the gold nuggets. Explain to students that although the goal is to work toward a consensus, it is perfectly acceptable for members to disagree with that conclusion. Tell them that you will have a large group discussion at the end of the period in which dissenting views will be heard.

When the groups of four have reached their conclusions, select a spokesperson for each group or have them select their own. Give each group about 3 minutes to choose the one reason that best supports the group's conclusion, and have the spokesperson jot it down. When each group has chosen its reason, call on the different spokespersons to report their group's decision. At this time ask the spokesperson to also give any dissenting viewpoints and the support for these positions.

As a follow-up activity to the discussion web, you might want to have students write their individual answers to the question "Should Matthew have taken the gold nuggets?" and post these in the classroom for others to read.

Adapting the Activity: The *Both Sides* activity can be used any time students read material that raises a question that might evoke dissenting viewpoints. For example, in *In the Year of the Boar and Jackie Robinson* by Bette Bao Lord, Emily, the sixth-grade class president, is supposed to present Jackie Robinson with the key to P.S. 8, but instead she gives the honor of presenting the key to Shirley Wong, the protagonist in the story. Students might use the discussion web to decide the answer to the question "Should Shirley have allowed Emily to give her the honor of making the presentation to Jackie Robinson?" After reading *The Kids From Kennedy Middle School: Choosing Sides* by Ilene Cooper, sixth-grade students might discuss the question "Should Jon have quit the basketball team?" After reading Barbara Park's *The Graduation of Jake Moon,* about a boy dealing with a beloved grandfather who develops Alzheimer's disease, fourth-grade students might discuss the question "Should Jake have stopped inviting friends over because of his grandfather's behavior?" The discussion web can also be modified to use across the curriculum. Suppose eighth-grade students have read a selection on the Civil War that discusses Stephen A. Douglas and Abraham Lincoln and their opposing views on the slavery issue. As a postreading activity, you might substitute the names *Douglas* and *Lincoln* for the *yes* and *no* columns of the discussion web, write *slavery* in the box where the question usually goes, and have students discuss the two men's different views on the issue.

Reflection: Although the primary purpose of this activity is to discuss the pros and cons of an issue before drawing conclusions, in many cases this activity can generate further discussion that leads to the consideration of a story's theme. Such a discussion might be prompted by a question such as "Why did the author include this episode?" This in turn might lead to these considerations: "Was he trying to show the contrast between what has value in a wilderness survival situation contrasted to the values of civilization?" or "Was he making a statement about the cost of individual greed on collective survival?"

Quality literature and nonfiction serve the purpose of generating and communicating ideas about what humans need to survive, to make strides personally and collectively. Discussion provides not only a forum to make ideas accessible to students but also a way to make sparks and create flames.

Writing

E. M. Forster said, "I don't know what I think until I see what I said." For many of us, that adage rings true. Writing is the twin sister of reading—a powerful way to integrate what you know with the information presented in a text as well as to find out what you really understand and what you don't. Writing is powerful because it requires a reader to actively manipulate information and ideas. Unfortunately, the significance of the link between reading and writing has been adequately recognized only in the past two decades (Atwell, 1998; Calkins, 2001; Nelson & Calfee, 1998; Shanahan, 1990), and only recently has this powerful relationship affected instruction in a large number of classrooms.

Obviously, writing does not lie exclusively in the domain of postreading activities. Writing has its place as both a prereading activity—a tool for motivating, for activating background knowledge, and for relating a selection to students' lives—and as a during-reading activity, a device for guiding students' thought processes as they build meaning from a text. As a postreading activity, writing can serve all the purposes we listed at the beginning of the chapter: demonstrating understanding of the information and ideas presented in a text; applying, analyzing, synthesizing, evaluating, and elaborating text information and ideas; and connecting information and ideas in a logical way. Writing also provides opportunities for students to extend ideas; to explore new ways of thinking, doing, and seeing; and to invent, evaluate, create, and ponder (Ryder & Graves, 2003).

In discussing writing activities, we focus on two issues that go hand in hand: purpose and audience. Why are we encouraging students to write, or what purpose does the writing serve? For whom is the student writing—him- or herself or someone else?

Dividing the purposes of writing into two broad categories—writing to learn and writing to communicate with others—can help you to identify the kinds of writing you might encourage students to do after they read a selection, as well as to determine the appropriate audience for their writing. However, it is important to keep in mind that whether students are writing to learn, to explore, or to communicate, they are actively manipulating ideas and language. Thus, learning is always taking place.

Table 6-2 shows writing activities appropriate for each of these purposes.

Table 6-2.   Writing Purposes and Activities

Writing Activities for Learning About Oneself or the World

Audience: Self

Informational Writing

Personal journals
Diaries of daily events
Free writing
Learning logs
Charts and diagrams
Notes, summaries, time lines,
 and outlines

Creative Writing

Stories
Poems
Free writing

Writing Activities for Communicating With Others

Audience: Teachers, other students, authors, family members, prospective
employers, and the greater community of readers

Informational Writing

Letters
Reports
Charts and diagrams
Dialogue journals
Essays

Creative Writing

Poetry
Stories
Plays
Creative nonfiction
 Memoirs
 Biographies
 Essays

The two sample writing activities described here illustrate just a few of the
many types of writing that can be fruitfully incorporated into reading experiences.

Writing Sample Activity 1: *Compare and Contrast*

In *Compare and Contrast,* after completing a Venn diagram students write three
paragraphs to compare and contrast two topics.

Selection: The chapter "Members of Our Solar System" in *Science in Your
World* by John Hackett and Richard Moyer. The last section of this chapter,
"Other Members of Our Solar System," explains how comets and meteoroids
are both members of our solar system. Comets, which come from the far outer
edges of the solar system, have very large orbits and are composed of ice
mixed with dust particles. Meteoroids are small pieces of metal or rock that are
scattered in different orbits around the sun.

Students: Fifth grade students of mixed abilities; three gifted students.

Reading Purpose: To understand the concepts of comets and meteoroids, what part they play in the solar system, the differences between them, and their similarities, in order to appreciate the intricacies and diversity of the universe as well as the laws that govern it.

Goal of the Activity: To help students organize the textual information on comets and meteoroids, showing similarities and differences in order to better understand what comets and meteoroids are and how they function as members of our solar system.

Rationale: Although they may have heard the terms, most students will probably not have a good understanding of exactly what comets and meteoroids are—in fact, they may well lump the two together. After having read the first part of the chapter, they will have learned about the planets, their different orbits, and how the planets themselves are different as well as similar. Having students organize the textual information on comets and meteoroids by using a graphic aid such as a Venn diagram will aid them in internalizing and remembering these two concepts. Completing a Venn diagram requires students to classify information to highlight differences and similarities. They then use the completed diagram to write three paragraphs: one describing the unique qualities of comets, one the unique qualities of meteoroids, and one the qualities they have in common.

Procedure: After students have finished reading the chapter on the solar system, briefly discuss some of the similarities and differences they found among the planets. Next tell them that there is a good device, the Venn diagram, they can use to look at the similarities and differences between things. Draw a sample Venn diagram such as that shown in Figure 6-4 on the board. Show students how they can use it to compare and contrast Venus and Earth, and have them refer to their texts as you complete the diagram together.

   After this, explain that the Venn diagram is also useful in organizing their thoughts for writing an essay or writing to get a better understanding of a sub-

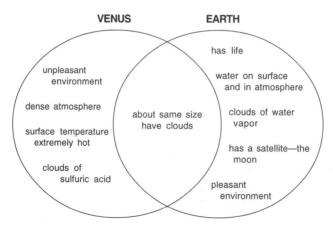

Figure 6-4.   Venn Diagram for Comparing and Contrasting Venus and Earth

ject. Together with students, compose a three-paragraph composition on Venus and Earth, using the information recorded on the Venn diagram. Tell students that the audience for this composition is themselves—they are writing to get a better understanding of the two planets, not to communicate this information to anyone else. As they write, they should add anything that connects the information they have written in the diagram with something they already know. Below is an example of what these paragraphs might look like.

> Venus is not a planet I'd want to live on. Its environment is very unpleasant. It's extremely hot and smelly because the atmosphere is thick with clouds of sulfuric acid. (I think I remember sulfur has the smell of rotten eggs. Yuck!)

> In contrast to Venus, Earth has a great atmosphere. One reason is that it has water—water on the surface and water in the air (clouds). Also Earth has life on it—probably because it has water and a temperature that's not too hot or cold for people and animals. Earth also has a satellite, the Moon.

> Venus has been called Earth's twin because they are nearly the same size. Venus and Earth both have clouds. Other than that, I can't see too much the same about these two planets. Oh, I guess they both orbit the Sun!

Use the Venn diagram to compare and contrast as many other planets as you feel appropriate, and then compose three-paragraph expositions that use the information from the diagram. When students sufficiently understand the activity, have them develop a Venn diagram for comets and meteoroids and write three paragraphs using the information they have recorded on the diagram. Remind them that the audience for the composition is themselves—the purpose of writing is to better understand comets and meteoroids.

If this activity doesn't appear challenging enough for the three gifted students, have them do the same exercise, but have them take the information from chapters 1–2 and 4–5 in the trade book *Meteors and Meteorites: Voyagers from Outer Space* by Patricia Lauber.

Adapting the Activity: Venn diagrams are particularly useful for writing-to-learn with expository texts in which the author has presented material that can be compared and contrasted, but they can also be used with narratives. Students can use them to analyze differences and similarities between characters in the same story or to compare and contrast characters in different stories. For example, you might have students use a Venn diagram in writing about the two protagonists, Prince Brat and Jemmy, in Sid Fleishman's Newbery award-winning novel *The Whipping Boy*. The appropriate audience for this composition might be the teacher or classmates. Students might use a Venn diagram in writing an essay comparing and contrasting Patricia MacLachlan's *Sarah, Plain and Tall* and Pam Conrad's *Prairie Songs,* two stories about pioneer women and their experiences on the prairie, or in comparing and contrasting *Subira Subira* by Tololwa M. Mollel and *The Lion's Whiskers: An Ethiopian Folktale* by Nancy Raines Day, two variants of an African folktale in which the protagonist must perform the task of plucking whiskers from a lion. The audience for this composition might be the authors of these works. The students are attempting to communicate to the authors what they perceive as the similarities and differences in the two books. This will give students' writing a slightly different flavor compared to the writing they might do for themselves, their teacher, or their classmates.

Reflection: This activity, in which a Venn diagram is used to facilitate learning and writing, is only one of many graphic approaches that might be used in dealing with expository material. Instead of using a Venn diagram, students might record information in outline form using each of the members of the solar system as a subtitle and recording two or three important details about each member under the title. As they compose, students would then use the notes to write a paragraph on each topic. Students might also use a tree structure to show the hierarchical organization of a topic, producing a structure such as that in Figure 6-5. Then they could use the tree to organize their writing.

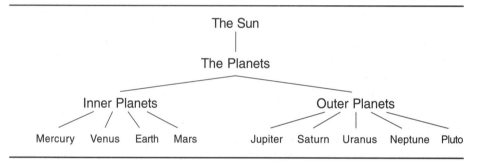

Figure 6-5. Tree Structure

One matter to consider, as you plan what graphic aids to suggest that students use to organize their writing, is how many different kinds of graphics you want to present. On the one hand, different graphics accomplish somewhat different purposes, and students appreciate variety. On the other hand, it takes time for students to learn to use different graphics, and introducing too many of them may take too much time or even be confusing for some students.

Whatever graphic students use, the audience can be the students themselves, students in other classes, parents, and any number of others. With any writing activity, students should be aware of its purpose as well as the audience for whom the writing is intended, and writing that is intended for an audience other than the student will require that the student revise the initial draft.

Writing Sample Activity 2: *What If?*

What If? is a creative writing activity that extends the concepts in a selection by allowing students to explore alternate possibilities. Students must take what they know and what they have learned about a topic to create a novel situation.

Selection: "Members of Our Solar System," the same chapter as in the above activity. This chapter discusses our solar system—the Sun and the space objects around it. These include the nine planets and their moons, as well as asteroids, comets, and meteoroids.

Students: Fifth-grade students of mixed abilities; three gifted students.

Reading Purpose: To understand the characteristics of the various members of our solar system, the parts they play, and their differences and similarities, in order to appreciate the intricacies and diversity of the universe as well as the laws that govern it.

Goal of the Activity: To encourage students to apply and extend concepts by proposing a situation in which one of the characteristics or laws they have read about in a selection is changed and to have them consider how that change would affect the other factors.

Rationale: Virtually all of our scientific advancements and discoveries have been achieved because someone was able to take what they knew and manipulate it in a way that no one else had ever considered. Students need to be encouraged to practice this kind of thinking with science material. Not only is it worthwhile and fun, but it is risk-free—there are no right answers. In this type of activity, students are not writing to learn what someone else already knows, they are writing to discover, which is a crucial component of creative thinking.

Procedure: Begin the activity by brainstorming with students, asking them to list facts about the solar system and scientific laws that they have learned from the chapter. Write their suggestions on the board. Some of their suggestions might include the following:

> *The force of gravity keeps each planet in orbit around the Sun.*
>
> *The tilt of the Earth causes seasons.*
>
> *Planets travel around the Sun.*
>
> *Venus contains dense clouds of sulfuric acid.*
>
> *There is no water on Venus.*
>
> *Earth has water.*
>
> *Earth has a moon.*
>
> *Mars has a thick atmosphere of carbon dioxide and a little water vapor.*
>
> *Oxygen is needed for life to exist.*

Next, create What If? questions for some of the facts and laws by changing those facts and laws. For example:

> *What if the Sun shrunk? What would happen to the planets?*
>
> *What if the Sun grew? What would happen to the planets?*
>
> *What if the Sun disappeared? What would happen to the planets?*
>
> *What if the Earth weren't tilted? How would life in our city be different?*

What if Venus contained clouds of water vapor instead of sulfuric acid? What might be different about that planet.

What if Earth had no moon? What would be different about our life?

What if Mars had oxygen instead of carbon dioxide?

Students can also suggest their own "what ifs" after you give them a few examples. After you have written a sufficient number of What If? statements on the board, have students write their responses either in their journals or on note paper. These responses can range from a phrase or two to a paragraph or more. Some students may be inspired by one prompt to write a whole story. They should be encouraged to follow whatever path these prompts suggest for them. The idea is to stretch the imagination, not crimp it.

Students might write What if? responses just for themselves, to explore ideas just for the fun of seeing where it takes them, or they might like to share their ideas with others. If the latter is the case, create an audience for this activity by telling students that you will publish their responses in a What If? book for their classroom science library. Therefore, as they write they should keep their classmates in mind. Also, remind them that the latter type of writing—published writing—will require more than just one draft.

Students might also enjoy proposing additional "what ifs" and exploring those ideas. Also, besides writing their own stories, gifted students might be posted at computers to serve as editors and publishers of What If? stories that students compose.

Adapting the Activity: Having students write their responses to "what if" questions is readily adaptable to nearly any reading selection: expository texts, narratives, or poetry. After reading Virginia Hamilton's *The People Could Fly*, students might compose stories prompted by the question "What if you could fly?" After reading the poems of Patricia Hubbell in *A Green Grass Gallop*, a student might write a poem in response to "What if you had a horse?" The title of the poem might be "If I Had a Horse" or perhaps "Racing the Wind." After reading *If I Were President* by Catherine Stier, students could write what they think their day would be like if they were president.

Reflection: This example illustrates one possibility for getting students to think creatively or to extend their thinking about concepts found in informational texts. Obviously, there are as many more as there are creative teachers to dream them up. Narratives also abound in opportunities to inspire creative writing. A few of these are as follows:

- Select a scene from a book and rewrite it to show what might happen if a character did something differently than was done in the book. For example, in the scene from the Katherine Paterson novel *The Great Gilly Hopkins* in which Gilly first meets William Ernest, students might develop the scene showing an assertive instead of a passive William Ernest.
- Write an alternative ending to a story.
- Write a sequel to a story.

- Present the events of a book in newspaper format.
- Rewrite a contemporary story as a fairy tale: "Once upon a time there was a girl named Galadriel Hopkins, but most everyone called her Gilly."
- Write a scene from the perspective of another character. For example, in *The Great Gilly Hopkins,* any one of the scenes that include Gilly and William Ernest might be written from William Ernest's viewpoint instead of Gilly's.
- Write What If? stories for folktales by changing one aspect of the story. For example, in the Native American folktale *Big Thunder Magic* by Craig Kee Strete, in which Great Chief visits the "City" taking his sheep Nanabee with him, students could change the character Nanabee to a different type of animal and write their own tales based on the main story idea.

Writing with the purpose of exploring ideas and possibilities nurtures not only students' writing abilities but their spirits as well. Students need time to give their imaginations free reign. As Neil Postman reminds us in *The Disappearance of Childhood* (1982), this is particularly true for many students in today's world—students for whom the pressure to succeed, poverty, or uncertainty of what will come tomorrow bring adulthood all too soon. Also, for students who struggle with the basics, it also means a chance to do something whose success is measured only by the pleasure of riding an idea to see where it will take them.

Drama

Drama is a natural part of childhood. As soon as their language and social skills begin to develop, children play "house," "doctor," and "school" with their playmates. They enact dramas with their dolls, trucks, cars, or plastic figures of their favorite cartoon, movie, and TV characters. Not only are children participants in these playtime dramas, they are also their creators. Through drama, children translate what they know about the world into oral and body language.

Drama as a postreading activity encourages students to extend existing meanings and generate new ones. It is also fun, a highly motivating way to involve students in all of the cognitive tasks we listed at the beginning of the chapter.

In postreading dramatic activities, students create settings, characters, dialogue, action, and props by combining the meaning they have constructed with the text, the resources available to them, and their own ideas to produce a "play," using their bodies and voices to communicate. This play might consist of a 1-minute pantomime involving just one "actor," or a 50-minute production of *The Best Christmas Pageant Ever* that involves the entire class, props, costumes, and lighting.

Dramatic activities can emerge from fiction, nonfiction, or poetry. Two fifth graders might play the parts of Gilly and Miss Ellis, Gilly's caseworker, and dramatize the opening scene from Katherine Paterson's *The Great Gilly Hopkins*; an entire class of second graders might dramatize Indian tigers after reading or listening to Ted Lewin's informational picture book *Tiger Trek*; and small groups of first through third graders might gather to dramatize their favorite poems in Jack Prelutsky's *Tyrannosaurus Was a Beast*.

As students dramatize informally, they are involved in all sorts of decision making. What will I say? How will I say it? What actions and facial expressions will I use? What costumes or props will I need? Will I need to play more than one part? To illustrate the last question, let us say two first graders are dramatizing "The Kite" from Arnold Lobel's *Days With Frog and Toad*, which has two main characters, Frog and Toad, and a choir of minor characters, the Robins. One student might take the part of Frog and the other Toad, and both might assume the roles of the Robins. Problem solving, which requires them to use available resources to devise their own unique interpretations of a selection, is part of the creative process.

Although an audience is sometimes appropriate, dramatizations don't require one. The audience may consist of only the students who are enacting the drama. After reading a chapter in a social studies text, students might pair up, choosing two historical figures to portray. After reading a chapter that discusses the 1960s, for example, two seventh or eighth graders might decide to portray Martin Luther King, Jr. and Lyndon Johnson. First they need to collect data on these individuals—policies, actions, attitudes, style of speech–and then select a topic or topics to discuss. What would Martin Luther King and Lyndon Johnson say to each other? For the dramatization, students carry on a conversation posing as these individuals. This dramatization could end here, or students might choose to perform it for other students or for an even greater audience, such as another class or parents. Drama doesn't have to, but it can, move beyond the school walls to places such as day care centers and nursing homes.

With dramatic activities the teacher will play a variety of roles that depends on the students, the selection, and the purpose of the activity. Occasionally, a teacher might need to assume the role of director or producer, but more often the job will be that of facilitator and encourager. In that capacity, he might find himself stepping in to fill the role of the troll in *Three Billy Goats Gruff*, reading passages from *The Magic School Bus* series by Joanna Cole, helping to build a puppet stage or sew puppets, or showing students how to make "princess" hats for Ruth Sanderson's version of *The Twelve Dancing Princesses*.

Drama has great potential for showing students that language can be transformed and ideas can be seen, heard, and felt, as the next sample activity demonstrates.

Drama Sample Activity: *History Comes to Life*

In History Comes to Life, groups of students dramatize scenes from a biography.

Selection: *Harriet Tubman: Call To Freedom* by Judy Carlson. (See description on page 88.)

Students: Third and fourth graders of high abilities.

Reading Purpose: To learn more about the plight of Black Americans during the mid-1800s and to appreciate and be inspired by the courage, resourcefulness, and commitment of Harriet Tubman.

Goal of the Activity: To provide students with an opportunity to practice their problem-solving and decision-making skills; to come to a better understanding of Harriet Tubman and the times and conditions in which she lived.

Rationale: To successfully dramatize a scene from the biography, students must combine their knowledge of what they know about dramatizing events and portraying characters in general with the specific information in the text. They need to make decisions about what events to portray, what characters to include, who will play these characters, what action will take place, what will be said, which props (if any) will be used, and a number of smaller matters. These are the sorts of cognitive tasks in which students are continually involved, in and out of school. Providing a supportive setting in which children can succeed at these tasks is one way to increase their confidence and encourage risk taking—certainly a desirable goal, as children's willingness to take risks is crucial to their growth in skill and knowledge.

Procedure: After the students have read the biography and you have spent some time discussing its main themes and issues, explain that students are going to form small groups and dramatize various events in the book. Have them suggest incidents from the biography that might work as dramatizations, and write these on the chalkboard. Along with these incidents, write the number of actors required for each. Some of these incidents might include the following:

- Harriet being sent off at age 6 to work for the Cooks, getting the measles, and being brought home sick. Roles needed: Mr. and Mrs. Cook, Harriet, Harriet's mom.
- Harriet working for Miss Susan, trying to dust and take care of the baby, stealing the sugar cube, running away. Roles needed: Miss Susan, Miss Emily, Harriet.

- Harriet's family life—eating together, singing, talking, listening to Bible stories. Roles needed: Harriet, Old Rit, Ben, brothers and sisters.
- Harriet trying to help a slave escape and getting hit with the 2-pound weight. Roles needed: Harriet, slave, overseer, Old Rit, Ben.
- Harriet leading her brother James and two friends to freedom. Roles needed: Harriet, James, two friends, search party, Thomas Garrett.

As a class, discuss why these incidents would or wouldn't work as dramatizations (interesting action to portray, too much action, not enough action, good speaking parts, not enough dialogue, too much dialogue, reasonable number of characters in scene, too many characters, not enough characters, workable setting or settings, too many changes of scene).

Divide the class into groups of two to six students to work on a dramatization of their choice. Remind students that they will need to cooperate in assigning roles. Explain that for a successful dramatization they will need to be thoroughly familiar with the incident they are dramatizing and that each person will need to know what he or she is to say and do. They may want to write scripts that detail the dialogue and summarize the action.

Be available as the groups are working. Encourage creative thinking, praise cooperative behavior, and supply resources. Use one or two class periods for students to prepare the dramatization and another to present them.

Adapting the Activity: This kind of activity, in which students are re-creating through drama the events from a specific selection, can be used with any number of expository or narrative works that contain memorable characters and vivid, portrayable scenes: biographies, history texts, contemporary stories, folktales and fairy tales. Some of the scenes from *Fourth Grade Rats* by Jerry Spinelli might be fun for third or fourth graders to enact because they will be able to identify so well with the protagonist, Suds, and his need for peer approval, his desire to "grow up" and have some status, and his feelings of self-doubt. Fourth to sixth graders might enjoy dramatizing scenes from the action-packed fantasy novel *Amy's Eyes* by Richard Kennedy, and first and second graders might enjoy dramatizing *The Five Silly Fishermen* by Roberta Edwards or *Henny-Penny* by Jane Wattenberg. For the latter, Judy Freeman (2000) suggests first reading the story aloud, encouraging students to chime in on the repeated refrains, "especially Foxy's wicked little rhymes, such as 'Looking JUICY, Goosey,' and 'You're in luck, Duck.'"

Reflection: Prerequisite to dramatizing scenes is spending some time discussing character and theme as well as pinpointing those events and scenes that are dramatizable. Also, students are bound to get frustrated if they don't know or can't do what is expected of them. Thus, giving them clear explanations of what it is they are to do and how they are to do it before they form their groups is imperative for success. In addition, students need to know the purpose of these dramatizations. Are they to work out a scene that can be presented to other students, or are they doing it simply for the enjoyment and understanding it will bring to them?

The chance of a successful experience can also be enhanced by putting students into heterogeneous groups. Dispersing your leaders, competent readers, creative thinkers, diplomats, and good followers among the groups can help to ensure that groups achieve their goals. Each student should be aware of the unique contribution that he or she is able to make to the group effort and that this contribution is both necessary and appreciated. Adam may not be "the best reader," but he has a heck of a voice and can be a model of "good voice projection" for the rest of the group. Adam's gift should be recognized and encouraged. Kudos should not be given exclusively to those who "know the most" or "read the best." If throughout the year students are encouraged to discover what their particular talents are and are given opportunities to hone and polish these talents, when it comes time for group work they will be ready to put these talents to work in achieving the group goal. Working toward achieving a common goal with their peers helps students to realize that each person's contribution is important in achieving that goal—in this case, putting together a dramatization that makes sense in terms of its faithful rendition to the text and students' expectations of what drama should achieve.

Dramatizing scenes from historical pieces immerses students in a powerful context for understanding unique times and people. In putting themselves in the roles of historical characters, students can discover some common threads that weave through different ages, stories, and characters, such as the human desire for respect, love, freedom, and justice. They may discover the attributes that allow individuals to achieve these goals, such as courage, diligence, and concern for others, and they may also identify those attributes that work against achieving them, such as greed, self-interest, ignorance, and hatred.

Artistic, Graphic, and Nonverbal Activities

In this category, we include the visual arts, music, and dance—each a specialized language that can be used in response to printed and spoken communication. In this section, too, we include response activities that involve the creation of media productions such as audiotapes, videos, and slide shows; visual displays such as bulletin boards, artifacts, and specimens; and visual representations of information such as graphs, maps, and charts. Each of these various forms of expression provides students with a special way to deepen and broaden their understanding of the ideas and information found in the texts they read.

To illustrate how the languages of art, music, and dance can be connected to written and spoken language, we present the following example. Suppose that your third-grade class has just finished a unit on animals. Over a 4-week period, they have read numerous fiction and nonfiction tradebooks, and you have read *Dr. Doolittle* by Hugh Lofting aloud to them as well. As a culminating activity, you read William Jay Smith's book of poems *Birds and Beasts*. Next, you divide the class into three heterogeneous groups and assign them one of the three nonverbal expressive languages: art, music, or dance. Each group then decides which animal it will portray in their appointed "language" and brainstorms about what materials and approach they might take. For example, the art group might suggest watercolor painting, collages, scratch boards, paper sculpture, clay modeling, papier-mâché, or wood sculpture. After the students have brainstormed and decided on their animal and some possibilities for depicting this animal in a visual way with the resources available, they then work individually, in subgroups, or in pairs to create their animals using whatever medium they think will best capture the essence of their animal.

The music group's goal is to create an instrumental piece to depict their animal. During their brainstorming session, students think about the musical resources available to them as well as the characteristics of their particular animal. They consider rhythm and percussion instruments and those that produce melody. Some of their suggestions might include drums, cymbals, sticks, sandpaper blocks, recorders, song flutes, xylophone, bells, piano, and keyboard. After they think about what animal they are going to depict and how they might depict this animal through music, they begin working in pairs or small groups to re-create their animal through music.

The dance group's goal is to depict their chosen animal through movement. During their brainstorming session, students offer suggestions about what body movements represent this animal. Their discussion involves both showing and telling, with these sorts of words describing the characteristics and movements of their chosen animal: slow, steady, heavy, swinging, head moving, tail swishing, or clomp, clomp, clomp. The group might decide to work together to create one dance that represents their animal, or they might choose to work in pairs or subgroups.

After their brainstorming sessions, students spend an hour or so over 2 or 3 days to come up with nonverbal expressions of their chosen animals. On the fourth day, they present their work; their animals come to life in visual art, in music, and in dance, and other students guess the animals they are depicting.

A similar approach might be used for any number of subjects or selections. A few possibilities for connecting art, music, and dance to reading are as follows:

- After fourth-grade students have read several books on Native American culture, read *Dancing Teepees* by Virginia Driving Hawk Sneve and have students chose a tribe or nation to depict in art, music, and dance.

- After sixth graders have read folktales from many cultures, read the poem *Lord of the Dance: An African Retelling* by Veronique Tadjo and choose one culture to illustrate in art, music, and dance.

- After a unit on seasons with second graders, read Myra Cohn Livingston's *A Circle of Seasons* and have students choose one of the four seasons to illustrate in art, music, and dance.

• After a unit on feelings with middle-grade students, read Cynthia Rylant's *Waiting to Waltz: A Childhood* and have students choose one of the emotions of growing up to depict in art, music, and dance.

Books, journals, and periodicals abound with suggestions for artistic and non-verbal activities that students can do in your classroom. Because it is impossible to even begin suggesting all the possibilities or to describe the ones that might work best for you—in your particular situation, with your particular students—we can offer only a sampling of ideas. Undoubtedly you can think of many more immediately and will discover even more as time goes on.

Tables 6-3 through 6-6 show some of our ideas for implementing visual art, music, dance, and audiovisual presentations and displays, respectively. Think

Table 6-3. Potpourri of Visual Arts Activities

Learning Activities

After reading about art or an artist:
    Invite a guest artist to demonstrate a technique a children's
      book illustrator uses.
    See a film about an artist you have read about.
    Visit an art museum or gallery.
    Borrow reprints of paintings from the library.

Creating Activities

Kinds of Activities	**What to Make**
sculpting	masks
origami	murals
weaving	dioramas
painting	collages
drawing	mats
carving	quilts
etching	posters
macramé	baskets
	totem poles
What to Use	pottery
finger paint	puppets
watercolors	costumes
chalk, crayons	props
clay	scenery
wood	jewelry
paper	
magazines	
objects from nature	
material scraps	
yarn, straw	

of these tables as formative. Use them to write down your own ideas as you read through the categories and examples. When you run across another idea someplace else, you might want to jot it down here also.

Table 6-4. Potpourri of Musical Activities

Learning Activities

Learn

- to sing or play a song—period songs after historical fiction
- to play an instrument
- about the instruments—go to hear an orchestra play, listen to recordings, invite a musician to class
- about composers—listen to recording of their works, do research on a composer
- about the kinds of music—contemporary, classical, jazz, rock, rap, country, gospel—go to a concert, listen to recordings

Creating Activities

Experiment with

- rhythm and tempo
- percussion
- melody and harmony
- instruments, voices, and computer synthesizers

Create a song or poem about

- horses (after reading *Misty of Chincoteague* by Marguerite Henry)
- a famous person (after reading about Abe Lincoln or Michael Jordan)
- a time in history (after reading about the expansion of the West)
- a place (after reading about Japan)
- a story character (after reading about Pippi Longstocking or Huckleberry Finn)
- a feeling or mood (after reading poetry)

Create different kinds of songs about story characters: a jingle, a ballad, a funny song, a sad song, a happy song.

Table 6-5. Potpourri of Dance Activities

Learning Activities

See a dance

Invite a person from an ethnic group to perform a dance.

Watch a film or video of a dance.

Go to a dance production—notice dance titles.

Invite a dancer to talk about "dance language."

Learn a dance

- ethnic dances: Native American, Russian, Scottish, Polish, Hawaiian (invite a person from an ethnic group to teach a dance)

- other kinds of dances: square dance, period American dances from the 1920s, '30s, '40s, '50s, '60s, '70s, '80s, and '90s.

Creating Activities

Invent a dance to show:

- scene from a story

- a poem

- a character from a story

- a culture you have read about

- a subject you have read about—wind, turtles, exploration, dinosaurs, robots

- an abstract idea from a story you have read about—love, friendship, courage, personal growth

Table 6-6. Potpourri of Audiovisual Displays

Create

videotapes	models
audiotapes	displays
filmstrips	scrapbooks
bulletin boards	photo albums
charts	board games
maps	posters
graphs	time lines
diagrams	computer presentations

Artistic, Graphic, and Nonverbal Sample Activity: *Postcards*

In *Postcards,* after hearing a chapter or chapters in a novel read aloud, students draw small sketches—illustrations or designs—that capture or symbolize the essence of those chapters.

Selection: *The Wanderer* by Sharon Creech, illustrated by David Diaz. Thirteen-year-old Sophia is enamored by the sea, so she sets out on a journey, one that takes her across the Atlantic Ocean with a crew of which she is the only girl. However, this journey aboard a sailboat named *The Wanderer* turns out to be more than just an exciting sail across the Atlantic. It is a journey of self-discovery not only for Sophie but also for each of *The Wanderer's* crewmembers, Sophie's three uncles and two cousins. Through two travel logs, Sophie's and her cousin Cody's, the reader experiences all the excitement, wonder, and dangers of an ocean crossing on a sailboat as well as the personal growth and discoveries of two seemingly very different teens.

Students: Sixth graders of average ability; two English language learners.

Reading Purpose: To expose students to a well-crafted, beautifully written novel.

Goal of the Activity: To provide an opportunity for creative thinking and responding by encouraging students to create visual images for an engaging and evocative narrative.

Rationale: Drawing sketches or designs that capture the essence of the chapters in a novel requires students to use both their creative and critical thinking skills. In an activity such as this one, they are required to make decisions about what to include in a very spare drawing, as they must choose designs or symbols that are the most important and appropriate for a particular chapter. It also gives those students who are more adept at thinking visually than verbally a chance to shine.

Procedure: Tell students that for the next several days you are going to be reading a book called *The Wanderer* by Sharon Creech aloud to them, two or three chapters a day. (The 78 chapters in this 303-page book are short—some only a page long—journal entries by the two protagonists, Sophie and Cody.) Give a brief description or preview of the story. Tell students that at the beginning of each chapter there is a small black-and-white sketch by the artist, David Diaz. In these miniature drawings (the largest of which are 2" x 1"), the artist has captured the essence of the chapter. Discuss with students what is meant by *essence*.

Provide students with a blank 8½ x 11 sheet of paper. Have them fold the paper in half three times so that they have made eight 4¼ x 2 sections (see Figure 6-6). At the top of the page, across the first two sections, have students write *The Wanderer* by Sharon Creech and illustrated by Jane Q. Student (student's name), and in the remaining six sections have them write the chapter titles as shown.

Tell the students that you are going to read aloud the first chapter, entitled "The Sea," which is only three paragraphs long. While you are reading, they

---

The Wanderer by Sharon Creech
Illustrated by Jane Q. Student

The Sea	Three Sides
Slow Time	The Big Baby
Afloat	Slugs and Banana

Figure 6-6. Artistic Response Sheet

should think about how they might illustrate this chapter with one small drawing or design. Explain that after you have finished reading, they will have the opportunity to draw a small sketch in pencil or ink that they feel captures the essence—the narrative content and mood—of this chapter, kind of like a postcard snapshot.

Read the first chapter aloud. After you have finished the first chapter, give students about 5 minutes to draw their first postcard sketch. After about 5 minutes, ask them to put down their pencil or pen. If some students haven't completed their drawings, tell them they can do so later.

Read the second chapter, "Three Sides." Again, after you have finished reading, give them about 5 minutes to complete their drawings.

Take a few minutes to let students share their two drawings, to discuss what they drew and how successfully they were able to capture the essence of the chapter. Show them David Diaz's drawings for the chapter and also briefly discuss. Do they think Diaz did a good job capturing the essence of the chapter with his drawing? Why or why not?

The next day, read chapters 3 and 4 in the first section of the novel and have students draw postcards sketches for each. Before you begin reading, say something like "As you hear the story, imagine you are right alongside the main characters, Sophie and Cody, seeing, feeling, and experiencing what they are. Think about how you would capture what you are experiencing in a visual way. Each of your drawings for the chapters will be like a postcard you might send to your parents, friends, or relatives, capturing in a visual way what you are experiencing—what you are seeing, feeling, and thinking."

Continue with this activity for as long as student interest holds, or read the first three sections of the novel (22 chapters, 106 pages) and let students finish the book on their own.

Adapting the Activity: Instead of using an 8 ¹/₂ x 11 paper folded into rectangles, students could make actual postcards by drawing their sketches on 3 x 5 blank index cards. On the flip side of their sketch, have them draw a line down the center. (On the right side they will write the address, and on the left side they can write a note to the addressee.) In small letters on the side where the note goes, have students write "Chapter 'The Sea' from *The Wanderer* by Sharon Creech" (see Figure 6-7). Also, instead of using pencil and ink, students might like to use colored markers. They could send these postcards to friends or the author or illustrator with a note.

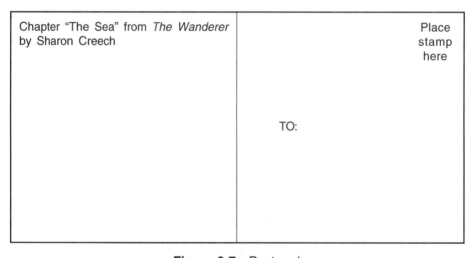

Figure 6-7 Postcard

The *Postcards* activity can be adapted to use with almost any chapter book or novel, especially those with exotic or historical settings and those with chapter titles. Two good examples are *Our Only May Amelia* by Jennifer L. Holm, the story of a rambunctious 12-year-old, May Amelia, the only girl in the Finnish town of Nasel, Washington, circa 1899, and *Esperanza Rising* by Pam Muñoz Ryan, a novel that traces Esperanza's journey from a privileged life in Mexico to the farm labor camps of California.

Reflection: Because we assumed that the sixth graders in this example had some instruction in the techniques for creating an aesthetically pleasing composition, we said little about it. If students have had no instruction in what makes for a pleasing two-dimensional design—balance, contrast, and repetition, for example—then these ideas will have to be discussed. To help students develop an understanding of the difference between designs that "work" and those that "don't work," you can show them examples of eye-pleasing designs as well as nonexamples (shapes pasted haphazardly onto the paper, no repetition in shape or color, no unifying point of interest). Providing students with plenty of exposure to the quality art that abounds in children's literature is one way to provide students with excellent models. (That is one good reason why picture books should be made accessible to students of all ages.) David Diaz's own illustrations in *The Wanderer* are excellent examples of designs that "work." Another way is to display artwork in your classroom. Reprints of well-known works are available at a relatively low cost at most discount stores and also through loan programs at many libraries. Wall calendars and appointment calendars are another good source for art reprints. Around December, you might want to encourage students to check with their parents to see if they have any of these types of calendars and ask them to bring them to school in January. Display the calendar art around the room or create a bulletin board. Collecting old calendars is a wonderful way to build your own reprint library. Not only can these prints be used as examples of good art, but often their subject matter is appropriate to use for other reading activities.

Application and Outreach Activities

Books open doors. They invite us to step out, to go beyond the text to see for ourselves, to act on our newfound knowledge, and to apply it in a unique way. In this sense, all of the previously mentioned categories in one way or another reflect the idea of going beyond the text to explore other realms and other applications of information and ideas.

Activities that we are labeling specifically as application and outreach endeavors are those in which students take the ideas and information from a text and deliberately test, use, or explore it further. Students might read an article on how to make friends, but the information has little value unless students try out the author's ideas to see if they work. Students might read a story about making ice cream or an article describing several science experiments, but it's not quite as much fun as actually following the steps and eating the ice cream or doing the experiments in Sandra Markle's *Science Mini-Mysteries* to see if they actually work. The logical next step after reading about something is to try it out in the real world.

It is not just how-to books that invite real-world applications, however. A chapter on the environment in a science text may inspire students to do something themselves to better care for the Earth. Or, after finishing a novel in which the main character has a disability, a reader might change his or her attitude about persons with disabilities and begin to act differently toward them. Application activities invite and encourage many different kinds of personal and social action.

The fiction, nonfiction, and poetry that students read can open doors to the wider world. Mary Ann Hoberman's poem "Cricket" in her collection *Bugs* might send them into summer fields to find out for themselves if a cricket's wing can really "sing a song" or to the science museum to explore the entomology exhibit to find out if "a cricket's ear is in its leg." Or, after reading Jane Yolen's *Owl Moon*, 7- and 8-year-olds might beg their parents or grandparents to take them "owling" in the night woods.

Outreach activities not only take children beyond the school walls to explore a topic or idea further or to discover more, they can also inspire them to social action. After third graders read Chris Van Allsburg's *Just a Dream*, in which a child dreams of a future wasted due to poor management of the environment, students might decide to write letters to state and local representatives encouraging them to support environmental legislation or develop an environmental ad campaign for their school or neighborhood. Barbara Huff's *Greening the City Streets: The Story of Community Gardens* might inspire urban seventh graders to plan and develop community gardens in their neighborhood. Or after reading Mem Fox's touching picture book *Wilfrid Gordon McDonald Partridge,* in which a young boy discovers a unique way to help the forgetful Miss Nancy recapture her memories, first or second graders might be inspired to share the story with residents in a nursing home or to try this memory-recapturing approach with an elderly relative or friend.

Students will not always make the connections necessary to transfer ideas from the text to the real world on their own. By providing activities that demonstrate this connection, you can drive home a critical aspect of the nature of text: We should not be the same after we have read it. We are a little more than we were before. Our new selves contain new information and ideas that we can now use. The following activity shows one way students might apply what they have discovered in a text by reaching out to others.

Application and Outreach Sample Activity: *Getting to Know You*

In *Getting to Know You,* students think about ways to get to know senior citizens better and plan ways to achieve this.

Selection: *Anastasia Again!* by Lois Lowry. In *Anastasia Again!*, 12-year-old Anastasia Krupnik moves from her apartment in the city to the suburbs, taking with her some rather negative assumptions about the people who live there. Her next door neighbor, Gertrude Stein, turns out to be an eccentric old recluse who looks like a witch. However, as Anastasia gets to know Gertrude Stein, she discovers much to admire and like in this woman. On an outing to the library one day, Anastasia happens upon the Senior Citizens' Drop-in Center. She invites the people at the center to a party at her house with the idea of introducing Gertrude to some new friends. On the day of the party, two of Anastasia's old friends from Cambridge arrive at Anastasia's house, as does a potential new friend from her new neighborhood. Many a myth about the young, old, city dwellers and suburbanites are dispelled at this delightful, if somewhat outlandish, gathering.

Students: Fifth graders of mixed abilities.

Reading Purpose: To understand and enjoy an engaging story.

Goal of the Activity: To help students see how ideas found in literature can be applied to the real world and to encourage an understanding and appreciation for people who are a number of years older than they are.

Rationale: This novel is a wonderful springboard for activities that provide opportunities to dispel stereotypes and to build bridges of understanding, especially between generations. Anastasia's idea for the party comes very much out of her desire to get the reclusive Gertrude Stein involved with life and people again. Ideally, after reading this book and participating in this activity, students might come up with their own ideas of ways to reach out to others, in addition to having some of their stereotypes dispelled.

Procedure: After students have read the story, talk about Anastasia's first impressions of Gertrude Stein. (She looked like a witch and acted grouchy and unfriendly, although she was nice to Anastasia's brother, Sam.) Ask how Anastasia felt about Gertrude Stein after she got to know her. (She thought she was very interesting, nice, and funny. Anastasia learned that when Gertrude acted brusquely, it wasn't because she was mean, but because she was scared—scared of being rejected.) You might want to talk about the idea of stereotypes and why people have them. Talk about the stereotypes Anastasia had and how some of her ideas about the suburbs and older people had changed by the end of the story.

Encourage students to talk about the older people in their own neighborhoods, houses of worship, or families. Ask if they are friends with any of these people, then discuss what Anastasia did that helped her to become friends with Gertrude Stein. Talk about some things students have done to get to know people who are much older than they are. Next, discuss what Anastasia wanted to do for Gertrude Stein after they became friends (help her get new friends).

Talk about what students might do as a group or as individuals to bring together seniors and young people. Record their suggestions on the chalkboard or a chart. (You may have to remind students that they will need their parents' permission do some things on their own, such as visiting or giving gifts.) If having a party—such as the one Anastasia had—for seniors is one of the students' suggestions, you may want to do this as a class activity. Students could invite seniors from their neighborhood, house of worship, family, or from a nearby nursing home. Together students can plan a time and a place for their party and the refreshments, activities, and decorations.

Adapting the Activity: This type of activity can be used after reading any story in which the protagonist begins by having mistaken assumptions about a person or group of people and ends up changing her views after getting to know that person or group of people. Postreading discussion would focus on what the protagonist did, or what things happened to the protagonist, that made her think differently at the end of the story. The discussion could then move to what students might do in similar situations. However, parties and other outreach activities such as letters, gifts, and visits should come out of a sincere spontaneous desire by the students, not as a teacher assignment. Outreach activities that focus on a changed perspective or attitude might include having third or fourth graders invite a class of younger (or older) students to a "Getting to Know You" party after reading *Fourth Grade Rats* by Jerry Spinelli, or inviting a guest from the Native American community to come to talk about Native American rites and traditions to a class of second graders after they have read the mystical story *Bring Back the Deer* by Jeffrey Prusski, or inviting guests that represent different occupations after reading Andrew Clement's *The Janitor's Boy,* a 140-page novel in which Jake learns some surprising things about his janitor dad when Jake is accidentally locked in the town's steam tunnel.

Reflection: Outreach activities can be preplanned, but often the best ones are generated from the students themselves as they respond to a selection. This is the ultimate goal of this kind of activity: to get students to make their own connections, to see how a text can build bridges to other ideas and other places.

Nevertheless, the central theme here is scaffolding, and many students will require scaffolding to move from passive to active modes of responding to what they read—to reaching outward as a result of the inward effect reading has had on them.

Building Connections

The category of activities just discussed obviously offers students many opportunities to build connections; so why, you might ask, do we also include a section on building connections? We do so because a huge amount of what we have learned about students' learning over the past 20 years—from David Rumelhart's early work on schema theory (1980) to contemporary reports on teaching and learning (Bransford, Brown, & Cocking, 2000; National Reading Panel, 2000; National Research Council, 1999; Snow, 2001; Snow, Burns, & Griffin, 1998)—highlights the huge importance of children's store of organized knowledge to their learning and success in and out of school. Building connections—establishing links among the vast array of schemas that students internalize—is important whether students are involved in reading narratives or exposition, factual material or fiction, history, science, English, or any other subject.

Moreover, we want children to build connections in several directions. First, we want students to realize that the wealth of their out-of-school experiences, which they bring to school when they enter first grade and which are constantly enriched each year, are relevant to understanding and making sense of what they are learning in school. For example, the pride they felt when they were first allowed to go to the grocery store alone can provide insight into a story character's feelings when she successfully meets some challenge, and it may also be a useful experience that they can use in their writing. Second, we want students to realize that the various subjects they deal with in school are interrelated in many ways. For example, the understanding of the Revolutionary period that they gain in social studies can be used in understanding some of the motives of Johnny in Esther Forbes's *Johnny Tremain.* Third, we want students to realize that ideas and concepts learned in school are relevant to their lives outside school. For example, when a character finds that persistence paid off in meeting her goal, this suggests that similar persistence may pay off for the students in getting their younger siblings to quit leaving their toys scattered all over the bedroom they share.

Very little that we do as teachers is more important than helping students to build these sorts of connections. The following activity provides one example of how we can do so.

Building Connections Sample Activity: *Problems and Solutions*

In *Problems and Solutions,* students identify the problems and solutions of a story's protagonist and compare and contrast those with problems and solutions from their own lives.

Selection: *Taking Care of Trouble* by Bonnie Graves. In this humorous chapter book, 11-year-old Joel is coerced by his best friend's older sister into watching her babysitting charge, Tucker (aka Trouble) while she goes to the mall to hear her favorite rock group perform. Joel, the only kid in Junior Adventurers who hasn't earned his emergency preparedness badge because he panics in emergency situations, is sure there's going to be some sort of emergency he can't handle—just what he doesn't need the day before he's to take the emergency preparedness test for the umpteenth time. And pass it he must in order to go on the Junior Adventurer's mountain-biking adventure in the Rockies later that summer. Joel's worse fears, of course, come true. Tucker's toddler antics challenge him with a minor emergency at every turn. However, surprising himself, Joel rises to each challenge, proving to himself that he is capable of handling emergency situations and giving him the confidence he needs for the upcoming test.

Students: Fourth graders of average ability.

Reading Purpose: To enjoy a light-hearted piece of literature and to make personal connections with the text.

Goal of the Activity: To help students better understand the connections between literature and life and, more specifically, to connect the problems and solutions in a story with the problems and solutions that occur in their own lives.

Rationale: One of the characteristics of literature is that it allows readers to vicariously experience life's challenges and the rewards of meeting those challenges along with a story's protagonist. Taking students through an activity such as *Problems and Solutions,* in which they compare and contrast the character's problems and strategies for solving them with their own problems and problem-solving strategies, can help students to realize that they are not alone in the kinds of challenges they face. It can also, perhaps, give them insights into how they might go about solving similar problems in their own lives.

Procedure: After students have finished reading this short chapter book, say something like "Joel, the main character in this story, sure had his share of problems, didn't he? How many of you have found yourselves in situations that caused *you* problems?" Your typical group of fourth graders will certainly answer affirmatively.

Ask "What is a problem, anyway?" Have students discuss what constitutes a problem (a situation that requires a solution). Have students give examples of problems that have come up in their own lives.

"Let's look at some of the problems Joel faced in the story *Taking Care of Trouble.*" Tell students you are going to read the first part of the story aloud, and as soon as they hear what they think constitutes a problem for the main character, they are to raise their hands. Read a page or so aloud until several students have identified a problem and have raised their hands. Ask students to share what they thought Joel's first problem was and why it was a problem. (For example, it was a problem for Joel when he heard the girl next door scream, because he thought it was an emergency of some sort and that he might be required to do something, and Joel always freaks out in emergency situations.)

Next ask, "What did Joel do about the problem?" (He tried to duck out of sight.) "Did Joel's solution solve his problem? Why or why not?" (He didn't solve it by trying to hide, because the girl saw him, called to him, and asked him for help.)

Place Problems and Solutions Chart 1 (Table 6-7) on an overhead projector and fill in the first row of blanks with students' responses for the first problem encountered in the story.

Table 6-7. Problems and Solutions Chart 1

Character's Problem	Why was it a problem?	How did the character try to solve the problem?	Was the problem solved? Why or why not?
He hears a girl scream.	He's afraid he'll be asked to help.	He ducks out of sight.	No, because the girl sees him and asks for help.

Ask students if they've ever found themselves in problem situations, what they did to try solve the problem, and whether their actions were successful in solving the problem. Briefly discuss. Put Problems and Solutions Chart 2 (Table 6-8) on the overhead and write their responses in the blanks.

Table 6-8. Problems and Solutions Chart 2

Your Problem	Why was it a problem?	How did you try to solve the problem?	Was your problem solved? Why or why not?
Mom asked me to go to the store for her.	I wanted to watch my favorite TV show.	I asked if I could go later.	No, because she needed tortillas right away so she could fix our supper.

Read the next page or so of *Taking Care of Trouble* aloud and have students raise their hands when they hear what they think is the next problem the main character encounters. Fill in the chart as before.

Explain that literature often shows people dealing with problems that are similar to problems readers encounter. In *Taking Care of Trouble,* although Joel had lots of problems to deal with throughout the story, one problem was larger than the others, and he finally solved it in the end. What was it? Discuss. (Not being able to handle emergency situations, or lacking the confidence that he could do so.) How did Joel solve the problem? (He used his head and the resources at hand, he didn't give up, and he took his babysitting job seriously. In doing those things, he proved to himself that he was capable of handling emergency situations.) Explain that one of the things that literature does sometimes is to show us people dealing with situations similar to ones in which we find ourselves. Sometimes, seeing the hero of a story solve problems can inspire us to try and solve our problems in a similar way.

Ask students what were some of the things Joel did to solve his main problem. Write their suggestions on the board.

> *Didn't give up. Worked hard. Used his head.*
> *Used the resources he had.*
> *Tried to solve problem on his own.*

"Think of a problem in your own life you are trying to solve. Would any of the things Joel did be helpful in solving your problem?" Briefly discuss.

Adapting the Activity: Because most literature portrays a character faced with at least one main problem, with several smaller problems to overcome as they try to solve the big one, this activity can be used with almost any piece of fiction. This activity could be modified to use with primary grade children after reading the picture book *Lilly's Purple Plastic Purse* by Kevin Henkes. In this delightful tale, Lilly causes problems for herself when she brings her purple plastic purse to school and can't resist showing it off to everyone. Another good choice for primary students is *The Circus Dog* by Andrew Clements and illustrated by Sue Truesdell. Here, Old Grumps, a circus dog, has a cushy life that is turned upside down when a younger dog, Sparks, bursts onto the circus scene. In adapting the activity for younger students, you may want to pare the problems listed on the chart to three, the one major one and two others that the protagonist faces in trying to solve the big one. For upper grade students, a good choice for the *Problems and Solutions* activity is Will Hobbs's gripping survival story *Far North*, a 226-page novel in which two Native American boys struggle to survive in the Canadian wilderness after their plane crashes and the pilot dies.

Biographies for any grade level are also excellent choices for this activity, because the subjects of most biographies are prime examples of problem solvers, people who have overcome numerous challenging obstacles in their noteworthy lives. For sixth- through ninth-grade students, this activity could be adapted to use after reading *Ida B. Wells: Mother of the Civil Rights Movement* by Dennis and Judith Fradin, for fourth- and fifth-grade students who have read *Who Was Ben Franklin?* by Dennis Brindell Fradin or *Who Was Albert Einstein?* by Jess Braillier, and for primary grade students reading Robert Coles's *The Story of Ruby Bridges,* illustrated by George Ford, a picture book that recounts the hostilities faced by 6-year-old Ruby Bridges, the first African American girl to attend the Frantz Elementary School in New Orleans in 1960.

Reflection: Because students don't always make the connection between their lives and the literature they read, it is helpful to provide an activity such as *Problems and Solutions* that will help them to make these connections. During the discussion portion of the activity, when students are talking about themselves and their own problems and solutions, sometimes they will forget the relevance of the story or will not, see how their problems and solutions are connected to those of the story characters at all. Because this is often the case, we have found it necessary to help students to make these connections by asking questions such as "How is the problem you just told us about similar to the one faced by our story character? How is it different? What did you do to solve your problem that was similar to the character's? Was there anything the character did that might have helped you in solving your problem?" Questions such as these help to connect students' lives to the literature.

Because some students may be reluctant to share their own problems, we have also found it helpful to invite students to suggest problems and solutions "from people they know—anonymous family members or friends." They don't need to identify these people, just the problems and solutions.

Reteaching

One of the advantages of categorizing ideas is that it allows us to focus our thoughts, to structure and order them so that we can see relationships among ideas. Through this mental effort, logical patterns of organization will often emerge, and with them a workable framework, a structure that will help us to move ideas from the abstract to the concrete and suggest ways of implementing them in real-life situations—in this case, the classroom. The disadvantage is that categorizing can sometimes lure us into thinking that ideas can be pigeonholed. They cannot. When dealing with such a complex and organic process as teaching, we need to search for models that will help to guide our thinking and suggest ways for effectively designing and implementing instruction in the classroom. Because teaching is so complex and organic, any kind of order, structure, or model can only serve as a guide, a beginning, or a framework. Coming at last to the final category of our postreading activities, reteaching, we are reminded of that truth.

In our ordering of activities, we have placed reteaching in the postreading category. However, as anyone who has spent even an hour in the classroom knows, reteaching is an ongoing process. Teachers, as the artists they are, are constantly assessing the efficacy of their instruction. "Are the students understanding what I'm saying and doing? Do I need to try another approach?" Teachers are continually using the feedback they receive from students to modify their approach even as they teach. Sometimes, however, after the entire lesson has been completed and the teacher has tried her best to ensure that all students are succeeding, some still fall short of their goals. When this happens, reteaching is called for.

Reteaching might be necessary when students, after reading a selection and engaging in various activities, have not reached their reading goals. If the goal was for them to recall the organs of the human body and understand their functions, and the discussion, questioning, or writing activities indicate that students did not achieve this goal, then reteaching is in order.

Reteaching will often focus on encouraging students to self-evaluate, to become metacognitive readers. Although the teacher is there to encourage and assist, it is the student who is ultimately responsible for his or her own learning. Activities that encourage students to ask questions for themselves can help to nudge them in the direction of being responsible, active readers. Here are some of the questions students might be asked to consider after not understanding the information in a text about the organs of the body.

- Why didn't I understand what the author said about the way the heart functions? Were there too many words I didn't know? Was I reading too fast? What might I do to understand the information?

- Was I concentrating on what the author was saying, or was my mind wandering? What might I do to help myself concentrate?

Help students to see the importance of asking these sorts of questions and suggest possible strategies for students to use:

- Adjust your reading speed to reflect the difficulty of the material.
- Write down key words or phrases.
- Draw a map to show the relationship between ideas in the chapter.

Such assistance will foster the development of readers who know how to construct meaning from text, how to be copartners with the authors. Let students know that their job is just as important as the author's. Without their own effort, no communication takes place, no meaning is born, no idea comes to life. The words exist as mere marks on a page.

In addition to encouraging metacognitive thinking in students, reteaching activities might include retracing the steps of a specific activity with students to see what went wrong and where. Perhaps students had difficulty completing a reading guide or answering postreading questions. In these cases, reteaching might include discussing with student the problems they had and why they had them, and then reviewing the purposes and steps involved in completing the guide or answering the questions. During this review process, you might decide to alter the approach of the original activity to reflect the new insights the discussion revealed or to create a totally different activity. Alternately, you might have students simply repeat the original activity with their new level of understanding. The purpose of this approach—discussing the problem and then modifying the activity, creating a new activity, or repeating the original one—is to give students another opportunity to succeed.

Reteaching Sample Activity: *Play It Again, Sam*

In *Play It Again, Sam,* a previous lesson is repeated with those students who didn't achieve the goals of the activity.

Selection: *Frozen Fire* by James Houston. (See description on page 68.)

Students: Sixth graders of mixed abilities.

Reading Purpose: To understand and enjoy an exciting survival adventure story.

Goal of the Original Activity: To help students understand how literature can be a medium for understanding the various ways people have of responding to similar situations and issues, and to provide all students with the opportunity to voice their opinions and reach their own conclusions.

Goal of the Reteaching Activity: To make sure that all students have the opportunity to successfully draw their own conclusions about ideas presented in the text.

Rationale: In the Both Sides postreading discussion, a handful of students had problems coming up with more than one or two reasons to support their responses to the question "Should Matthew have taken the gold nuggets?" By repeating this activity in a supportive setting, students have the opportunity to review procedures or concepts not grasped in a previous lesson and to achieve success.

Procedure: On the chalkboard, on an overhead, or in a handout, provide students with a copy of the original discussion web. Then read the section from the novel aloud in which Matthew finds the gold nuggets. After each page or so, pause and let students think about the question "Should Matthew have taken the gold nuggets?" and have them suggest why Matthew should have taken the nuggets or why he shouldn't have. Write these on the chart or have students record them.

For example, below is an excerpt from the text that might support the position that Matthew shouldn't have taken the nuggets and therefore belongs in the no column.

> Matthew pushed up the right sleeve of his parka shirt and sweater as far as he could and, lying on the ice, reached down into the water.
>
> "Wahh! You're acting crazy," whispered Kayak. "You'll freeze your arm off, freeze yourself to death."

Reasons

_____			_____
_____			_____
_____	**NO**	Should Matthew have taken	**YES**
_____		the gold nuggets?		_____
_____			_____
_____			_____

Conclusions

Figure 6-8. Reteaching the Both Sides Activity

Write a word or phrase in the *no* column that supports the position that Matthew should not have taken the nuggets, as shown in Figure 6-8.

Proceed similarly with the remaining pages, encouraging each student to participate in giving responses. After you have finished reading aloud and students have provided several responses for each column, have each student write a conclusion based on the chart you have constructed together. Then have each student choose the reason that best supports his or her answer. Let students tell what reason they have chosen and why, and be sure to commend them for their efforts.

Adapting the Activity: *Play It Again, Sam* can be used whenever students haven't achieved their reading goals and repeating that activity with assistance from you will help to ensure a successful experience. For example, let us say some students had problems answering some of the questions in *The Yellow Brick Road* postreading questions. Meet with those students, find out which questions posed problems, and read aloud parts of the story that might provide the answers, leading students to discover the answers. Alternately, if some students had difficulty writing paragraphs using the Venn diagram in the *Compare and Contrast* activity, meet with them and review the procedures for gathering information on the diagram and for using that information in their writing.

Reflection: A reteaching activity of this sort, in which you are primarily repeating the original procedure with students, is helpful when they are likely to profit from additional exposure and practice of a particular activity. Sometimes, however, a reteaching activity will involve trying a whole new approach. In this case, you will toss out your original activity and return to your primary reading purpose.

Postreading Activities: A Final Word

Many of the postreading activities described in this section have been traditionally thought of as "enrichment" activities. Indeed they are, for they do enrich the reader. However, we need to be careful, when we use this label, that we are being inclusive and not exclusive in selecting the students who will be enriched. If we think of *all* students who read as "rich"—those who soar as well as those who flounder—then we need to be certain to provide activities that will enrich them all. Sometimes, those students who struggle with the basics, those who are lacking in traditional literacy skills, have been left out of these activities and thus have not been allowed the opportunities for the growth that enrichment activities can provide. We believe that all students deserve and will benefit from a variety of postreading activities and should be given the opportunity to explore as many of them as possible. Activities that students engage in after reading drive home the point that reading has a purpose, that they can actually *do* something with the ideas in books. They can make connections between what they know and what they discover in texts and apply that new knowledge so that their lives become more enjoyable, more productive, and more meaningful—enriched, if you will.

References

Alvermann, D. E. (1991). "The discussion web: A graphic aid for learning across the curriculum." *Reading Teacher, 45,* 92–99. A complete description of this very useful graphic aid and the teaching procedures that accompany it.

Alvermann, D. E., Dillon, D. R., & O'Brien, D. G. (1987). *Using discussion to promote reading comprehension.* Newark, DE: International Reading Association. Much of this is particularly useful for discussion of informational texts.

Anderson, L. W., & Krathwohl, D. R. (2001). *A taxonomy for learning, teaching, and assessing.* New York: Longman. A very substantial revision of Bloom's taxonomy of educational objectives.

Atwell, N. (1998). *In the middle: New understandings about writing, reading, and learning* (2nd ed.). Portsmouth, NH: Heinemann. Presents the author's influential views on teaching adolescents through connecting reading and writing.

Beach, R. W. (1993). *A teacher's introduction to reader-response theories.* Urbana, IL: National Council of Teachers of English. A thorough and quite sophisticated introduction to reader response.

Beck, I. L., & McKeown, M. G. (1981). Developing questions that promote comprehension: The story map. *Language Arts, 58,* 913–918. Discusses problematic approaches to selecting and sequencing and offers a valuable alternative.

Beck, I. L., & McKeown, M. G. (2001). Text talk: Capturing the benefits of read-aloud experiences for young children. *Reading Teacher, 55,* 10–20. Suggests a read-aloud procedure that scaffolds children's efforts and keeps the focus on important text ideas.

Beck, I. L., McKeown, M. G., Hamilton, R. L., & Kucan, L. (1997). *Questioning the author: An approach for enhancing student engagement with text.* Newark, DE: International Reading Association. An in-depth description of the questioning-the-author approach to fostering deep and thorough understanding of a text.

Beck, I. L., McKeown, M. G., Hamilton, R. L., & Kucan, L. (1998). Getting the meaning. *American Educator, 22* (1–2), 66–71, 85. Describes a specific approach, questioning the author, to fostering deep and thorough understanding of text.

Bransford, J. D., Brown, A. L., & Cocking, R. R. (2000). *How people learn: Brain, mind, experience, and school.* Washington, DC: National Academy Press. Excellent summary of cognitive research on learning.

Calkins, L. M. (2001). *The art of teaching reading.* New York: Longman. A personal yet scholarly description of the author's approach to leading students to literacy.

Collins, P. M. (1992). Before, during and after: Using drama to read deeply. In C. Temple & P. Collins (Eds.), *Stories and readers: New perspectives on literature in the elementary classroom* (pp.141–155). Norwood, MA: Christopher-Gordon. Excellent discussion of ways in which dramatic activities can help children to explore literature deeply.

Fosnot, C. T. (1996). *Constructivism: Theory, perspectives, and practice.* New York: Teachers College Press. Collection of essays examining constructivism and its relationship to teaching and learning.

Freeman, J. (2000, April). Talk to the animals. *Scholastic Instructor,* pp. 12–17. Annotations and suggested classroom activities for 13 books about quirky and colorful animal characters.

Galda, L., & Guice, S. (1997). Response-based reading instruction in the elementary grades. In S. A. Stahl & David A. Hayes (Eds.), *Instructional models in reading* (pp. 311–330). Mahwah, NJ: Erlbaum. An overview of the reader-response approach.

Galda, L., & West, J. (1992). Enriching our lives: The humanities in children's literature. *Reading Teacher, 45* (7), 536–545. Reviews children's books dealing with music, opera and dance, theater and film, the visual arts, and architecture.

Johnson, D. W., Johnson, R. T., & Holubec, E. J. (1994). The *new circles of learning: Cooperation in the classroom and school.* Alexandria, VA: Association for Supervision and Curriculum Development. This book describes a specific form of cooperative learning and presents a great deal of useful information on group work in general.

Marshall, J. (2000). Response to literature. In M. Kamil, P. Mosenthal, P. D. Pearson, & R. Barr (Eds.), *Handbook of reading research,* (vol. 3, pp. 381–402). Mahwah, NJ: Erlbaum. A thoughtful overview and analysis of reader-response research.

Nagy, W. E. (1988). *Using vocabulary to improve reading comprehension.* Newark, DE: International Reading Association. This brief and inexpensive publication describes a variety of ways of displaying information graphically, including semantic maps, semantic feature analysis charts, Venn diagrams, hierarchical arrays, and linear arrays.

National Reading Panel. (2000). *Teaching children to read.* Bethesda, MD: National Institute of Child Health and Human Development. A major review of research on teaching reading.

National Research Council. (1999). *Improving student learning.* Washington, DC: National Academy Press. A plan for research that would, as the title indicates, improve student learning.

Nelson, N., & Calfee, R. C. (1998). *The reading-writing connection.* Chicago: National Society for the Study of Education. Major collection on reading and writing.

Pearson, P. D., & Duke, N. K. (2002). Comprehension instruction in the primary grades. In C. C. Block & M. Pressley (Eds.), *Comprehension instruction: Research-based practices* (pp. 247–258). Collection on related to teaching comprehension strategies.

Perkins, D. N. (1999). The many faces of constructivism. *Educational Leadership, 57* (3), 6–11. Describes a practical approach that teachers can take to create constructivist instruction.

Phillips, D. E. (1995). The good, the bad, and the ugly: The many faces of constructivism. *Educational Researcher, 24* (7), 5–12. Explores several meanings of this complex and often difficult concept.

Phillips, D. E. (Ed.). (2000). *Constructivism in education.* Chicago: National Society for the Study of Education. A recent major collection on constructivism as it applies to education.

Postman, N. (1982). *The disappearance of childhood.* New York: Delacourte. Thought-provoking discussion of the fate of childhood in the modern world.

Rosenblatt, L. (1938). *Literature as exploration.* New York: Appleton-Century. Rosenblatt's original presentation of her response theory.

Rosenblatt, L. (1978). *The reader, the text, the poem: The transactional theory of the literary work.* Carbondale, IL: Southern Illinois Press. Another presentation of Rosenblatt's response theory; both this and her 1938 book have had enormous influence on the teaching of literature.

Rumelhart, D. E. (1980). Schemata: The building blocks of cognition. In R. J. Spiro, B. C. Bruce, & W. F. Brewer (Eds.), *Theoretical issues in reading comprehension* (pp. 33–58). Hillsdale, NJ: Erlbaum. One of the earliest descriptions of the concept of schemata, detailed and revealing.

Ryder, R. J., & Graves, M. F. (2003). *Reading and learning in content areas* (3rd ed). New York: Wiley. Comprehensive text on teaching reading in the content areas.

Sebesta, S. L. (1992). Enriching the arts and humanities. In B. E. Cullinan (Ed.), *Invitation to Read: More children's literature in the classroom* (pp. 50–63). Newark, DE: International Reading Association. Examines ways of giving students aesthetic experiences by linking literature with the visual arts, drama, and music.

Shanahan, T. (Ed.). (1990). *Reading and writing together: New perspectives for the classroom.* Norwood, MA: Christopher-Gordon. An excellent collection of essays exploring the relationships between reading and writing.

Sipe, L. R. (2000). "Those two gingerbread boys could be brothers": How children use intertextual connections during storybook readalouds. *Children's Literature in Education, 31* (2), 73–90. A study showing how children use intertextual connections during storybook read-alouds.

Snow, C. E. (2001). Reading for understanding: Toward an R&D program in reading comprehension. Santa Monica, CA: Rand Education. Also available online at http://www.rand.org/multi/achievementforall/reading/. A plan for research on reading comprehension.

Snow, C. E., Burns, M. S., & Griffin, P. (Eds.). (1998). *Preventing reading difficulties in young children.* Washington, DC: National Academy Press. Seminal review of research on what makes early reading instruction and experiences effective.

Vacca, R. T. & Linek, W. M. (1992). Writing to learn. In J. W. Irwin & M. A. Doyle (Eds.), *Reading/writing connections: Learning from research* (pp. 145–159). Newark, DE: International Reading Association. Another good source on using writing to promote learning; the book itself contains other useful articles on the relationship between reading and writing.

Children's Literature

Armstrong, J. (2000). *Spirit of endurance: The true story of the Shackleton expedition to the Antarctic.* New York: Crown. 32 pages.

Asimov, I. (1983). *How did we find out about our genes?* New York: Walker. 61 pages.

Brailler, J. (2002). *Who was Albert Einstein?* New York: Grosset & Dunlap. 112 pages.

Bunting, E. (2001). *The summer of Riley.* New York: HarperCollins. 170 pages.

Carlson, J. (1989). *Harriet Tubman: Call to freedom.* New York: Fawcett Columbine. 116 pages.

Cleary, B. (1991). *Strider.* New York: Morrow. 179 pages.

Clements, A. (2000). *Circus family dog.* New York: Clarion. 32 pages.

Clements, A. (2000). *The janitor's boy.* New York: Simon & Schuster. 140 pages.

Cole, J. (1990). *The magic school bus: Lost in the solar system.* New York: Scholastic. 32 pages.

Coles, R. (1995). *The story of Ruby Bridges.* New York: Scholastic. 32 pages.

Compestine, Y. C. (2001). *The runaway rice cake.* New York: Simon & Schuster. 32 pages.

Conrad, P. (1985). *Prairie songs.* New York: Harper & Row. 167 pages.

Cooper, I. (1990). *The kids from Kennedy Middle School: Choosing sides.* New York: Morrow. 218 pages.

Creech, S. (2000). *The wanderer.* New York: Joanna Cotler Books. 305 pages.

Davidson, M. (1986). *I have a dream: the story of Martin Luther King, Jr.* New York: Scholastic. 127 pages.

Day, N. R. (1995). *The lion's whiskers: An Ethiopian folktale.* New York: Scholastic. 32 pages.

Edwards, R. (1989). *The five silly fishermen.* New York: Random House. 32 pages.

Fleischman, S. (1986). *The whipping boy.* New York: Greenwillow. 90 pages.

Forbes, E. (1971). *Johnny Tremain.* New York: Dell. 269 pages.

Fox, M. (1985). *Wilfrid Gordon McDonald Partridge.* New York: Kane/Miller. 32 pages.

Fradin, D. B. (2002). *Who was Franklin?* New York: Grosset & Dunlap. 112 pages.

Fradin, D. B., & Fradin, J. B. (2000). *Ida B. Wells: Mother of the civil rights movement.* New York: Clarion. 178 pages.

Fritz, J. (1987). *Shh! We're writing the Constitution.* New York: Scholastic. 64 pages.

Graves, B. (2001). *Taking care of trouble.* New York: Dutton. 70 pages.

Hackett, J. K., & Moyer, R. H. (1991). *Science in your world.* New York: Macmillan/McGraw-Hill.

Hamilton, V. (1985). *The people could fly: American black folktales.* New York: Knopf. 178 pages.

Henkes, K. (1996). *Lilly's purple plastic purse.* New York: Greenwillow. 32 pages.

Henry, M. (1947). *Misty of Chincoteague.* New York: Macmillan. 190 pages.

Hobbs, W. (1996). *Far north.* New York: Morrow. 226 pages.

Hoberman, M. A. (1976). *Bugs.* New York: Viking. 32 pages.

Holm, J. L. (1999). *Our only May Amelia.* New York: HarperCollins. 253 pages.

Hong, L. T. (1991). *How the ox star fell from heaven.* Chicago: Whitman. 32 pages.

Houston, J. (1977). *Frozen fire.* New York: McElderry. 149 pages.

Hubbel, P. (1990). *A green grass gallop.* New York: Atheneum. 32 pages.

Huff, B. A. (1990). *Greening the city streets: The story of community gardens.* New York: Clarion. 75 pages.

Kennedy, R. (1985). *Amy's eyes.* New York: Harper & Row. 112 pages.

Lauber, P. C. (1989). *Meteors and meteorites: Voyagers from outer space.* New York: Crowell. 74 pages.

Lewin, T. (1990). *Tiger trek.* New York: Macmillan. 32 pages.

Livingston, M. C. (1982). *A circle of seasons.* New York: Holiday House. 32 pages.

Lobel, A. (1979). *Days with frog and toad.* New York: Scholastic. 64 pages.

Lofting, H. (1988). *The Story of Doctor Doolittle.* New York: Delacorte. 156 pages.

Lord, B. B. (1984). *In the year of the boar and Jackie Robinson.* New York: Harper & Row. 164 pages.

Lowry, L. (1981). *Anastasia again!* Boston: Houghton Mifflin. 145 pages.

MacLachlan, P. (1991). *Journey.* New York: Delacorte. 85 pages.

MacLachlan, P. (1985). *Sarah, plain and tall.* New York: Harper & Row. 64 pages.

Markle, S. (1988). *Science mini-mysteries.* New York: Atheneum. 64 pages.

McCurdy, M. (1997). *Trapped by the ice!: Shackleton's amazing Antarctic adventure.* New York: Walker. 41 pages.

Mollel, T. M. (2000). *Subira subira.* New York: Clarion. 32 pages.

Park, B. (2000). *The graduation of Jake Moon.* New York: Atheneum. 115 pages.

Parker, S. (1989). *Touch, taste, and smell.* New York: Franklin Watts. 40 pages.

Paterson, K. (1977). *The great Gilly Hopkins.* New York: Crowell. 148 pages.

Peck, R. (2000). *A year down yonder.* New York: Dial. 130 pages.

Prelutsky, J. (1988). *Tyrannosaurus was a beast.* New York: Greenwillow. 31 pages.

Pringle, L. (2002). *Strange new animals, new to science.* Tarrytown, NY: Cavendish. 112 pages.

Prusski, J. (1988). *Bring back the deer.* San Diego: Harcourt Brace Jovanovich. 32 pages.

Ryan, P. M. (2000). *Esperanza rising.* New York: Scholastic. 262 pages.

Rylant, C. (1984). *Waiting to waltz: A childhood; poems.* New York: Bradbury. 45 pages.

Sanderson, R. (1990). *The twelve dancing princesses.* Boston: Little, Brown. 32 pages.

Smith, W. J. (1990). *Birds and beasts.* New York: Godine. 32 pages.

Sneve, V.D.H. (1989). *Dancing teepees: Poems of American Indian Youth.* New York: Holiday House. 32 pages.

Spinelli, J. (1991). *Fourth grade rats.* New York: Scholastic. 84 pages.

Souhami, J. (2000). *No dinner!: The story of the old woman and the pumpkin.* New York: Cavendish. 32 pages.

Steptoe, J. (1987). *Mufaro's beautiful daughters.* New York: Lothrop, Lee & Shepard. 32 pages.

Stevens, J. (1989). *Androcles and the lion.* New York: Holiday House. 32 pages.

Stier, C. (1999). *If I were president.* Morton Grove, IL: Whitman. 32 pages.

Strete, C. K. (1990). *Big thunder magic.* New York: Greenwillow. 32 pages.

Tadjo, V. (1989). *Lord of the dance: An African retelling.* New York: Lippincott. 32 pages.

Uchida, Y. (1985). *The happiest ending.* New York: Atheneum. 111 pages.

Van Allsburg, C. (1990). *Just a dream.* Boston: Houghton Mifflin. 32 pages.

Wattenberg, J. (2000). *Henny-Penny.* New York: Scholastic. 32 pages.

Yep, L. (1991). *The star fisher.* New York: Penguin. 150 pages.

Yolen, J. (1987). *Owl moon.* New York: Philomel. 32 pages.

Chapter

7

Comprehensive Scaffolded Reading Experiences

In each of the preceding three chapters, we focused on a single segment of the Scaffolded Reading Experience (SRE) framework: prereading, during reading, or postreading. This allowed us to take an in-depth look at each segment. However, it did not allow us to discuss or demonstrate one essential feature of the SRE framework. An SRE is a carefully coordinated, integrated, and sequenced set of prereading, during-reading, and postreading activities. What you do in any segment of an SRE is very strongly influenced by what you do in the other segments. In fact, this point should be made more emphatically: What you do in any segment of an SRE really makes sense only in terms of what you do in the other segments. Moreover, the prereading, during-reading, and postreading activities in an SRE are strongly influenced by the factors that you consider during the planning phase: the students, the text, and the purpose(s) for which students are reading. Creating the most effective possible SRE for your students requires the careful reflection and decision making we discussed in chapter 3.

In this chapter, we provide examples of four complete SREs, illustrating how pre-, during-, and postreading activities are interrelated and influenced by the students, the text, and the purposes of the reading. Figure 7-1 shows the basic SRE framework.

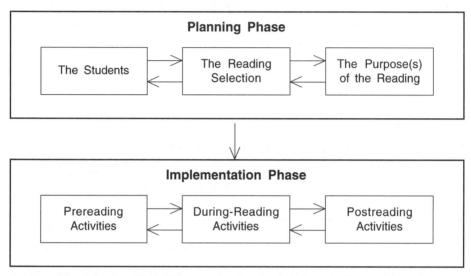

Figure 7-1.　Two Phases of a Scaffolded Reading Experience

In each of the four samples of complete SREs, we include an overview of the entire SRE, a detailed day-by-day description of possible pre-, during-, and postreading activities, and a brief reflection on the entire SRE.

Guide to SREs for Chapter 7

Sample 1: Earthquakes (p. 209)

Students: Fourth-grade students with low to average reading ability in an ethnically diverse classroom in California, five English language learners.

Selection: *Earthquakes* by Seymour Simon.

Purpose: To learn about earthquakes, what causes them, what effect they have on people and property, and what might be done to prepare for them.

Sample 2: Because of Winn Dixie (p. 218)

Students: Sixth-grade students of mixed abilities.

Selection: *Because of Winn-Dixie* by Kate DiCamillo

Purpose: To understand, enjoy, and make connections with an award-winning middle grade novel and to help foster students' awareness of character development in novels.

Sample 3: Eleanor Roosevelt: A Life of Discovery (p. 234)

Students: Eighth-grade students of mixed abilities.

Selection: *Eleanor Roosevelt: A Life of Discovery* by Russell Freedman.

Purpose: To learn about one of the most influential women in the world, to understand how she achieved such stature, and to give students the experience of critically analyzing a nonfiction text.

Sample 4: Real-Life Heroes (p. 245)

Students: Third-grade students reflecting a variety of abilities and ethnic backgrounds.

Selections: Self-selected books reflecting the theme "real-life heroes."

Purpose: To understand how real-life heroes are made, how they have met challenges and achieved their goals, and what makes them heroes.

A Complete SRE for *Earthquakes*

This SRE uses the K-W-L procedure developed by Donna Ogle (1986; Ogle & Blachowicz, 2002). K-W-L includes pre-, during-, and postreading activities in which students actively consider what they *know*, what they *want to know*, and what they *learn.*

Students: Fourth-grade students with low to average reading ability in an ethnically diverse classroom in California; five English language learners.

Selection: *Earthquakes* by Seymour Simon. This informational book gives a dramatic photographic account of the cause and effect of earthquakes around the globe.

Reading Purpose: To learn about earthquakes, what causes them, what effect they have on people and property, and what might be done to prepare for them.
    Table 7-1 outlines the activities of this SRE.

Table 7-1. *Earthquakes* Overview

Students	Selection	Purpose
Fourth-graders of average to low ability; 5 English language learners	*Earthquakes* by Seymour Simon	To learn more about earthquakes
Day 1 **Prereading** • Motivating and Relating; Reading to Students' Lives (10 min.) • Activating Background Knowledge (10 min.) • Prequestioning and Direction Setting (5 min.)	**During-Reading** • Guided Reading • Reading to Students	**Postreading** • Discussion • Questioning
Day 2 **Prereading** • Prequestioning and Direction Setting	**During-Reading** • Modifying the Text • Guided Reading and Silent Reading (30 min.)	**Postreading** • Discussions • Application and Outreach

Prereading for Day 1

Motivating and Relating Reading to Students' Lives: *What's Your Story?*

In this activity, an event relating to the topic of the text is described and then students relate their own similar experiences.

Goal of the Activity: To pique students' interest in a topic and activate their background knowledge.

Rationale: Describing an event in a way that requires students to infer what is happening can be an effective way to stimulate interest and introduce a topic at the same time. Having students then discuss their own experiences requires that they access relevant knowledge, which will help them to build meaning from the text.

Procedure: Begin by describing a scenario similar to the following: "Imagine yourself in this situation. You are asleep in bed. Suddenly the bed begins to move back and forth. Half awake, you say to the sister or brother in the bed next to yours, 'Stop shaking the bed.'" Ask students to explain what is going on. Tell students that this was an experience you had with earthquakes and encourage them to talk about their own experiences.

Activating Background Knowledge: *What I Know*

In this activity, students brainstorm to find out what they know about a topic and then generate categories of information that are likely to be found in the text they will read.

Goal of the Activity: To have students activate their prior knowledge about a topic and consider what information on that topic might be included in a specific text.

Rationale: These California students are likely to have some knowledge of earthquakes. Activating this knowledge before reading can help to establish a framework that will aid them in understanding and remembering.

Procedure: On the chalkboard, write the title *Earthquakes.* Underneath that title and to the left, write the heading *What I Know*. Ask students to give some of the facts they know about earthquakes. Jot their responses under the heading *What I Know.*

EARTHQUAKES

What I Know

Can cause damage

Are unpredictable

Are scary

Happen in California

Not all are the same

Shake the earth

Don't happen at night

Are getting worse

As you will notice, not all of the students' responses are accurate. During this brainstorming session, you might ask students various questions such as "How did you learn that?" or "How could you prove that?" Later, during the postreading discussion, you can clear up any remaining misconceptions.

After students have given a variety of responses, show them the cover illustration on the book *Earthquakes.* Ask them to think about the kind of information that might be included in the book, and write their suggestions on the board to the left of their initial responses. Some of their suggestions might include how earthquakes happen, where they happen, what we can do about them, how much damage they do, why they happen, and descriptions of some of the worst quakes.

Prequestioning and Direction Setting: *What I Want to Know*

In this activity, students consider what they would like to know about a topic that might be discussed in a specific text.

Goal of the Activity: To turn students' interest in earthquakes into a desire to read about them.

Rationale: Having students think about what they would like to know about a topic sets up a purpose for reading. If students have questions in mind, they will be looking for answers to those questions as they read, and comprehension will be facilitated.

Procedure: Explain that informational books such as *Earthquakes* are written to give us information that we might need or want. Ask students to think about what they would like to know about earthquakes—things they don't already know or aren't quite sure of. Write their responses on the board in a column to the right of the *What I Know* column.

EARTHQUAKES

What I Know	What I Would Like to Know	What I Learned
Can cause damage	*What causes earthquakes*	
Are unpredictable	*How earthquakes are measured*	
Are scary	*What places have earthquakes*	
Happen in California	*What was the worst earthquake*	
Not all are the same	*Where most earthquakes are*	
Shake the earth	*What we can do about earthquakes*	
Don't happen at night		
Are getting worse		

During Reading for Day 1

Guided Reading: *What I Learned*

In this activity, students write down answers to the questions they posed prior to reading that are given in the text, and then they consider which of their questions still need answers.

Goal of the Activity: To have students transform questions into answers and thoughts into writing.

Rationale: Having students search for answers to their questions requires active reading on their part. Transforming what they learn into writing requires and promotes even deeper understanding. Having students go a step further and check what questions still need answering lets them know that the information an author chooses is selective and that they may need to check other sources to get their answers.

Procedure: On the chalkboard to the right of the previous two headings, write *What I Learned.* Explain to students that this will be the last part of the K-W-L procedure, which they can use when they read informational books and articles. They have already completed the first two steps, thinking about and writing down what they know about earthquakes and what they would like to know. The last step is to record what information they do learn.

Direct students' attention to the information they wanted to know. Explain that as they read they will look for the answers to these questions.

Reading to Students: *The Appetizer*

In this activity, you read the first few pages of an informational book aloud to students.

Goal of the Activity: To interest students further in the topic of the book and motivate them to read it on their own.

Rationale: Reading aloud helps to ease students into the material. A good enthusiastic rendition can also be an enticement for students to read on their own. In addition, this shared experience allows you to complete the third step of the K-W-L procedure as a group and to provide clarification of the task before students read and record answers on their own.

Ask students to listen carefully as you read the first five pages in the book aloud. They should be thinking about the questions they had listed on the board and decide whether or not they are answered in these pages.

Postreading for Day 1

Discussion: *Questions Answered?*

In this activity, students decide which questions were answered in the text.

Goal of the Activity: To have students realize that even though a specific text may answer some of their questions, it may not answer all of them, and they will need to seek other sources for some questions.

Rationale: To become critical thinkers and readers, students need to realize that our questions about a topic might be answered in a text or they might not be. Authors have to be selective in what they include. What we may wish to know may not be in the scope of the text, and therefore we need to consult others.

Procedure: Draw students attention to the questions asked in the prereading activity.

EARTHQUAKES

What I Want to Know

What causes earthquakes

How earthquakes are measured

What places have earthquakes

What was the worst earthquake

Where most earthquakes are

What we can do about earthquakes

Begin by asking students if the first question was answered in the first five pages of the book. If students answer yes, ask them to tell you what the answer is and write that answer in the column *What I Learned.* Proceed in a similar manner with each of the questions. If questions aren't answered, tell students that these questions might still be answered in the remainder of the text or that they may not be answered in this particular text at all and they will need to consult other sources for the answers.

Prereading for Day 2

Prequestioning and Direction Setting: *K-W-L*

In this activity, students record what they know about a topic, what they want to know, and what they learned from reading a text. This prereading activity prepares students to use the K-W-L procedure independently.

Goal of the Activity: To have students access their knowledge on a topic, think about what they would like to learn about that topic, and better understand and remember the information that interests them most.

Rationale: Having students access appropriate knowledge before reading a text, posing their own questions, and writing down the answers to those questions can help them to better understand and remember text material.

Procedure: Hand out the "What I **KNOW**—What I **WANT** to Know—What I **LEARNED**" chart shown below.

What I Know	What I Would Like to Know	What I Learned

When students have their charts, review the three types of information they will record. First they will think about and record what they **know** about earthquakes, then write down what they **want** to know in the second column. As they read the book, they will write the answers to their questions or what they **learned** in the third column. Remind students of what they had done as a group the day before and explain that today they will have the opportunity to focus on their own knowledge and interest in earthquakes as they read.

Remind students that not all of their questions will be answered in the text. This might be a good opportunity to talk about other resources for finding answers if this particular text doesn't provide them.

Explain that when they finish they will get a chance to share what they learned about earthquakes.

During-Reading for Day 2

Modifying the Text: *Tape It*

In this activity, an audiotape recording is made available for students to listen to as they follow along in the text.

Goal of the Activity: To make the concepts in the text accessible to readers who might have difficulty reading the text on their own.

Rationale: Although this text is richly illustrated and not particularly dense, some students, particularly English language learners still in the process of mastering English, may have difficulty with it. Having an audiotape available will help to make the concepts accessible for those students whose oral skills are more developed than their reading skills.

Procedure: Make a recording of the story on an audiotape or have an older or more competent student do it. Make as many copies as necessary or hook up one tape player to several receivers.

Guided Reading: *What I Learned*

Students read the text silently (or while listening to a tape), guided by the questions they have written on their K-W-L chart, and write any answers to their questions as they find them in the text as well as other information they would like to record.

Goal of the Activity: To actively engage students with the text and to encourage and facilitate meaning-building.

Rationale: Having students search for answers to their questions requires active meaning-building on their part. Transforming that meaning into writing requires and promotes even deeper understanding of the information and ideas in the text.

Procedure: Have students read the entire book silently, recording what they learn about earthquakes as they read. Students who are following along in the text while listening to a taped version also write what they learn on their K-W-L charts.

Postreading for Day 2

Discussion 1: *What Did You Learn?*

Students meet in small heterogeneous groups to discuss what they learned from the text.

Goal of the Activity: To give students the opportunity to express their ideas to an audience and hear other students' ideas as well.

Rationale: Expressing themselves in an informal small-group setting gives students the opportunity to clarify their thoughts and also receive new information and insights from their classmates.

Procedure: After students have finished reading the text and have completed their K-W-L charts, have them meet in groups of three to six. Appoint a facilitator and a recorder for each group. In the groups, students take turns telling what their questions were, which ones were answered, and what the answers were. The facilitator's job is to make sure that everyone gets a chance to speak and that the recorder keeps an account of the questions that were not answered in the text.

Discussion 2: *Research It*

The recorders from each small-group discussion session report to the class what questions are still left to be answered, and then each group takes a question to research.

Goal of the Activity: To have students work in small groups to check multiple sources in order to find answers to a question.

Rationale: As previously mentioned, students need to realize that finding the information they want sometimes requires searching in additional sources. Working in heterogeneous groups to locate these sources and answers requires that group members support one another in their efforts. Learning to work cooperatively is a skill that is necessary not only in school but in many aspects of life.

Procedure: After the groups have met to discuss what they learned in *Earthquakes*, have the recorders report to the entire class what questions their group members still have. Write these questions on the chalkboard. Have each group choose one question to research. That group is then responsible for finding the answer and reporting their findings to the entire class.

This may also be a good time to compare the statements students listed in the *What I Know* activity with what they actually did learn from the text. For example, one student had said, "They are getting worse." Ask students if the idea that earthquakes are getting worse was validated by the text. If the consensus is no, the student who offered this initial comment may concur or perhaps decide to pursue independent research to try to confirm the statement.

Since this class is familiar with library research techniques, students need only be reminded at this time on how to proceed. This may require a brief discussion to activate students' prior knowledge and to review the guidelines they might follow.

Application and Outreach: *Let's Jigsaw*

Students form cooperative jigsaw groups (Aronson & Patnoe, 1997) and take a topic that emerged from their readings to make posters that will be displayed in the school cafeteria, library, or other public places.

Goal of the Activity: To help reinforce the concepts that students learned in their reading and to provide the opportunity for students to apply their knowledge in a practical, helpful way.

Rationale: Having groups of students work together to create posters designed to communicate information they learned from reading about earthquakes can provide students with practice in working cooperatively, recalling, analyzing and summarizing information, and thinking creatively—how to present information in a clear, concise, yet eye-catching way. It also demonstrates that information garnered from reading can be shared with others and can be important and useful.

Procedure: After students have met in their discussion groups, bring the entire class together again. Discuss some of the major points of interest in their reading about earthquakes and ask students to think about what information might be of interest to other students in the school. Have students offer their suggestions and write these on the board. Some of their suggestions might include:

> How earthquakes are measured
> What you should do to prepare for an earthquake
> What you should do when an earthquake happens
> How earthquakes happen
> Where earthquakes happen

Assign (or let each group choose) one of the topics for making a poster. If sample posters are available, show them to students, or clip appropriate advertisements from magazines and discuss what makes these informative and eye-catching.

Each group will then meet to decide what information, graphics, and illustrations will go on their poster. Next, they will use the resources available to them to produce a poster that will communicate information on their topic in the most interesting way possible. Finally, they will publicly display their poster.

Adapting the Activity: The *K-W-L* activity can be used any time students' purpose for reading is to learn information. Students might use this procedure while reading content-area textbooks, magazine articles, or any number of informational trade books. For example, students might use a K-W-L chart to help them learn more about Benjamin Franklin while reading *The Many Lives of Benjamin Franklin* by Mary Pope Osborne, to learn more space exploration in *Can You Hear a Shout in Space?* by Melvin and Gilda Berger, or to discover what it means to be president when reading the Caldecott-winning picture book *So You Want to be President?* by Judith St. George and illustrated by David Small, or to learn more about the California condor and the efforts to save this very endangered species when reading *California Condor: Flying Free* by Bonnie Graves.

Reflection: This SRE is based primarily on the K-W-L teaching model developed by Donna Ogle (1986). Although it is not the only procedure that might be used with *Earthquakes,* it's a good one. The prereading and postreading activities, of course, will reflect the material students are reading and their purposes for reading it. The essence of the model, however, includes three phases: brainstorming, purpose-setting through asking questions, and finding answers to those questions. The procedure provides a scaffold that helps to support students' own interests and inquiries. According to Ogle, K-W-L

> helps students keep control of their own inquiry, extending the pursuit of knowledge beyond just the one article. The teacher is making clear that learning shouldn't be framed around just what an author chooses to include, but that it involves the identification of the learner's questions and the search for authors or articles dealing with those questions.

A Complete SRE for *Because of Winn-Dixie*

This is adapted from an SRE created by Lauren Liang, a Ph.D. student at the University of Minnesota.

Students: Sixth graders of mixed abilities.

Selection: *Because of Winn-Dixie* by Kate DiCamillo. In this engagingly told Newbery Honor book, 10-year-old India Opal, a lonely child who has recently moved to a new town with her father, searches for friends and makes them with the help of a homeless mutt whom she befriends and names Winn-Dixie. The diversity of the friends she gradually makes—from an elderly librarian to a guitar-playing ex-felon who works in the local pet store—and the way she brings them together as a community make an entertaining and compelling tale.

Reading Purpose: To understand, enjoy, and make connections with an award-winning middle grade novel and to help foster students' awareness of character development in novels.

Table 7-2 outlines the activities of this SRE.

Table 7-2. *Because of Winn-Dixie* Overview

Students	Selection	Purpose
Sixth graders of mixed abilities	*Because of Winn-Dixie* by Kate DiCamillo	To understand, enjoy and make connections with an award-winning middle grade novel and to help foster students' awareness of character development in novels
Day 1		
Prereading	**During-Reading**	**Postreading**
• Building Text-Specific Knowlede (5 min.) • Relating the Reading to Student's Lives (20 min.)	• Reading to Students (20–25 min.) • Silent Reading (homework)	None
Day 2 **Follow-up on Homework for Day 1** • Discussion and Questioning (15 min.)		
Prereading	**During-Reading**	**Postreading**
• Preteaching Concepts (20 min.) • Direction Setting (15 min.)	• Silent Reading (homework)	• Writing (homework)
Day 3 **Follow-up on Homework for Day 2** • Discussion (10 min.)		
Prereading	**During-Reading**	**Postreading**
• Predicting (10 min. before Reading to Students) • Predicting (5 min. just before the Silent Reading homework assignment)	• Reading to Students (15 min.) • Silent Reading (homework)	• Writing (homework)

(Continued on next page)

Table 7-2. *Because of Winn-Dixie* Overview (*Continued*)

Day 4		
Follow-up on Homework for Day 3		
• Graphic Activity (15 min.)		
Prereading	**During-Reading**	**Postreading**
• Building Background Knowledge (5 min.)	• Silent Reading (homework)	• Writing (homework)
Day 5		
Follow-up on Homework for Day 4		
• Discussion (5 min.)		
Prereading	**During-Reading**	**Postreading**
None	• Reading to Students (15 min.)	• Discussion (20 min. after Reading to Students)
	• Silent Reading (homework)	• Writing (homework)
Day 6		
Follow-up on Homework for Day 5		
• Writing and Drama (40 min.)		
• Discussion (5 min.)		
Prereading	**During-Reading**	**Postreading**
• Predicting (5 min. just before Silent Reading homework assignment)	• Silent Reading (homework)	• Writing (homework)
Day 7		
Follow-up on Homework for Day 6		
• Discussion (10 min.)		
Prereading	**During-Reading**	**Postreading**
• Predicting (5 min. just before Silent Reading homework assignment)	• Reading to Students (25 min.)	• Writing (homework)
	• Silent Reading (homework)	

Day 8 **Follow-up on Homework for Day 7** • Discussion (10 min.)		
Prereading • Building Background	**During-Reading** • Reading to Students (15 min.)	**Postreading** • Questioning (20 min. after Reading to Students)
Day 9–10 **Prereading** None	**During-Reading** None	**Postreading** • Graphic and Artistic Activities and Writing (1–2 hours as homework) • Discussion (20 min. as homework)

Prereading for Day 1

Building Text-Specific Knowledge: *Stepping Into the Story*

In *Stepping Into the Story,* students are given a preview of the selection. The preview includes questions that encourage students to connect incidents in their lives with what happens to the main character, India Opal. It also provides a brief introduction to what the story is about and what might happen in it.

Goal of the Activity: To serve as a bridge from the students' experiences to those of the story's character and to give students an initial framework for the story.

Rationale: To get students to think about events in their lives that relate to the story's character through a few focused questions and then provide specific information about the story—the character, setting, and problem. This will help students to quickly make their own connections and build meaning as they read.

Procedure: Read the following preview to students slowly and with expression. Treat most of the questions in the first paragraph as rhetorical, and then pause after the last question to get a few responses, but take only a minute or two with these. The purpose of the questions is to get students thinking, not to promote an extended discussion.

Preview for *Because of Winn-Dixie*

Have you ever moved to a new town? Or transferred to a new school with very few people you know? Or maybe gone to a summer camp away from home? Most people at one point or another have experienced what it is like to be new to a place. Perhaps the biggest challenge of being the newcomer is making friends. Think back to a time when you were the new person. How did it feel to not know anyone? Did you try to start conversations with others? Did you watch people closely? Can you remember what it felt like when you first met someone who might be a friend?

In *Because of Winn-Dixie,* you will meet India Opal, a 10-year-old girl who has just moved to a new town in Florida. You'll go along with her as she begins to get used to her new home and make friends. You'll hear her first impressions of the people she meets, and you'll see if any of those impressions change. You may see that moving to the new town could change Opal, too.

Relating the Reading to Students' Lives: *5 x 2 x 2*

In *5 x 2 x 2,* students write for 5 minutes about an experience they've had that is similar to the main character's, share their writing with a partner for 2 minutes, and ask questions of their partner for 2 minutes.

Goal of the Activity: To bring to consciousness through writing and discussion ideas and issues that are relevant to appreciating and understanding the situation and motivations of the characters in a story.

Rationale: Although the experiences of India Opal are her own, they represent a very common situation: finding oneself in a situation in which you are the newcomer. A writing, discussion, and questioning activity such as *5 x 2 x 2* encourages students to think about times when they found themselves this type of situation, to write about the specifics of their experience, and to hear similar experiences from their peers. Having thought about, written about, and talked about these times serves as a terrific link from their lives to the character and promotes empathy and understanding.

Procedure: After you give students the preview, have them write in their journal for 5 minutes about a time they experienced moving or being the newcomer in a situation such as camp or school.

After 5 minutes of writing, have students share their writing with a partner in a 2-minute pair-share. (In a 2-minute pair-share, each student has 2 minutes to talk without interruption about what he or she wrote.) After each partner has had 2 minutes, allow 2 minutes for them to ask each other questions or offer comments.

Next, gather students together as a class and invite them to share their ideas with their classmates. Then, as a whole class brainstorm ways to make new friends when you are new to a place. After students have generated some ideas, tell them that the book they are about to read is about a 10-year-old girl who moves to a new town in Florida and the experiences she has as she gets used to her new surroundings, seeks new friends, and begins to deal with some of her past experiences.

During-Reading for Day 1

Reading to Students

Have students open their books and follow along as you read aloud the first two chapters. Discuss the definition of *missionary* when you come across the word. You may also need to explain that Winn-Dixie is a supermarket chain.

During-Reading Homework for Day 1

Silent Reading

Have students read chapters 3 and 4 for homework.

Follow-up on Homework for Day 1
(This activity occurs at the beginning of Day 2)

Discussion and Questioning: *The Top Ten*

In *The Top Ten* activity, you ask students, "What are the 10 things that Opal learned about her mother?" and write their responses on the board; then students prioritize the list, beginning with what they think is the least important (10) and ending with the most important (1).

Goal of the Activity: To encourage students to recall story details and to foster critical thinking.

Rationale: Details help to make a story believable, and recalling the details about a character highlights this aspect of good fiction. Also, encouraging students to prioritize details for their importance and to justify their choices helps to hone their critical thinking skills and prepares them for the next activity, which they will be involved in throughout the novel.

Procedure: After students have read chapters 3 and 4 as homework, ask them why Opal wanted her father to tell her 10 things about her mother and briefly discuss. Next, say something like "Let's make a list of those 10 things," and write students' responses on the board or overhead. Do not number these. When you have all 10 details about Opal's mother on the board or transparency, read them aloud, then say something like "I wonder if we can arrange these in order of their importance to Opal? What do you say we try, beginning with the least important?"

As students give their suggestions, accept all answers in the order they are given and write them on the board that way. Whenever students disagree about the order of importance, have them justify their choices. When all 10 are listed in order from least important (10) to most (1), let students who disagree give their opinions. Tell students there is no "correct" order. You weren't trying to get them to reach a consensus, just to think about which details about Opal's mother may have been the most important to Opal. Here's what their list might look like:

10.   *She had red hair and freckles.*
9.   *She couldn't cook. She burned everything, including water.*
8.   *She knew all the constellations.*
7.   *She could run fast.*
6.   *She could make just about anybody laugh.*
5.   *She loved stories.*
4.   *She liked to plant things.*
3.   *She hated being a preacher's wife.*
2.   *She drank.*
1.   *She loved Opal very much.*

Prereading for Day 2

Preteaching Concepts: *Physical Traits and Personal Attributes*

In the *Physical Traits and Personal Attributes* activity, students identify the physical traits and personal attributes of story characters by finding examples of these in the text.

Goal of the Activity: To help students gain an understanding of the difference between physical traits and personal attributes and to learn how authors develop story characters by using both of these types of attributes.

Rationale: Understanding the difference between the physical traits and personal attributes of story characters and learning how authors develop their characters by using both of these will foster students' appreciation of a storytelling technique that will help them better appreciate the fiction they read and enhance their storytelling abilities.

Preparation: Before class, make copies of Table 7-3.

Table 7-3. Possible Personal Attributes

Agreeable	Enthusiastic	Kind	Self-Sacrificing
Aggressive	Fearless	Lazy	Self-centered
Ambitious	Flexible	Loyal	Selfish
Angry	Foolish	Merciful	Sensible
Appreciative	Friendly	Mischievous	Serious
Arrogant	Generous	Modest	Servile
Bashful	Gentle	Narrow-minded	Shy
Boastful	Grouchy	Noble	Stubborn
Brave	Gullible	Obedient	Subservient
Calculating	Hard-working	Observant	Superstitious
Candid	Honest	Overconfident	Suspicious
Cautious	Honorable	Patient	Thoughtful
Clever	Humble	Perceptive	Thoughtless
Conceited	Humorous	Persistent	Timid
Confident	Imaginative	Proud	Trusting
Considerate	Impatient	Reasonable	Uncooperative
Cooperative	Impulsive	Reliable	Understanding
Courageous	Inconsiderate	Responsible	Unreasonable
Curious	Independent	Rigid	Unselfish
Deceitful	Industrious	Sarcastic	Wise
Determined	Insecure	Scornful	
Dishonest	Insincere	Self-conscious	

Procedure: Ask students which of the 10 items they listed in The Top Ten activity are physical traits, things that describe Mama's physical appearance. Label these items PT for physical traits. Then have students look at the remaining items. Explain that these items describe Mama in a different way: They are all examples of personal attributes of Mama. Tell students that when we describe a person, we often use both physical traits and personal attributes. For example, Brian is tall with brown hair and is very patient with young children.

Next, ask students how an author helps a reader to get to know a character. Brainstorm ideas, ultimately leading students to see that most of the time authors develop characters through physical descriptions, dialogue with others, inner thoughts, and actions. Through these ways, we get a picture of that character and his or her personality. Tell students that as they read *Because of Winn-Dixie* over the next several days, they'll be looking for and talking about the character traits of the characters. They'll also be finding quotes in the story that show physical traits and personal attributes of each character.

Have students practice using physical traits and personal attributes for description by choosing a person they know well (their mom or dad, brother or sister, or best friend) and writing a list of five physical traits and five personal attributes of that person. Circle the room, and check students' work to see if they have the right idea. Invite students to share some of the personal attributes they listed. Then hand out Table 7-3. Explain that this is only a partial list and that they should add more ideas to it.

Now ask students to think about Opal. Based on what they have read so far, what personal attributes does Opal have? As students suggest ideas using the Possible Personal Attributes list to help them, ask them to explain why they think each attribute fits and to back up their reason with a specific quote from the book. You will most likely need to guide students to find quotes. For example, if a student suggests that Opal is brave because she saved Winn-Dixie from the pound, have students look at pages 9 and 10 and find the quote that supports this idea:

> "Wait a minute!" I hollered. "That's my dog. Don't call the pound." All the Winn-Dixie employees turned around and looked at me, and I knew I had done something big. And maybe stupid, too. But I couldn't help it. I couldn't let that dog go to the pound.

Other attributes, not on the list, that students might suggest for this quote might be *caring* and *compassionate*. These could be then added to the list.

Direction Setting: *The Double-Entry Journal*

In *The Double-Entry Journal* activity (Vaughn, 1990), students look for passages in the novel that reveal the personal attributes of story characters and record both the attribute and the quote that shows this attribute in a double-entry journal.

Goal of the Activity: To focus students' attention on characters' personal attributes by requiring them to identify both the attribute and how the author reveals that attribute with a specific example.

Rationale: An activity such as this one, which focuses students' attention on a specific literary technique and requires that they not only identify a personal attribute but determine the passages in which that trait is revealed, requires students to read critically, to use textual evidence to support opinions, and to explore thoughts underlying feelings and feelings underlying thoughts of story characters.

Preparation: Before class, put Table 7-4 on the board or a transparency and make enough copies of it for students to write entries for chapters 6 and 7.

Procedure: Using the board or overhead, show students a copy of Table 7-4 and demonstrate how to complete an entry in the journal, using the personal attribute for Opal that was suggested in the previous activity.

Next, explain that for each chapter of Winn-Dixie, students will complete a page in their character double-entry journal. Then hand out the journal assignment guide. Read through the guide with students and explain that they will be responsible for doing an entry for each chapter that is assigned for homework. Remind them to look for personal attributes rather than physical traits, and ask them to record two for each chapter.

Table 7-4. *Winn-Dixie* Double-Entry Journal Page

For each chapter of Kate DiCamillo's *Because of Winn-Dixie* you will create a page in your character double-entry journal. Use the format below and the example to help you.

Today's Date:

Chapter:

CHARACTER'S NAME AND PERSONAL ATTRIBUTE	Quote From Text Showing This Personal Attribute
Name of Character: Personal Attribute:	Page Number of Quote: Quote: Why This Quote Works:
CHARACTER'S NAME AND PERSONAL ATTRIBUTE	Quote From Text Showing This Personal Attribute
Name of Character: Personal Attribute:	Page Number of Quote: Quote: Why this Quote Works:

During Reading—Homework for Day 2

Silent Reading

Have students read chapters 5 and 6 for homework.

Postreading Homework for Day 2

Writing: *Double-Entry Journals*

As homework, have students write in their double-entry journals for each chapter (two personal attributes with textual evidence per chapter.)

(*Note:* Because many of the activities for days 3–8 revolve around the same activity—identifying personal attributes and the quotes that show these attributes and recording these in a double-entry journal—or are basically self-explanatory, we do not give the Goal of the Activity or the Rationale as we typically have done. We give just the directions necessary to carry out the activity.)

Follow-up on Homework for Day 2
(*This activity occurs at the beginning of Day 3*)

Discussion

Begin by having students briefly share their double-entry journal assignments, either with partners or in small groups. Ask a few students to volunteer examples to the class.

Then, as a whole class, briefly discuss Opal's adaptation to her new town so far. Does it seem like she has made any new friends?

Prereading for Day 3

Predicting

Give students 3 or 4 minutes to write down their predictions of what Miss Fanny's story might be. Share a few of these ideas as a whole class.

Have students make predictions in preparation for their homework assignment about Amanda and the role she will play in the book.

During-Reading for Day 3

Reading to Students

Read aloud chapter 7 to the students while they follow along.

During Reading Homework for Day 3

Silent Reading

Have students read chapters 8, 9, and 10 for homework.

Postreading Homework for Day 3

Writing

Students should write in their double-entry journals for each chapter as homework (two personal attributes with textual evidence for each chapter).

Follow-up on Homework for Day 3
(This activity occurs at the beginning of Day 4)

Graphic Activity

Have students in pairs create a list of all the characters in the book so far. For each character, have them list two personal attributes next to the character's name. Next to these two traits, have them draw the character, showing two physical traits in the picture. Finally, have pairs share their work in groups of six or so.

Prereading for Day 4

Building Background Knowledge

Discuss briefly with students how animals often react to storms.

During-Reading Homework for Day 4

Silent Reading

Have students read chapters 11, 12, and 13 for homework.

Postreading Homework for Day 4

Writing

Have students write in their double-entry journals for each chapter (two personal attributes with textual evidence for each chapter).

Follow-up on Homework for Day 4
(This activity occurs at the beginning of Day 5)

Discussion

Ask students to share one of the personal attributes they discovered in last night's reading, and give the supporting quote they wrote down as the textual evidence.

Prereading for Day 5

There is no prereading activity for this day.

During-Reading for Day 5

Reading to Students

Read aloud chapter 14 to students for 15 minutes as they follow along.

Postreading for Day 5

Discussion

After reading to students, have them reread the line on page 96 that says "Judge them by what they are doing now." Then ask students if they would rather be judged by what they are doing right now or by what they were like in the past. Have students debate this idea in small groups and then as a whole class.

During-Reading Homework for Day 5

Silent Reading

Have students read chapters 15, 16, and 17 for homework.

Postreading Homework for Day 5

Writing

Have students write in their double-entry journals for each chapter as homework (two personal attributes with textual evidence for each chapter).

Follow-up on Homework for Day 5
(This activity occurs at the beginning of Day 6)

Writing and Drama

On the board or overhead, write the word *bittersweet*, and define it if necessary. Give students 10 to 15 minutes to write about an experience in their lives that they would call bittersweet. After the writing time is over, have students share their stories with small groups. Then, have each small group choose one story to act out in a brief skit and prepare their skit. Finally, ask for volunteers to act out their stories for the class.

Discussion

As a whole class, briefly discuss why India Opal's life is bittersweet.

Prereading for Day 6

Predicting

Have students predict, for 5 minutes, what they think will happen next in the story.

During-Reading for Day 6

Silent Reading

Have students read chapters 18, 19, and 20 for homework.

Postreading Homework for Day 6

Writing

Have students write in their double-entry journals for each chapter as homework (two personal attributes with textual evidence for each chapter).

Follow-up on Homework for Day 6
(This activity occurs at the beginning of Day 7)

Discussion

Have students review their double-entry journal notes from start to finish, looking for characters who have changed and show different personal attributes than they did before. Then have volunteers discuss characters who have changed and give textual support demonstrating these changes.

Prereading for Day 7

Predicting

Have students predict what will happen at the party.

During-Reading for Day 7

Reading to Students

Read aloud chapters 21 and 22 to your students.

During Reading Homework for Day 7

Silent Reading

Have students read chapters 23, 24, and 25 for homework.

Postreading Homework for Day 7

Writing

Have students write in their double-entry journals for each chapter as homework (two personal attributes with textual evidence for each chapter).

Follow-up on Homework for Day 7
(This activity occurs at the beginning of Day 8)

Discussion

Have students share with partners their favorite parts of the last four chapters in the book, then have volunteers share a few of these with the whole class, for 10 minutes.

Prereading for Day 8

There is no prereading activity for this day.

During-Reading for Day 8

Reading to Students

Read aloud chapter 26, the final chapter in the book, to students.

Postreading for Day 8

Questioning

Have students respond in writing to two questions:

1. Why are 10 things not enough for Opal?
2. Do you think the ending is positive or negative? Why?

If time allows, you may want to discuss these questions orally.

(There are no prereading or during-reading activities for Days 9–10.)

Postreading In Class and Homework for Days 9-10

Graphic and Artistic Activities and Writing

As a final activity for the book, have students work on the following assignment in class and as homework: Make a poster featuring one of the characters in the story. The poster must contain a picture of the character exhibiting three physical traits that were mentioned in the story. These traits should be labeled, and a quote from the text should be given with each label as "evidence." Underneath the picture, list five personal attributes of the character with a quote from the text to support each attribute. At the very bottom of the poster, describe what is bittersweet for that character.

Discussion

Allow students to view one another's posters and make positive comments. One way you can do this is to have students place their posters on their desks and rotate seats every few minutes. A piece of paper left on the desk can be used for the "visiting" students to write a positive comment.

Optional Culminating Activities

- Have students write an essay about an experience they have had that was bittersweet.

- Encourage students to read Kate DiCamillo's book, *The Tiger Rising*. Ask them to consider how is it bittersweet and to compare India Opal to Rob.

- Suggest that students draw a picture of one of the scenes in *Because of Winn-Dixie* that they think is very important in revealing one of the character's personality traits. Then have them explain in writing why they think this scene is important for that reason.

- Invite students to write a song (lyrics only to a tune they know or a tune and lyrics) that Oliver might sing to his pets in the store. Have them then explain in writing why they think Oliver would sing this song.

Adapting the Activity: A similar SRE might be built around any number of novels with well-developed characters. Any one of Barbara O'Connor's delightful novels—*Beethoven in Paradise, Me and Rupert Goody,* and *Moonpie and Ivy*—all of which are peopled with well-drawn, unforgettable characters, would work well with this activity. Another good possibility is Marie Lee's *Necessary Roughness,* about Chan and his sister, Kim, who must adjust to living in a small town in northern Minnesota as well as come to terms with their father's strict rules, which seem out of step with modern America.

Reflection: The purposes of these 10 days of activities have been to help students successfully read and enjoy *Because of Winn-Dixie*; introduce them to two types of character traits (personal attributes and physical traits), give them experience using textual quotes to support an opinion or judgment, provide experience making predictions in fiction stories, and to help develop their awareness of character development in novels. With these objectives in mind, several higher order reading and comprehension skills have been emphasized:

- Making plausible inferences, predictions, and interpretations about a fiction text

- Reading and listening critically

- Using textual evidence to support opinions

- Exploring thoughts underlying feelings and feelings underlying thoughts

In addition, it would be our hope that at the completion of this SRE, students will have come away from the experience with a few new insights about themselves and the world as portrayed through literature.

A Complete SRE for
Eleanor Roosevelt: A Life of Discovery

(This is adapted from an SRE created by Sharon M. Scapple, an English education professor at Minnesota State University, Moorhead, and a specialist in adolescent literature.

Students: Eighth graders of mixed abilities.

Selection: *Eleanor Roosevelt: A Life of Discovery* by Russell Freedman. In this "memorable portrait" of First Lady Eleanor Roosevelt (*Publisher's Weekly,* 1993) and Newbery Honor book, readers meet a woman in the making, a woman who stood tall in her convictions and against her fears, who opened her heart to humanity, and who accomplished rather courageous acts to do the right thing. Readers will also encounter a master storyteller and researcher who lives with the subject of his writing day and night until the writing is done, who brings integrity to the writing, and who sees in his research that Eleanor Roosevelt was a woman who made an impression on people. Freedman cites one of Eleanor's friends who captured what was so remarkable about her: "She [Eleanor] gave off light," the woman said. "I can't explain it better." This was Freedman's intention, to capture that light. It was the light within Eleanor Roosevelt that enabled her to do the unthinkable.

Reading Purpose: To introduce students to one of the most influential women in the world, to help them understand how she achieved such stature, and to give them the experience of critically handling and analyzing a nonfiction text, the literature of fact.

Table 7-5 outlines the activities of this SRE.

Table 7-5. *Eleanor Roosevelt* Overview

Students	Selection	Purpose
Eighth graders of of mixed abilities	*Eleanor Roosevelt: A Life of Discovery* by Russell Freedman	To learn about one of the most influential women in the world, to understand how she achieved her stature, and to critically read and analyze a non-fiction text
Day 1 **Prereading** • Building Background Knowledge—about author (20 min.) • Relating the Reading to Students' Lives (20 min.) • Building Background Knowledge—relevant to the story (10–15 min.)	**During-Reading** None	**Postreading** None
Day 2 **Prereading** • Building Background Knowledge—about historical setting (20 min.) • Providing Text-Specific Knowledge—preview (10 min.)	**During-Reading** • Reading to Students— recorded reading of chapter 1 (10 min.)	**Postreading** • Discussions— Think-Pair-Share (10 min.) *(Continued on next page)*

Table 7-5. *Eleanor Roosevelt* Overview (*Continued*)

Days 3–7		
Prereading	**During-Reading**	**Postreading**
None	• Silent Reading (several days)	• Questioning—Story Map (several days)
Day 8		
Prereading	**During-Reading**	**Postreading**
None	None	• Writing and Graphic Activity (50 min.)

Prereading for Day 1

Building Background Knowledge: *About the Author*

In *About the Author,* students are introduced to the author and given an overview of his work.

Goal of the Activity: To provide students with information about the author and his work.

Rationale: The students are not only reading *Eleanor Roosevelt* to know about her and her times; they are also making judgments about quality writing and the construction of nonfiction, and for this Russell Freedman is the model. Talking about Freedman's reasons for writing about Roosevelt and the process he goes through constructing a text (including doing his own photographic selection and design) will enhance the readers' appreciation and understanding of the subject.

Procedure: Begin the class by talking a little about Freedman and his work; he has at least 40 nonfiction books for adolescents to his credit. Display several of Freedman's books and identify a couple in detail. Let students gather in small groups to examine the books for their physical and visual design.

As students examine the books, point out how nonfiction text is laid out and discuss how an author establishes credibility for his writing.

If you have the time and think that your students might benefit from it, you might do a slide show of how Freedman constructs his texts. The narrational quality of his writing almost breathes life into the historical figure and the times. Freedman's art and craft of writing biographies is as important as the subject of Eleanor Roosevelt herself.

Relating the Reading to Students' Lives: *Whom Do You Admire?*

In *Whom Do You Admire?* students brainstorm a list of people they admire, choose a single "most admired" person from that list, and create a list of words that describe that person.

Goal of the Activity: To get students thinking about the qualities that make a person admirable and choosing words that describe those qualities.

Rationale: By having students think about the admirable people in their lives and what makes them admirable, you are preparing them to make connections with Eleanor Roosevelt, a person who was admired throughout the world.

Procedure: Ask students to consider why we admire the people in our lives the way we do. Lead them toward recognizing admirable people in their own lives, Eleanor Roosevelt being regarded by so many as a woman to be admired, and Freedman's conviction that she was a "most inspiring woman."

First ask students to brainstorm a list of people in their lives whom they admire. Then ask them to circle one person they most admire. They are then to create another list by placing their chosen person at the top of a sheet of paper. They are to create a list of words they would use to describe the qualities of the person they admire.

After giving students time to construct their lists, ask for volunteers to share those qualities that make someone admirable. It would be a good idea to ask a student volunteer to record these on the board or for you to record them on an overhead transparency and keep that record to use later when students draw from the reading those characteristics that made Roosevelt so admired.

Building Background Knowledge: *About the Times, A Slide Show*

In *About the Times, A Slide Show,* you present a slide show depicting the historical periods in which Eleanor lived.

Goal of the Activity: To provide students with background knowledge with visuals that depict the relationship between Eleanor Roosevelt and her environment, and to prepare them to understand the strides she made as a woman, as a president's wife, and as a person within such an environment; also, to give students visuals to compare with the photographs Freedman presents in his text.

Rationale: Providing students with visual images of the times in which Roosevelt lived will give them important background knowledge necessary to understand what motivated Roosevelt to think as she did and do what she did.

Procedure: Give students a slide show presenting the historical backdrop to Roosevelt's life. Include slides that show life at home in America and in the fields during World Wars I and II, slides during the Great Depression, and slides during the time of peace and the Cold War. Briefly discuss what life must have been like during each of these periods.

During Reading for Day 1

There are no during reading activities for this day.

Postreading for Day 1

There are no postreading activities for this day.

Prereading for Day 2

Building Background Knowledge: *About the Times, A Time Line*

In *About the Times, a Time Line,* you draw a time line depicting the historical periods of Roosevelt's life and have students brainstorm a list of words that describe various aspects of life during each of those periods.

Goal of the Activity: To provide students with information about the life and times in which Eleanor Roosevelt lived.

Rationale: In order to understand the whys of a person's actions, statements, and beliefs, it is important that students realize what was going on in the world during that person's lifetime. Accessing students' knowledge of the time periods spanned by Roosevelt's life with a brainstorming activity can aid them in this understanding.

Procedure: Draw a time line on the board showing the historical periods that Roosevelt lived through: World War I, the Great Depression, World War II, peace, and the Cold War.

Beginning with the first period, ask students to write a list words that describe some aspect of life during each of those periods.

Keep the brainstorming short, allowing a minute or two for students to write words for each historical period. Then, ask students to share the results of their brainstorming as you record these results under the appropriate headings.

As you discuss these periods in American history, talk briefly about how people may have felt living in those times.

Providing Text-Specific Knowledge: *Stepping Into the Story*

In *Stepping Into the Story,* you give a preview of the selection designed to gain students' attention, serve as an overview of the text up to a suitable stopping place, and provide brief directions for reading. A preview (Graves, Prenn, & Cooke, 1985) is a well-crafted introduction to a text that is read to students prior to their reading the text itself.

Goal of the Activity: To provide students with knowledge specific to the text and to pique their interest in the upcoming selection and motivate them to want to read.

Rationale: Providing students with a preview to the selection they are going to read not only gives them information specific to the text that will aid them in making connections with the text when they read it; it also serves to pique their interest and reveal how a person of the stature of Eleanor Roosevelt was a human being with fears and obstacles to overcome, just as they are. It is important to recognize the life of Roosevelt as significant to adolescent readers, particularly as a female role model; clearly, she is an example of "somebody who took control of her own life" (*Publisher's Weekly,* 2000). She did what she believed needed to be done, and for that she will always be regarded as a great humanitarian, a most admired woman.

Procedure: After doing the Time Line Activity, present the preview of *Eleanor Roosevelt* given below. Do so with enthusiasm and an earnestness that inspires students to want to read on.

Preview for *Eleanor Roosevelt: A Life of Discovery*

Imagine that you are living during the time of World War I, when, for the first time, American combat troops were sent to fight in Europe (1917–1918). Imagine that you are seeing women casting their votes at the polls for the first time (1920). Imagine that you are living during the Great Depression (1930s), the worst economic period in American history, when businesses, factories, and banks closed and numerous people were unemployed after the stock market collapsed, struggling to be fed and clothed. And imagine the Second World War, when Hitler reigned in Germany and Nazi sirens wailed and when America ended the war with Japan by dropping atomic bombs on Hiroshima and Nagasaki.

Finally, imagine that you are stepping into the shoes of Eleanor Roosevelt, a woman who has lived the life of world wars, a depression, and women's and civil rights. Imagine you are entering the White House as the wife of President Franklin D. Roosevelt; it is 1933—all the while you are dreading the prospect of being pegged as the "White House hostess." How do you maneuver a life independent of the presidency and manage a career?

Eleanor Roosevelt was raised in privilege, although she lost her parents by age 10 and grew up in a time when a woman's life was predominantly domestic and dominated by her husband's interests and needs. Not until midlife did Eleanor have the courage, as she says, to develop interests of her own, outside the duties to her family. In this she was unique, defying convention and moving well beyond anyone's expectations of a timid and uncomely child and an obedient society matron, particularly as directed by her mother-in-law. Eleanor took up her pen and voice as teacher, writer, journalist, and humanitarian and wielded a personal and political power all her own.

As you read Russell Freedman's biography of Eleanor Roosevelt, step into her life and her times and observe and listen to how Eleanor, a woman who had perceived of herself as a timid and fearful child and as an "ugly duckling," became honored in her adult life as the "First Lady of the World." What did Eleanor do to be regarded so highly? How did she accomplish this honor?

Leave students to consider questions about Eleanor posed at the end of the preview as you tell them they will be hearing a recording of the first chapter.

During-Reading for Day 2

Present a recorded reading of the chapter "Poor Little Rich Girl," as students follow along in the text.

Postreading for Day 2

Discussion: *Think-Pair-Share*

In *Think-Pair-Share,* students pair up to discuss the chapter they just heard read aloud and record their musings to share with the whole group.

Goal of the Activity: To give students the opportunity to reflect on the significant events in Roosevelt's early life, to share these ponderings in a low-stress situation (with a partner), and to hear the musings of their fellow students as well.

Rationale: Providing students with the opportunity to reflect on a reading, share their views, and listen to others' ideas not only gives students practice in distinguishing the important themes from the details in a selection, it also adds to their knowledge of the topic of the selection.

Procedure: After students have heard the chapter read, group them in pairs. Give them about 10 minutes to comment aloud to each other about the significant experiences in Roosevelt's childhood that they learned from the chapter "Poor Little Rich Girl." Also, encourage them to think about how those experiences might have formed her character. One partner should serve as a recorder so the ideas can be shared with the larger group later.

During the large-group sharing of these, ask students to consider the later changes in Roosevelt's character and how she worked to overcome her fears, things that they will discover as they read the book.

Prereading for Days 3–7

There are no prereading activities for these days.

During-Reading for Days 3–7

Silent Reading

Have students read the book on their own, either in class or as homework. As they read, have them answer the questions on the story map that corresponds with the chapter they are reading. With upper grades, you can realistically ask that this book be read in a week's time out of class and that students answer the story map questions individually. If this is not feasible, an alternative is to read some or all of the book in class and have students work in groups to answer the story map questions, the postreading activity described below.

Postreading for Days 3–7

Questioning: *The Story Map*

In *The Story Map,* questions are developed that follow in sequential order the information that is central to understanding the selection. A story map (Beck & McKeown, 1981) is a set of questions whose answers reveal the essence of the selection. The story map questions follow the text's chronology, focusing on events of central importance to the text and requiring both a reader's understanding of factual knowledge and the ability to draw inferences. A set of extension questions follows the story map questions. These are intended to be answered after readers have arrived at a basic understanding of the selection.

Goal of the Activity: To focus students' attention on the important events of Roosevelt's life in the order in which they take place.

Rationale: This biography, as is the case with many biographies, is written primarily in chronological order. Thus, the story map questions are divided into the parts of Roosevelt's life chronologically, as Freedman reveals them. Having students answer questions about important story events in the sequence in which they occur can help to promote comprehension of this particular narrative as well as to develop their schema for narrative sequence.

Procedure: Hand out the story map questions to students shown in Table 7-6. Depending on your students, you may not want to give them the entire set of questions at once; rather, give them to students in increments that are matched to what they can most successfully handle. For example, you might give them the questions from Roosevelt's childhood and adolescence as the first set, marriage as the second, and terms as First Lady and post-presidency years as the third.

Have students write answers to the story map questions on a separate sheet of paper.

Table 7-6. Story Map for *Eleanor Roosevelt: A Life of Discovery*

Childhood

1. Eleanor Roosevelt was raised in privilege and wealth and in a society where beauty mattered. Eleanor tells us that her mother was troubled by Eleanor's lack of beauty. How did Eleanor see herself as a child?

2. What kind of relationship did Eleanor have with her father?

Adolescence

3. Eleanor believed that the three years she spent in London (ages 15–18) as a student of Mademoiselle Souvestre—a woman of liberal mind and strong personality—had changed her life. In what ways did Eleanor change?

4. As a rite of passage, Eleanor's grandmother introduced her into society (social debut). How did Eleanor fare?

5. Why, at age 19, does Eleanor describe herself as "a curious mixture of extreme innocence and unworldliness with a great deal of knowledge of some of the less agreeable sides of life" (p. 34)?

Marriage

6. During the Victorian era, the early 1900s, when Eleanor was just entering her twenties, what rules governed meetings between men and women? How did these rules affect Eleanor's courtship with and marriage to Franklin Delano Roosevelt?

7. In what ways did Eleanor's role as the wife of a statesman and politician enable her to venture outside the duties of her family and find a personal voice?

8. After 13 years of marriage and six children, Eleanor learns of her husband's affair with her social secretary, Lucy Mercer. For Eleanor, this was a life-changing event and one that Russell Freedman states he included because it is honest to do so and because it significantly changed both Franklin's and Eleanor's lives. How did Eleanor manage her life after discovering her husband's infidelity?

9. Franklin Delano Roosevelt contracted polio in 1921. How did his paralysis affect and influence Eleanor's roles as wife and mother, and her eventual role as First Lady?

Terms as First Lady of the Nation

10. In 1933, FDR took the oath as 32nd president of the United States. What were Eleanor's deeply felt feelings about her husband's presidency, and what actions did she take to pursue her own career?

11. Freedman reveals some of the controversy Eleanor faced as a social and political First Lady; he writes that she had a strong "sense of injustice and felt in a very deep personal sense that there were things that . . . [were] wrong that had to be fixed" (p. 15). What opinions did Eleanor hold regarding social reform, segregation, and discrimination? What did she do to spark attacks branding her as a socialist or a communist?

(Continued on next page)

Table 7-6. Story Map for *Eleanor Roosevelt: A Life of Discovery (Continued)*

12. Eleanor's admirers saw her as an "inspirational figure, a woman of compassion who listened with sympathy and understanding to the concerns of ordinary people" (pp. 112–113). Why did they regard her so in this ennobled way? Why was it that during the Great Depression many American parents considered that naming a child Eleanor was like "bestowing the name of a saint" (p. 113)?

13. At the end of FDR's second term as president (1940), Eleanor was listed as one of "the Ten Most Powerful People in Washington" (p. 118). Why did political commentator Raymond Clapper include Eleanor on his list?

14. After witnessing Europe's battlefields after World War I (1918), Eleanor returned home "with a deeply felt hatred of warfare that remained a ruling passion for the rest of her life" (p. 127). As First Lady, she experienced yet another world war as totalitarian regimes seized power in Nazi Germany, Fascist Italy, and Imperial Japan. What efforts did Eleanor Roosevelt make toward promoting peace in the nation and in the world? With what success did she meet these efforts?

15. After realizing how vulnerable she was as First Lady performing a government job, that of co-director of the Office of Civilian Defense, Eleanor rerouted her efforts toward becoming a goodwill ambassador, making wartime trips to England and the South Pacific. Admiral William Halsey, chief of all naval operations in the Pacific, at first criticized Eleanor's trips but later proclaimed that "she alone accomplished more good than any other person, or any group of civilians, who had passed through [this] area" (p. 138). What was Eleanor doing that changed his first opinion?

Post-Presidency years

16. Franklin Delano Roosevelt died in his fourth administration as president on April 12, 1945. Shortly after, Eleanor had told a reporter that "the story was over," that she doubted she could be instrumental in the "postwar world" (p. 147). This was not the case, however. What became of Eleanor Roosevelt at the end of her husband's presidency?

Extension Questions

1. At her death on November 7, 1962, at the age of 78, Eleanor Roosevelt was barely slowing her public and political life; 16 years after her husband's death, she was still regarded as America's "Most Admired Woman" (p. 166). Looking back along the journey that Eleanor Roosevelt made in her life, can you identify some of the battles she fought, both public and private, and the victories she won?

2. Critics claim that Russell Freedman has candidly and authentically encapsulated the life of Eleanor Roosevelt, illuminating this historical figure, "casting her in the flesh," as it were; his conviction all along was that Eleanor Roosevelt was an "inspiring figure" (*Publisher's Weekly*, 2000). What do you know and understand about Eleanor Roosevelt after reading Freedman's biography—about Eleanor as a woman, a wife, a First Lady, a politician, and a humanitarian? In what ways was she a person you would admire or not admire?

Postreading for Day 8

Writing and Graphic Activity: *Charting the Journey*

In *Charting the Journey,* students work in groups of three to five to create a chart that presents a summary statement describing who Roosevelt was—what she did, said, and believed, and how she felt—for one of the major segments in her life as listed on the story map. The combined efforts of the groups result in a time line charting Roosevelt's life.

Goal of the Activity: To help students hone their critical thinking skills of summarizing, distinguishing between relevant and irrelevant facts, transferring insights into new contexts, and exploring thoughts underlying feelings and feelings underlying thoughts.

Rationale: Having students create a statement that summarizes Roosevelt's character based on the incidents in her life described in the text requires that students use critical thinking skills, which will serve them well, not only in the future reading they do but also in real-life situations.

Procedure: As a whole group, ask students to name the major periods of Roosevelt's life and the chronological order in which they occurred. (These are the categories listed on the story map: childhood, adolescence, marriage, four terms as First Lady, and post-presidency years.) Write these on the board.

Next, assign small groups of three to five students to be responsible for one time frame. Give each group the corresponding story map questions (which they have already answered). Tell them they are to reconsider each question and the textual information that surrounds the question, thinking about how Roosevelt lived her life at that time. They are to identify what she did, what she said, what she believed, and how she felt during that specific time period.

Give each group a sheet of butcher-block paper. Tell them they are to record the information they generate on the Charting the Journey sheet (shown in Table 7-7). At the bottom of each sheet, they are to write a summary statement that describes who Roosevelt was at that time in her life. Model this process, using one of the time frames as an example, recording relevant information and coming up with a summary statement.

After about 30 minutes of group work, have a representative from each group put their sheet on the board so that they create a time line of Roosevelt's life. Representatives from each group then explain why the group listed certain points and who Roosevelt was at that time in her life.

After all time periods are revealed, have the class consider the time line as the stream of Roosevelt's life and draw conclusions about why she was regarded as the First Lady of the whole world.

Adapting the Activity: By providing more scaffolding and/or modifying these activities, this could be an effective SRE for students in grades 5 through 7 as well. Also, this SRE could be adapted to use with any of Russell Freedman's

Table 7-7. Charting the Journey

Childhood	Adolescence	Marriage	Four terms as First Lady	Post-Presidency Years
Eleanor was . . .	Eleanor was . . .	Eleanor was . . .	Eleanor was . . .	Eleanor was . . .
She felt . . .	She felt . . .	She felt . . .	She felt . . .	She felt . . .
She believed . . .	She believed . . .	She believed . . .	She believed . . .	She believed . . .
She said . . .	She said . . .	She said . . .	She said . . .	She said . . .
She thought . . .	She thought . . .	She thought . . .	She thought . . .	She thought . . .
Summary Statement	Summary Statement	Summary Statement	Summary Statement	Summary Statement

excellent biographies—*Lincoln: A Photobiography*; *Franklin Delano Roosevelt*; *The Life and Death of Crazy Horse*; *Out of Darkness: The Story of Louis Braille*; and *Babe Didrikson Zaharias: The Making of a Champion*—in addition to many of the excellent biographies of inspirational historical figures by other authors.

Reflection: Eleanor Roosevelt was a complex and multifaceted person, and although Russell Freedman has done an outstanding job rendering her life in a text that older middle grade students can understand and relate to, *Eleanor Roosevelt: A Life of Discovery* is still a complex text. For this reason, it deserves a sturdy and well-designed scaffold such as this one. With the scaffold, you markedly increase the likelihood that students will really understand and learn from the book, come to appreciate the remarkable life and contributions of Eleanor Roosevelt, and perhaps as a consequence seek out other books about outstanding historical figures.

A Complete SRE for the Theme "Real-Life Heroes"

This is a different type of SRE from the three previous ones in that it is built to support not a single selection but many different selections, which have been chosen to reflect a specific theme. In this SRE, the theme is real-life heroes. In the following example, we show how a theme-based SRE might be developed.

Students: Third graders reflecting a variety of abilities and ethnic backgrounds.

Selections: Some of the possibilities:

Stone Girl, Bone Girl: The Story of Mary Anning by Laurence Anholt, set in England at the beginning of the 19th century; a picture book that tells the story of Mary Anning's beginnings as one of history's most celebrated fossil finders.

Through My Eyes by Ruby Bridges. Ruby Bridges tells of her experiences as the first Black student to attend Franz Elementary, an all-white school in New Orleans.

Journey for Peace: The Story of Rigoberta Menchú by Marlene Targ Brill depicts the difficult journey of Menchu, who won the Nobel Peace Prize in 1992, as she struggled to free her native Mayans in Guatamala and all Native cultures from oppression.

Uncommon Traveler: Mary Kingsley in Africa by Don Brown, a picture book that tells of Kingsley's adventures on her two trips to West Africa in 1893 and 1894.

The Story of Ruby Bridges by Robert Coles, a picture book depicting the first Black student, first-grader Ruby Bridges, to attend Frantz Elementary School in New Orleans, Louisiana, in 1960.

Mandela: From the Life of the South African Statesman by Floyd Cooper, a picture book depicting the extraordinary life of Nelson Mandela from childhood until his election to presidency of the new government in South Africa in 1994.

Women Pioneers in Science by Louis Harber. Biographical sketches of inspiring women in science.

Heroes: Great Men Through the Ages by Rebecca Hazell, presents the extraordinary lives of 12 heroes, beginning with Socrates and ending with Martin Luther King, Jr. The author depicts real people, replete with strengths and weaknesses, who with courage and determination were able to change the world or the way in which we view it.

Maria's Comet by Deborah Hopkinson, a fictionalized account of America's first female astronomer and her childhood yearning for adventure.

Wilma Unlimited: How Wilma Rudolf Became the World's Fastest Woman by Kathleen Krull, tells of Rudolf's inspiring journey as a child stricken with polio to an Olympic legend.

Tomas and the Library Lady by Pat Mora, a fictionalized account of migrant worker Tomas Rivera, who eventually became a university chancellor, and the librarian who aided him.

Mount Everest and Beyond: Sir Edmund Hillary by Sue Muller Hacking tells of Hillary's ascent of Mt. Everest in 1953 and his subsequent goodwill efforts and challenges.

Starry Messenger: Galileo Galilei by Peter Sis, a picture book detailing the triumphs and tragedies of this early astronomer.

Danger Marches to the Palace: Queen Lili'uokalani by Margo Sorenson, a fictionalized account of the bravery of Hawaii's Queen Lili'uokalani in overcoming would-be traitors.

Flight by Robert Burleigh and illustrated by Mike Wimmer, a picture book telling of the determined Charles Lindbergh's exciting solo flight across the Atlantic Ocean.

Reading Purpose: To understand how real-life heroes are made, how they have met challenges and achieved their goals, and what makes them heroes.
Table 7-8 outlines the activities of this SRE.

Table 7-8. *Real-Life Heroes* Overview

Students	Selection	Purpose
Third graders of mixed abilities and ethnic backgrounds	*The Story of Ruby Bridges* by Robert Coles, plus a variety of selections reflecting the theme "real-life heroes"	Enjoyment and new insights into what makes a hero
Day 1 **Prereading** • Motivating (10 min.) • Relating Reading to Students' Lives (10 min.)	**During-Reading** • Reading to Students—Coles' book (20 min.)	**Postreading** • Discussion and Questioning (10 min.)
Day 2 **Prereading** • Direction Setting (10 min.) • Building Text-Specific Knowledge (15 min.)	**During-Reading** • Silent and Oral Reading* • Modifying the Text— audio recordings available*	**Postreading** • Writing—graffiti board and journal entries* • Artistic Activity— illustrations*
Day 3—End of Unit—Postreading Culminating Activities		
Prereading None	**During-Reading** None	**Postreading** • Discussion—small group (20 min.) • Drama, Artistic, and Nonverbal—music, dance* • Writing*
Time will vary with individual students and what they are reading.		

Prereading for Day 1

Motivating: *Let's Talk About You!*

In this activity, students talk about the challenges they've faced and the problems they've encountered and how they dealt with these.

Goal of the Activity: To encourage students to think about problems and challenges and what can be done about them.

Rationale: Because youngsters at this age are still quite egocentric, they always enjoy thinking and talking about themselves. Getting them to ponder and discuss their own life experiences is the first step in leading them to make connections between themselves and the real-life heroes in the biographies they will read.

Procedure: Encourage students to talk about what problems or challenges they have encountered and how they solved them. For example, students might talk about something that was hard for them to do but they were able to do it. Also, try to get them to talk about how they felt about themselves as they tried to solve the problem. What were some of the obstacles they encountered? What made them keep going? How did they feel when things went wrong? What did they do to correct things that went wrong? Did they learn anything new about themselves? Elicit the problem-solving strategies they used and the feelings they had.

Relating Reading to Students' Lives: *They Did It! Real-life Heroes*

In this activity, students discuss stories they have read in which the people triumphed over difficult situations.

Goal of the Activity: To move students' thinking from themselves to story characters and to help them make the connection between real life and literature.

Rationale: Students need to know that they are not alone in what they think, feel, and experience. People everywhere, in other times and other places, no matter what sex, religion, or ethnic background, have similar needs, emotions, and thoughts and similar ways of dealing with difficult situations. These common characteristics are expressed through literature. Biographies a particularly good examples of people who have overcome difficulties or achieved important goals.

Procedure: Ask students to think about books they have read in which the characters faced a situation they thought was difficult or impossible but were able to triumph over in the end.

Explain that there have been many stories written over the years that show the kind of situation in which a character has a problem to solve or a goal to achieve. Ask students to think about why this is so. (It is a situation that most people face many times in their lives. Life, it seems, is always presenting us with challenges—problems to solve, goals we want to achieve.) Some of the best of these kinds of stories are about real-life heroes—biographies. Ask students to name books in which the main characters were real-life heroes who were able to solve a problem or achieve a special goal. Ask students if they thought these people learned anything about themselves while they were working so hard or when they achieved (or didn't achieve) their goal. List students' suggestions on the board with the challenges they faced.

Ask students if they like to read about real people and their struggles, and if so, why. Keep the discussion lively and brief. Show students an assortment of biographies that represent real-life heroes. Discuss with students what they think makes a hero a hero and write their responses on the board.

During Reading for Day 1

Reading to Students: *A Shared Experience*

In this activity, a selection that represents a real-life hero is read aloud

Selection: *The Story of Ruby Bridges* by Robert Coles. For months, 6-year-old Ruby Bridges must confront the hostility of White segregationists when she becomes the first African-American girl to integrate Frantz Elementary School in New Orleans, Louisiana, in 1960.

Goal of the Activity: To give students the opportunity to hear noteworthy literature and to provide all students with a common literary experience.

Rationale: Because each student will be reading a different text for this SRE, providing one shared experience establishes a common source of background information on which future discussions might be based. It also gives students the opportunity to hear quality literature read aloud and is a way to focus their attention on the theme of real-life heroes.

Procedure: Tell students that *The Story of Ruby Bridges* by Robert Coles tells the true story of a 6-year old by the name of Ruby Bridges, who was the first Black person to go to a school in New Orleans that had only White students. Explain that schools in the South at that time, 1960, were segregated—the Blacks went to their schools, and the Whites went to theirs. Ask students to listen carefully and to see if they think Ruby was a hero or not on the day she went to school. Read the book aloud.

Postreading for Day 1

Discussion and Questioning: *Do You Agree?*

In this activity, the teacher suggests a story's theme and students discuss whether they agree.

Selection: *The Story of Ruby Bridges* by Robert Coles. (See description on p. 249.)

Goal of the Activity: To encourage students to think about themes and how themes are portrayed through the words and actions of the story's protagonist.

Rationale: Getting students to consider what a story says to them can help them appreciate their role as a reader and understand how the elements of character and theme are intertwined.

Procedure: After reading the story, discuss whether students think Ruby Bridges was a hero and why they think as they do. After students have given their opinions, have them consider the following questions.

Did Ruby have a problem or problems? What was that problem or problems?

What did Ruby do about the problems she faced? Did she solve her problems? How?

Was Ruby different at the end of the story from what she was at the beginning? If so, in what ways was she different?

Did anyone else in the story change? Who? In what ways did they change, and why?

What did Ruby discover about herself? Do you think she thought of herself as a hero? Do you think of her as a hero? Why or why not?

Prereading for Day 2

Direction Setting: *Graffiti Board: Self Discovery and Personal Triumph*

In *Graffiti Board,* students write their personal responses to texts on a large sheet of butcher paper.

Goal of the Activity: To encourage students to think about and respond to what they read and to communicate those responses to others.

Rationale: Students need to know what they think has value. An activity of this sort can give students confidence in their ability to consider ideas and respond to them. It also provides an opportunity to learn how others respond to literature and to become aware of common issues and themes.

Procedure: Prior to beginning the SRE activities for the day, tack up a large sheet of butcher paper on one section of a wall. At the top of the sheet in bold letters write *Real-life Heroes.* Nearby, provide several colored felt tip pens for students to write their "graffiti." Display the biographies you have selected for students on a table or chalkboard ledge.

Begin your prereading discussion by reminding students of Ruby Bridges' special accomplishments and your previous discussions about how heroes solve problems or find ways to achieve their goals. Indicate the books on display and explain that each of them in one way or another expresses the theme of real-life heroes. Write *Hero* on the chalkboard and discuss what it means, drawing on the previous day's discussion and Ruby Bridges as examples. (How did Ruby triumph? What did she learn about herself? About others? Do you think Ruby is a hero? Why or why not?)

After the discussion, draw students' attention to the butcher paper on the wall. Tell them this is a "graffiti board," and ask them to speculate on what it might be for. Call on someone to read the heading and hold up the colored pens. Tell them the graffiti board has something to do with the books they will be reading and the theme of real-life heroes.

Next, explain that graffiti are sayings written on walls in public places. The graffiti they will write on the wall will be about the stories they read and the theme. Tell them about a book you have recently read, *The Impressionist* by Joan King, explaining that the book is about the famous impressionist painter Mary Cassatt, and that Mary began painting at a time when few women did. To achieve her goal of becoming a painter, she had many obstacles to overcome: first convincing her very obstinate and domineering father to send her to art school, then proving her competence to the world in an area dominated by men.

Tell students that while you were reading the story there were many thoughts that you had that you wanted to share with someone else, but no one else was around. If you had had a graffiti board nearby, you might have written on it. That's what gave you the idea of a graffiti board in class. On the chalkboard, model the activity by writing down the kinds of thoughts you might want to express on the graffiti board.

> *The Impressionist by Joan King.* I can't believe how persevering Mary Cassatt was, how determined she was to become a painter even though there were very few female painters at the time. Nothing came easily for her, yet she persisted. Her small successes and her intense love for the art must have kept her going. She learned that she did have what it takes to be an artist among men. Mrs. G.

Tell students they can use the graffiti board to write anything they choose, but ideally it will relate to the theme of real-life heroes. Students should write the title of the biography they're responding to, the author, their "graffiti" and their name. Copy your graffiti onto the graffiti board to serve as your contribution as well as a sample for the students. Ask students to suggest any graffiti they might create for *The Story of Ruby Bridges,* and let volunteers write it on the board.

Building Text-Specific Knowledge: *The Coming Attraction*

In *The Coming Attraction,* a preview of a selection is provided in which some of the most salient and interesting details of the selection are revealed. Previews of this sort have been described by Graves, Prenn, and Cooke (1985).

Goal of the Activity: To pique students' interest in various selections and give them background information on what the books contain.

Rationale: Using previews to introduce books can help students to decide which books to select. These brief sketches can also serve as enticements to read as well as schemata builders.

Procedure: Give a thumbnail description of each of the biographies—something about the person being written about and the setting. Explain that each in a different way shows a different kind of hero, but each of these heroes tries to solve a problem or achieve a goal. Let students peruse and select a biography to read.

During-Reading for Day 2

Silent and Oral Reading: *To Each His Own*

In this activity, students have the option to read their chosen selections in a variety of ways: alone silently, orally with partners or in small groups, or silently while listening to a tape recording of the story.

Goal of the Activity: To provide students with the opportunity to read books that interest them and that they can handle successfully.

Rationale: Providing students with a variety of texts, both in content and readability, and a variety of ways to build meaning from the text gives them many supports for an enjoyable and worthwhile reading experience.

Procedure: Tell students that they may read their books alone or with a partner and that a few of the books are available on tape, so that is also an option. You may want to make some specific recommendations to individual students—books that will have some special meaning for that student and is at his or her reading level—to ensure a successful experience. For instance, in a class of third graders you might enthusiastically suggest *Stone Girl, Bone Girl: The Story of Mary Anning* to Amanda, a rather shy student with adequate but not superior reading skills, and *Journey for Peace: The Story of Rigoberta Menchú* to Manuella, a good reader whose family has roots in Guatamala, and *Mount Everest and Beyond: Sir Edmund Hillary* to Michael, who is an average reader but who is always up to a challenge. You might recommend that two friends, Josh and B. J., read *Flight* together. You might also suggest that superior readers Emily, Monika, and Summer read *Women Pioneers in Science* and have a three-way discussion after each chapter, reading aloud some of their favorite scenes. You might let Natasha, an English language learner who is struggling with reading, know that you have made an audio recording of *Maria's Comet,* which she is welcome to listen to as she follows along in the text.

Before they begin reading, remind students that their purposes for reading the biographies are first to just enjoy the books and second to see how biographies reveal ways in which heroes from different times and places are similar in important ways. They also might want to think about what the central figure hoped to achieve or what problem he or she tried to solve. While they read, they are to feel free to write on the graffiti board, and journal writing is always an option. After they finish reading they will have a chance to talk about their ideas in small discussion groups.

The time it takes a student to read will vary tremendously. You will want to provide adequate time for the chapter-book readers and encourage the picture-book and easy-to-read-book readers to choose additional books to read, or respond to the stories by drawing pictures or writing responses on the graffiti board or in their journals. Tell students approximately the amount of class time they will have (3 days, 2 weeks, or whatever you decide is appropriate) to read books dealing with real-life heroes. Also, at this time or sometime during the SRE, you will want to prepare students for their self-selected postreading activities. (See *Express Yourself!* postreading activity on p. 255.)

Postreading for Day 2

Writing and Artistic and Non-Verbal Activities: *Now You Respond*

After students finish reading one of their selected texts, they respond to it by writing in their journals, writing on the graffiti board, or creating illustrations that communicate some aspect of self-discovery and personal triumph as illustrated in the story.

Goal of the Activity: To provide students with the opportunity to respond to the theme of a text in a personal way.

Rationale: In order to respond, students will need to have understood what they read, reflect on it, synthesize events and ideas, and decide how these events and ideas relate to the idea of self-discovery and personal triumph. This kind of reflective thinking and responding gives students an opportunity to grow in their ability to ponder, analyze, and draw thoughtful conclusions about the meaning of text.

Procedure: Explain to students that after they finish reading a story, they can write or create with a drawing, painting, collage, etc., something that communicates the theme of self-discovery and personal triumph in that particular story. They can write or draw on the graffiti board or in their journals or both. Explain that they will have a chance to share their ideas in small group discussion.

Postreading Culminating Activities: Day 3 to End of Unit

Discussion: *Let's Talk About Heroes: Self-Discovery and Personal Triumph*

In this activity, students gather in small groups to discuss the theme of "real-life heroes: self-discovery and personal triumph" as expressed through the subjects in the biographies they have read.

Goal of the Activity: To give students the opportunity to think about what makes a hero, to discuss what they have discovered through literature, and to listen to the responses of their classmates.

Rationale: Discussion provides an excellent forum for students to express, clarify, and expand their thinking. Hearing others' ideas can also give them new insights and perspectives. Discussing the problems real-life heroes grapple with and how they resolve these issues can help students to realize that problems have various aspects, are common to everyone, and can be solved in numerous different ways.

Procedure: After students have finished reading their selections, have them meet in groups of three to six to discuss the problems their heroes faced or the goals they were trying to achieve, what they did about these problems and goals, whether or not they triumphed in the end, and what these characters learned about themselves. If you think your students need extra support in focusing their discussion, you might provide the discussion leaders with questions similar to the ones you raised in *The Story of Ruby Bridges*.

> Did the hero have a problem or problems? What was that problem or problems?
>
> What did the hero do about the problems he or she faced? Did he or she solve the problems? How?
>
> Was the hero different at the end of the story from what he or she was at the beginning? If so, in what ways?
>
> Did anyone else in the story change? Who? In what ways did they change, and why?
>
> What did the hero discover about him- or herself? In what way did he or she triumph?

After the discussion, students might like to write their responses on the graffiti board. Also, after the small groups have had an opportunity to meet, you might want to conduct a whole-class discussion in which students can share the discoveries they made about their story characters with the whole class.

Drama, Artistic, and Nonverbal Activities: Writing—*Express Yourself!*

In the *Express Yourself!* activity, students select the ways they would like to respond to a story.

Goal of the Activity: To give students the opportunity to express themselves in a way that best suits them and the biography they read.

Rationale: Providing students with a number of options for expression can increase their chances for creating a response or application that is meaningful to them.

Procedure: Sometime during the SRE encourage students to think about how they might like to respond to the story or stories they are reading. Would they like to dramatize a scene with a partner or partners, or dress like the hero and do a pantomime or monologue?

Would they like to take a chapter book they have read and turn it into a picture book, diorama, or mural? Would they like to make a poster to advertise the book or the hero? Would a sculpture or collage be the best way to express their heroes?

Would they like to create a dance that would show how the hero developed from the beginning of the story to the end or a dance that expressed the mood of the biography?

Would an instrumental piece or a jingle or ballad express their hero? Could they compose a score to accompany the reading or dramatization of one of the scenes from the story?

Perhaps they would like to write something in response to the biography: a letter to the author or hero, a biography of a hero in their lives, or their own autobiography.

Ideally, the activities should allow for as much freedom to explore as possible, with the only restriction being that the students base their responses on the subject of their biographies and its themes of their stories, using the resources that they and you are able to supply.

Adapting the Activity: Instead of, or in addition to, focusing on biographies, you might have students read other types of expository selections that express the idea of solving a problem and that also provide the resources and the steps that are taken (or that might be taken) to solve it or fictional pieces where the main character turns out to be a hero.

Other Nonfiction

Kids' Computer Capers: Investigations for Beginners by Sandra Markle. History and workings of computers and computer programming.

Robotics by Stuart Paltorwitz and Donna Paltorwitz. How robots work and ways in which they are useful.

How to Think Like a Scientist by Stephen P. Kramer. Clear presentation of using the scientific method to solve several of life's everyday questions.

Science Mini-Mysteries by Sandra Markle. Twenty-nine short mysteries to be solved with science experiments.

Before the Wright Brothers by Don Berliner. Chronicles history of flight beginning in 400 B.C.

Totem Pole by Diane Hoyt-Goldsmith. Photos and text show techniques for creating a totem pole, their traditional designs, and the meanings of these designs.

Greening of City Streets: The Story of Community Gardens by B. A. Huff. Photo essay shows how Manhattan families and individuals develop and maintain urban garden plots.

Round Buildings, Square Buildings, & Buildings That Wiggle Like a Fish by Phillip M. Isaacson. Photographs and lyrical text describe elements that go into architectural planning and building.

Model Buildings and How to Make Them by Harvey Weiss. Text, photos, and drawings show just how to make model buildings.

The Furry News: How to Make a Newspaper by Loreen Leedy. Light-hearted picture book story illustrating through the character Big Bear how to start a newspaper.

Explorers and Mapmakers by Peter Ryan. Traces world exploration and the need for maps.

The President Builds a House by Tom Shachtman. Photo essay on Habitat for Humanity featuring the contributions of former President Jimmy Carter and First Lady Rosalynn Carter.

Thinking Big by Susan Kuklin. Describes through photographs how an 8-year-old girl copes with the problem of being a dwarf.

Mrs. Armitage on Wheels by Quentin Blake. An engaging picture book which illustrates in a comical way how inventions are precipitated by need.

Fiction

Cracker Jackson by Betsy Byars. Cracker takes responsibility for helping a babysitter who is a victim of physical abuse. Novel.

Stone Soup by John Warren Stewig. A young girl figures out a way to get stingy people to share. Picture book.

The Fourth Question: A Chinese Tale by Rosalind C. Wang. Yee-Lee figures out a way to solve his family's poverty as well as the dilemmas of many others. Picture book.

The True Confessions of Charlotte Doyle by Avi. A prim 13-year-old schoolgirl turns seasoned sailor in this historical novel of adventure and intrigue. Novel.

Hatchet by Gary Paulsen. Through his courage and ingenuity, 13-year-old Brian is able to survive for 54 days in the Canadian wilderness. Novel.

Amazing Grace by Mary Hoffman. Plucky Grace overcomes obstacles and earns the role of Peter Pan in the school play. Picture book.

. . . And Now Miguel by Joseph Krumgold. Set in the Sangre de Christo mountains of New Mexico, a young boy learns the joys and struggles of being a sheepherder. Novel.

Yossi Asks the Angels for Help by Miriam Chaiken. Yossi looks to angels for help in buying Hanukkah gifts after he looses his gift money. Chapter book.

How Sweetly Sings the Donkey by Vera Cleaver. Determined and resourceful teen Lily Snow works to improve her family's life. Novel.

The Sky Is Falling by Barbara Corcoran. Set during the Depression, Annah learns about growing up by accepting change. Novel.

Reflection: What we have suggested here is only one of many possible variations that may have arisen for a theme-based scaffold. Although there is a good deal of effort and skill involved in orchestrating a theme-based SRE, there are also great rewards: making discoveries along with your students and seeing them find in literature some new and special connections with their own lives and some insights that will stay with them long after they leave your classroom.

Comprehensive SREs: A Final Word

The chapter illustrating comprehensive SREs gives us an opportunity to make a point we have made before but one that we think deserves repeating. Students need and deserve a comprehensive and balanced reading program. The current major national reports on reading instruction—*Preventing Reading Difficulties in Young Children* (Snow, Burns, & Griffin, 1998), *Reading for Understanding* (Snow, 2001), *Teaching Children to Read* (National Reading Panel, 2000), *Teaching Reading Is Rocket Science* (Moats, 1999), and *Every Child Reading* (Learning First Alliance, 2000)—all note the importance of balanced programs. As David Pearson (2001) has pointed out, however, a close examination of many of these reports shows that what is presented is not as well balanced as it could be. In particular, lower level processes such as phonemic awareness and phonics receive considerably more attention than higher level processes such as comprehension and composition.

Even though SREs are only one part of a comprehensive reading program and by definition do not deal with matters such as phonemic awareness and phonics, SREs themselves ought to reflect balance. We believe that the comprehensive SREs in this chapter do that. They include examples of students working with easy texts and challenging texts, narratives and exposition, factual texts and fictional texts; texts that students will spend a lot of time on and texts that they will not spend much time on; situations in which students work under the careful guidance of a teacher and situations in which students are largely on their own. This sort of balance in what students read, in how teachers assist them in reading, and in the contexts in which they read is crucial. SREs can and should be used as one tool in achieving this balance.

References

Aronson, E., & Patnoe, S. (1997). *The jigsaw classroom: Building cooperation in the classroom* (2nd ed.). New York: Longman. A concise yet complete description of the powerful learning procedure.

Beck, I. L., & McKeown, M. G. (1981). Developing questions that promote comprehension: The story map. *Languate Arts, 58,* 913–916. Discusses problematic approaches to selecting and sequencing questions and offers a valuable alternative.

Graves, M. F., Prenn, M. C., & Cooke, C. L. (1985). The coming attraction: Previewing short stories to increase comprehension. *Journal of Reading, 28,* 549–598. A clear description of how to write previews and a summary of much of the research on previewing.

Learning First Alliance. (2000). *Every child reading: An action plan.* Washington, DC: Authors.

Moats, L. M. (1999). *Teaching reading is rocket science.* Washington, DC: American Federation of Teachers.

National Reading Panel. (2000). *Teaching children to read.* Bethesda, MD: National Institute of Child Health and Human Development.

Ogle, D. (1986). K-W-L: A teaching model that develops active reading of expository text. *Reading Teacher, 39,* 564–570.

Ogle, D., & Blachowicz, C. L. Z. (2002). Beyond literature circles: Helping students comprehend informational text. In C. C. Block & M. Pressley (Eds.), *Comprehension instruction: Research-based practices.* New York: Guilford Press. The authors consider K-W-L and other approaches to assisting students in understanding informational text.

Pearson, P. D. (2001). Learning to teach reading: The status of the knowledge base. In C. M. Roller (Ed.), *Learning to teach reading: Setting the research agenda* (pp. 4–19). Newark, DE: International Reading Association. Brief review of research on teacher education in reading.

Snow, C. E. (2002). *Reading for understanding: Toward an R&D program in reading comprehension.* Santa Monica, CA: Rand Education. Also available online at http://www.rand.org/multi/achievementforall/reading/. A review of our existing knowledge about reading comprehension and plan for future research.

Snow, C. E., Burns, S. M., & Griffin, P. (1998). *Preventing reading difficulties in young children.* Washington, DC: National Academy Press. Major review of research on beginning reading instruction.

Vaughn, C. L. (1990). Knitting writing: The double-entry journal. In N. Atwell (Ed.), *Coming to know: Writing to learn in the intermediate grades.* Portsmouth, NH: Heinemann. Description of the double-entry journal procedure.

Children's Literature

Anholt, L. (1999). *Stone girl, bone girl: The story of Mary Anning.* New York: Orchard. Unpaged.

Avi. (1990). *The true confessions of Charlotte Doyle.* New York: Orchard. 215 pages.

Berger, M. & Berger, G. (2001). *Can you hear a shout in space?* New York: Scholastic. 48 pages.

Berliner, D. (1990). *Before the Wright brothers.* Minneapolis: Lerner. 72 pages.

Blake, Q. (1988). *Mrs. Armitage on wheels.* New York: Knopf. Unpaged.

Bridges, R. (1999). *Through my eyes.* New York: Scholastic. 63 pages.

Brill, M. T. (1996). *Journey for peace: The story of Rigoberta Menchú.* New York: Lodestar. 56 pages.

Brown, D. (2000). *Uncommon traveler: Mary Kingsley in Africa.* Boston: Houghton Mifflin. Unpaged.

Burleigh, R. (1991). *Flight: The journey of Charles Lindbergh.* Illus. by Mike Wimmer. New York: Philomel. Unpaged.

Byars, B. (1985). *Cracker Jackson.* New York: Viking Kestrel. 147 pages.

Chaiken, M. (1985). *Yossi asks the angels for help.* New York: Harper & Row. 52 pages.

Cleaver, V. (1985). *How sweetly sings the donkey.* New York: Lippincott. 112 pages.

Coles, R. (1995). *The story of Ruby Bridges.* Illus. by George Ford. New York: Scholastic. Unpaged.

Cooper, F. (1996). *Mandela: From the life of the South African statesman.* New York: Philomel. Unpaged.

Corcoran, B. (1988). *The sky is falling.* New York: Atheneum. 150 pages.

DiCamillo, K. (2000). *Because of Winn-Dixie.* New York: Candlewick Press. 182 pages.

DiCamillo, K. (2001). *The tiger rising.* New York: Candlewick Press. 116 pages.

Freedman, R. (1987). *Lincoln: A photobiography.* New York: Clarion. 150 pages.

Freedman, R. (1990). *Franklin Delano Roosevelt.* New York: Clarion. 200 pages.

Freedman, R. (1993). *Eleanor Roosevelt: A life of discovery.* New York: Clarion. 198 pages.

Freedman, R. (1993). *The life and death of Crazy Horse.* New York: Holiday House. 166 pages.

Freedman, R. (1997). *Out of darkness: The story of Louis Braille.* New York: Clarion. 81 pages.

Freedman, R. (1999). *Babe Didrikson Zaharias: The making of a champion.* New York: Clarion. 192 pages.

Graber, J. (2000, November). *Thanksgiving gumbo.* Peru, IL: Cricket Magazine.

Graves, B. (2002). *California condor: Flying free.* Des Moines, IA: Perfection Learning. 48 pages.

Hacking, S. M. (1997). *Mount Everest and beyond: Sir Edmund Hillary.* New York: Marshall Cavendish. 48 pages.

Harber, L. (1979). *Women pioneers of science.* San Diego: Harcourt Brace Jovanovich. 171 pages.

Hazell, R. (1997). *Heroes: Great men through the ages.* New York: Abbeyville. 80 pages.

Hoffman, M. (1991). *Amazing Grace.* New York: Dial. Unpaged.

Hopkinson, D. (1999). *Maria's comet.* New York: Atheneum. Unpaged.

Hoyt-Goldsmith, D. (1990). *Totem pole.* New York: Holiday House. 30 pages.

Huff, B. A. (1990). *Greening of city streets: The story of community gardens.* Boston: Clarion. 61 pages.

Isaacson, P. M. (1988). *Round buildings, square buildings, & buildings that wiggle like a fish.* New York: Knopf. 121 pages.

Kramer, S. P. (1987). *How to think like a scientist.* Answering questions by the scientific method. New York: Crowell. 44 pages.

King, J. (1983). *The Impressionist.* New York: Beaufort. 312 pages.

Krull, K. (1996). *Wilma unlimited: How Wilma Rudolf became the world's fastest woman.* San Diego: Harcourt Brace Jovanovich. Unpaged.

Krumgold, J. (1953). *. . . And now Miguel.* New York: Crowell. 245 pages.

Kuklin, S. (1986). *Thinking big.* New York: Lothrop, Lee & Shepard. Unpaged.

Lee, M. G. (1996). *Necessary Roughness.* New York: HarperCollins. 228 pages.

Leedy, L. (1990). *The furry news: How to make a newspaper.* New York: Holiday House. Unpaged.

MacLachlan, P. (1991). *Journey.* New York: Delacorte. 83 pages.

Markle, S. (1983). *Kids' computer capers: Investigations for beginners.* New York: Lothrop, Lee & Shepard. 64 pages.

Markle, S. (1988). *Science mini-mysteries.* New York: Atheneum. 64 pages.

Mora, P. (1997). *Tomas and the library lady.* New York: Random House. Unpaged.

O'Connor, B. (1997). *Beethoven in paradise.* New York: Farrar/Foster. 153 pages.

O'Connor, B. (1999). *Me and Rupert Goody.* New York: Farrar/Foster. 105 pages.

O'Connor, B. (2001). *Moonpie and Ivy.* New York: Farrar/Foster. 151 pages.

Odijk, P. (1990). *The Incas, the Israelites, the Vikings.* Westwood, NJ: Silver Burdett. 64 pages.

Osborne, M. P. (1990). *The many lives of Benjamin Franklin.* New York: Dial. 127 pages.

Paltorwitz, S., & Paltorwitz, D. (1983). *Robotics.* New York: Jem Books. 76 pages.

Paulsen, G. (1987). *Hatchet.* New York: Bradbury. 195 pages.

Patrick, J. L. S. (2000). *The girl who struck out Babe Ruth.* Minneapolis: Carolrhoda. 48 pages.

Ryan, P. (1990). *Explorers and mapmakers*: Time detectives. New York: Lodestar. 48 pages.

St. George, J. (2000). *So you want to be president?* Illus. by David Small. New York: Philomel. 52 pages.

Shachtman, T. (1989). *The president builds a house.* New York: Simon and Schuster. Unpaged.

Simon, S. (1991). *Eathquakes.* New York: Morrow. Unpaged.

Sis, P. (2000). *Starry messenger: Galileo Galilei.* New York: Farrar, Straus & Giroux. Unpaged.

Sorenson, M. (1998). *Danger marches to the palace: Queen Lili'uokalani.* Des Moines, IA: Perfection Learning. 107 pages.

Soto, G. (1998). *Petty crimes.* San Diego: Harcourt Brace. 157 pages.

Stewig, J. W. (1991). *Stone soup.* New York: Holiday House. Unpaged.

Wang, R. C. (1991). *The fourth question: A Chinese tale.* New York: Holiday House. Unpaged.

Weiss, H. (1979). *Model buildings and how to make them.* New York: Crowell. 95 pages.

Chapter

8

Incorporating Scaffolded Reading Experiences Into Your Classroom

In preparing this chapter for the first edition of the book, we met with a number of elementary and middle school teachers and asked them about the principal decisions and challenges they faced in incorporating Scaffolded Reading Experiences (SREs) in their classroom. As we prepare the chapter for this second edition of the book, we have 10 years of experience observing teachers as they use SREs in their classrooms and talking to them and their students about doing so, teaching nearly 100 college classes and inservice sessions using the book, receiving feedback from scores of reviewers of the book and articles we have written on SREs, and conducting formal studies of the use of SREs (Cooke, 2001; Fournier & Graves, in press; Graves & Liang, 2001; Watts & Rothenberg, 1997). As a result, we have learned a tremendous amount about successfully incorporating SREs in classroom.

In this chapter, we focus on four broad issues that we believe are crucial in effectively using SREs. Each of these is considered in a separate section. In the first section, we discuss some of the principal decisions you face as you move to implement SREs in your classroom. In the second section, we consider using SREs to foster higher level thinking and deep understanding. In the third section, we consider assessing students, texts, and the effects of SREs. Finally, in the fourth section, we consider the place of SREs in a comprehensive literacy program and again stress that SREs are only one component of a comprehensive program.

Decisions and Challenges in Implementing SREs

Here, we consider the frequency of SREs, how much scaffolding to provide, how often to differentiate activities for different students, the importance of providing a balance between challenging reading selections and easier selections, adjusting and differentiating postreading tasks to ensure student success, and involving students in constructing SREs.

The Frequency of SREs

In chapter 2 we emphasized that SREs definitely do not constitute an entire reading program, and at the end of this chapter we discuss some other important components of a comprehensive literacy program. However, we have not yet directly addressed the question of how frequent SREs might be in your classroom. Of course, the answer to this question varies for different students, different teachers, different goals, different times of the year, and different grade levels—to name just a few of the myriad of factors affecting what takes place in any classroom. Nevertheless, we can suggest some considerations and guidelines.

We believe that SREs provide some of your best opportunities for extending students' zones of proximal development by supporting their efforts; helping them to succeed in their reading; and giving them some common experiences to talk about, write about, and know that they share. In this sense, SREs have an intrinsic value that would lead us to use them quite frequently for their own sake—for the stretching, success, and shared experiences they can provide. In order to take advantage of these benefits, we would generally include at least one SRE as part of reading instruction during most school weeks.

From another perspective, SREs are useful for the extrinsic reason that they facilitate students' reading and learning in various content areas. Because students need to do a good deal of reading in social studies, science, health, and the like—and because some of this reading is challenging—SREs are often called for in content reading. Although SREs used in content areas will sometimes be brief, most school weeks will call for several of them.

Finally, the question of how the frequency of SREs should differ at different grade levels is worth considering. Two somewhat opposing lines of reasoning come into play here. On the one hand, students obviously need to become increasingly independent and self-sufficient as they move toward adulthood.

This argues for SREs becoming less frequent over time. On the other hand, one very important purpose of SREs is to stretch students, enabling them to read material that would be too challenging without the assistance of an SRE. We certainly do not want to stretch students any less in later grades than in earlier ones.

The situation, then, appears to be this: Over time, students become increasingly competent. Over that same time, however, the materials students read and the tasks they complete with those materials become increasingly challenging. Thus, there continues to be a place for SREs throughout the middle grades and beyond. In fact, in our judgment, giving reading assignments without any scaffolding—the proverbial, "Read chapters 4 and 5 and come to class on Tuesday prepared to discuss them"—is generally inappropriate even in graduate school. Consequently, although SREs will certainly be different for older students than for younger ones, they continue to be an important component of a complete and balanced program, even in the upper grades.

How Much Scaffolding to Provide

We have already alluded to the matter of how much scaffolding to provide, but the topic is worth addressing directly. Our main point is that it is neither a case of the more the merrier, nor one of the less the merrier. The general rule is to provide enough scaffolding for students to be confident and successful in their reading, but not so much that they are not sufficiently challenged, feel spoonfed, or become bored. In general, then, the suggestion is to provide enough scaffolding but not too much. Further reinforcing the notion that you do not want to do more scaffolding than is needed is the fact that constructing scaffolds takes your valuable time, which is always at a premium. At the same time, there is no getting away from the fact that in today's classrooms many students need and deserve a significant amount of scaffolding if they are to succeed.

How Often to Differentiate Activities

Two sorts of differentiation are worth considering. On the one hand, you will sometimes want to differentiate SREs based on students' interests. For example, students can read different books while pursuing a common topic or theme. Thus, with a class of fifth and sixth graders exploring the themes of death and grieving, some students might read novels such as Marion Dane Bauer's *On My Honor*, others Katherine Paterson's *Bridge to Terabithia*, others *Pray Hard* by Pamela Walker, and still others Carol Carrick's *Upside-Down Cake*. Instead of fiction, students might read nonfiction books on these topics, such as *Death and Loss* by Sandra Giddens or *Death* by Barbara Sprung. Similarly, some students may choose to respond to a reading selection in writing, others with some sort of artwork, others with an oral presentation, and others by going to the library to pursue the topic further. The constraints on differentiation of this type are your time, ingenuity, and ability to orchestrate diverse activities. In addition, you need to keep in mind that the more different activities students are involved in, the less time you have to assist them with each activity. At the extreme, if 30 students are involved in different activities, you can give each of them less than 2 minutes of your time each hour. Thus, there are a number of practical limits on differentiating on the basis of student interest. However, if these limits are kept in mind, differentiation based on interest is very often desirable.

The other sort of differentiation to consider is based on students' ability or skill. Here, the same limits that influence differentiation based on interest apply. That is, constraints include your time, ingenuity, ability to orchestrate diverse activities, and ability to assist students when many activities are going on at once. Beyond these considerations, however, is that of the effect of being repeatedly placed in a group that receives more assistance. Being a member of the group that repeatedly receives more assistance certainly has the potential to weaken students' self image and motivation to learn. Singling out students for special, essentially remedial, assistance is not something we want to do any more frequently than necessary.

However, these are not the only facts to consider. There is also the fact that success begets success and failure begets failure. Thus, the suggestion that differentiation based on skill or ability should be infrequent because of the psychological effect it might have must be tempered by the realization that differentiation can make the difference between success and failure. With less skilled readers, it often is important to differentiate instruction to ensure success, even though that differentiation should be no more frequent than is necessary.

Providing a Balance of Challenging and Easy Reading

Consideration of differentiating SREs leads directly to the matter of providing a balance of challenging and easy reading. Every student needs and deserves opportunities to read easy material that can be understood and enjoyed without effort and challenging material that he or she needs to grapple with (Graves, 1998; Graves, Juel, & Graves, 2001). Reading easy material fosters automaticity, builds confidence, creates interest in reading, and provides students with practice in a task they will face frequently in their everyday lives. Reading challenging materials builds students' knowledge bases, their vocabularies, and their critical thinking skills. Reading challenging materials also provides students with practice in a task they will face frequently in school and college, in their work outside school, and in becoming knowledgeable and responsible members of a democratic society. Moreover, reading challenging materials builds students' confidence in their ability to deal with difficult reading selections—if you ensure that they are successful with the challenging material.

The point that needs to be stressed here is that students—more able, more skilled, and more knowledgeable ones as well as less able, less skilled, and less knowledgeable ones—need both challenging and easy reading. This condition cannot be met by providing only material that is of average difficulty for the average student. Assuming that classrooms are made up of students with various skills, knowledge, and abilities—and this description fits most classrooms—routinely providing only reading selections of average difficulty ensures that some students will repeatedly receive material that is very difficult for them, others will repeatedly receive material that is of average difficulty for them, and still others will repeatedly receive material that is easy for them. Such a situation is inappropriate for all students. Because the reading tasks we face in the world outside school vary and because the benefits of reading vary with the difficulty of the reading tasks, all students need frequent opportunities to read materials that vary in the challenges and opportunities they present.

Tailoring Postreading Tasks to Ensure Success

In constructing and using SREs ourselves and talking to teachers who have done so, we have found that sometimes—even after considering the students, the text, and the learning task, and arranging a series of prereading, during-reading, and postreading tasks—some students are still not likely to have a successful reading experience unless something more is done. In such cases, we recommend two approaches: simplifying postreading tasks and offering alternative postreading tasks. Five general approaches to simplifying postreading tasks are as follows:

- Asking students to do less rather than more
- Requiring recognition rather than recall
- Requiring assembly rather than creation
- Cueing students to the place where answers can be found
- Preceding production tasks with explicit instruction

Almost certainly the most straightforward approach to simplifying postreading tasks is to ask students to do less rather than more. We realize this sounds a bit flippant, but we are quite serious. Everything else being equal, tasks in which students answer fewer questions, construct less involved models, or write shorter pieces are distinctly easier. For example, after fourth-grade students read *The Island of the Blue Dolphins* by Scott O'Dell, you might ask them to identify two instances of courage and explain why these were courageous, rather than having them deal with four instances.

Requiring recognition rather than recall is another straightforward approach to simplifying postreading tasks. Any time you allow students to return to the text to find answers or present them with alternatives from which to choose rather than requiring them to construct answers, their task is simplified. In the case of *The Island of the Blue Dolphins,* for example, letting students return to the text to find instances of courage is likely to make the task markedly easier.

Requiring assembly rather than creation is quite similar to requiring recognition rather than recall. For example, fifth-grade students (and even some ninth grade students) might find it difficult to construct a time line of major events after reading a history chapter on the origins of the Revolutionary War. However, these students would be greatly aided if you gave them a list of those events and a list of dates out of order and asked them to reorder the events and dates to construct a time line.

Cueing students to the places where answers can be found is an easily implemented approach and a particularly powerful one to use when students are dealing with lengthy and challenging selections. This approach was first suggested by Harold Herber (1970) for use with secondary school students, but we believe it is equally or more applicable with elementary and middle school students. Depending on the difficulty students face, you can cue them to the chapter, page, or even paragraph in which the information needed to answer a question is found. For example, suppose some of your third-grade students have had a difficult time reading *California Condor: Flying Free* by Bonnie Graves, yet you want them to remember some of the ways in which California condors have become endangered. Giving them the pages on which the factors that have adversely affected the condors are discussed when you ask them to review these factors will increase the likelihood that they will successfully complete the review.

Our final suggestion here is to precede challenging production tasks with explicit instruction (Graves, Juel, & Graves, 2001). If you are going to ask students to summarize information, synthesize information, make inferences, and complete other activities that require them to construct new information, you may need to explicitly teach them how to do these tasks before asking them to complete them. Of course, some students will already have been taught the necessary procedures. However, even when students have been taught a procedure, it will sometimes be a good idea to review it. For example, if a group of sixth-grade students' task is to compare and contrast two boys growing up during the Revolutionary War—perhaps Johnny in *Johnny Tremain* by Esther Forbes with Tim in *My Brother Sam Is Dead* by James Lincoln Collier and Christopher Collier—you might review the notion of a compare-and-contrast essay, suggest some of the characteristics that they might compare and contrast in these two particular characters, and suggest some order for their essay, perhaps that of first listing the ways in which the two are the same and then listing the way in which the two differ.

At this point, you may be thinking that we have suggested a great deal of simplification and that what we are recommending amounts to spoonfeeding and thus robs students of the opportunity to grapple with difficult tasks. We want to stress that this is not our message. We are not recommending that postreading tasks always be simplified, and we are certainly not recommending that some students routinely be given simplified postreading tasks. On the contrary, the simplifications suggested here are fix-up strategies to be used sparingly, and only in cases in which students might otherwise fail. The essence of the SRE approach is to choose selections wisely and involve students in prereading and during-reading activities that will enable them to succeed with the postreading activities in which they engage. Occasionally, however, even with everything you have done to accomplish this, you will look at some students and some postreading activities and say to yourself, "Some of these kids aren't going to be able to do this." This is the point at which simplifying postreading tasks becomes both appropriate and advisable.

The other suggestion we have for tailoring postreading tasks to ensure success is to offer students alternative postreading options. The work of Robert Sternberg on types of thinking and that of Howard Gardner on multiple intelligences has been particularly insightful in this regard. Sternberg (Sternberg & Sperling, 1996) terms his approach a "triarchic theory of intelligence." The central thesis of Sternberg's theory is that there are three basic kinds of thinking: analytic, creative, and practical. Sternberg defines these three sorts of thinking as follows:

- *Analytic thinking* involves analyzing, judging, evaluating, comparing and contrasting, and examining.
- *Creative thinking* involves creating, discovering, producing, imagining, and supposing.
- *Practical thinking* involves practicing, using, applying, and implementing. (p. ix)

As Sternberg notes, schools typically focus on analytic thinking and largely neglect the other two sorts. This, he argues, is very unfortunate because all three sorts of thinking are important, both in the classroom and beyond it.

We have found it extremely useful to deliberately offer students all three types of thinking as options for postreading tasks.

Like Sternberg, Gardner believes that there is more than one sort of thinking and that schools largely neglect many of these. As you probably know, Gardner (1999) terms his types of thinking *intelligences* and describes eight of them: linguistic, logical-mathematical (these two are the most prevalent in schools), spatial, bodily-kinesthetic, musical, interpersonal, intrapersonal, and environmental. Our list of optional postreading activities for SREs suggests some of these alternatives, but we think that all of them deserve consideration. Again, our suggestion is that all of these ways of thinking and demonstrating understanding have a place in the classroom and ought to be considered as valid options.

Involving Students in Constructing SREs

One of the central themes of current thinking about learning and instruction, and a theme that we have repeatedly emphasized throughout the book, is that in order to really learn something students need to be actively involved in their learning. One approach to getting students actively involved in their learning is cross-age tutoring, involving older students in the instruction of younger students. Our experience as teachers, a substantial body of research and writing produced over a number of years (Block & Dellamura, 2000–2001, Cohen, Kulik, & Kulik, 1982; Juel, 1996), and common sense suggest that cross-age tutoring is extremely effective. We very much agree with the sentiments expressed by Wilbert McKeachie (McKeachie & Gibbs, 1999), a person who has spent more than 50 years studying instruction, in this statement:

> The best answer to the question, 'What is the most efficient method of teaching?' is that it depends on the goal, the student, the content, and the teacher. But the next best answer is, "Students teaching other students." There is a wealth of evidence that peer teaching is extremely effective for a wide range of goals, content, and students of different levels and personalities. (p. 81)

One way in which older students can assist in teaching younger students—and in doing so become actively involved in their learning—is by preparing SRE materials for younger students. Consider what the student who is going to prepare a preview, a set of discussion questions, or a map of a short story needs to do in order to construct first-rate materials. He or she needs to read the story, understand it, pick out what is important, pick out what is likely to be of interest to the younger students, decide what sort of language to use in addressing the younger student, and then prepare materials that will be interesting, informative, attractive, and engaging for the younger students. In other words, he or she needs to understand and appreciate the story fully, use his or her creative and problem solving skills to create material, and use his or her linguistic skills to communicate with a genuine audience.

It is hard to imagine a task that presents more opportunities for learning, for doing something useful, and for feeling a sense of accomplishment. Moreover, the possibilities are certainly not limited to previewing, mapping, or writing discussion questions. Many prereading, during-reading, and postreading activities require some sort of materials; with your help, older students are quite capable of constructing those materials. Selecting and teaching vocabulary and concepts, identifying the organization of a selection, recording parts of a selection on tape, developing a writing assignment, and many other scaffolded reading activities are within older students' range. Finally, not only will students learn more from creating SRE activities, but having students participate in constructing SRE materials will free up some of your time to work with students individually, prepare other interesting and enriching activities, or perhaps even take an evening off once in a while.

Usually, we agree with the adage that if something seems too good to be true, it probably is. However, we feel compelled to believe that students assisting teachers in constructing SRE activities is absolutely a win-win situation.

Using SREs to Foster Higher Level Thinking and Deep Understanding

As we have noted, SREs are intended to foster a variety of types of reading, not giving special consideration to any one type. Thus, for example, they can and should be used in situations in which you want students to gain only a rudimentary knowledge of a text as well as in situations in which you want them to gain rich and deep understanding. Here, however, we want to discuss the use of SREs to promote higher level thinking and deep understanding, a topic to which we have recently given a good deal of attention (Graves, 1999; Graves & Liang, 2001; Sales & Graves, 2001).

Actually, it is quite easy to use SREs to foster higher level thinking and deep understanding. Doing so simply requires objectives that necessitate such thinking and understanding and SRE activities that scaffold students' efforts to achieve those objectives. Here we first discuss what we mean by higher level thinking and what we mean by deep understanding.

We consider higher level thinking to be a broad and multidimensional concept, and a number of authorities have contributed to our understanding of the concept. These include philosophers such as Robert Ennis (1985), psychologists and cognitive scientists such as John Bransford and Anne Brown (Bransford, Brown, & Cocking, 2000), and critical-thinking proponents such as Arthur Costa (Costa & Kallick, 2000). We have gleaned valuable insights from each of them, but the most immediately useful information we have found comes from Lauren Resnick (1987) and from Lorin Anderson and David Krathwohl (2001).

After noting that higher level skills resist precise definition, Resnick lists some features of higher level thinking. Although lengthier than a typical definition, Resnick's list does an excellent job of providing a real feel for the concept. Higher level thinking has the following qualities:

- Higher order thinking is *nonalgorithmic*. That is, the path of action is not fully specified in advance.

- Higher order thinking tends to be *complex*. The total path is not "visible" (mentally speaking) from any single vantage point.

- Higher order thinking often yields *multiple solutions*, each with costs and benefits, rather than unique solutions.

- Higher order thinking involves *nuanced judgments* and interpretation.

- Higher order thinking involves the application of *multiple criteria*, which sometimes conflict with one another.

- Higher order thinking often involves *uncertainty*. Not everything that bears on the task at hand is known.

- Higher order thinking involves *self-regulation* of the thinking process. We do not recognize higher order thinking in an individual when someone else calls the plays at every step.

- Higher order thinking involves *imposing meaning*, finding structure in apparent disorder.

- Higher order thinking is *effortful*. There is considerable mental work involved in the kinds of elaborations and judgments required. (p. 3)

Anderson and Krathwohl (2001) take a different approach. With the assistance of a group of colleagues, Anderson and Krathwohl extensively revised the well-known and widely used *Taxonomy of Educational Objectives*, first published by Benjamin Bloom in 1956. Their revision encompasses an entire book, which we recommend highly. We will not, however, attempt to summarize the book here. Instead, what we describe here is seven types of thinking described in the revised taxonomy that we find particularly useful in working with SREs. The definitions of the first six types are taken nearly verbatim from Anderson and Krathwohl. The last definition reflects a mixture of their thinking and our own.

- *Remembering:* Retrieving relevant knowledge from long-term memory.

- *Understanding:* Constructing meaning from instructional messages, including oral, written, and graphic communications.

- *Applying:* Carrying out or using a procedure in a given situation.

- *Analyzing:* Breaking material into its constituent parts and determining how the parts relate to one another and to an overall structure or purpose.

- *Evaluating:* Making judgments based on criteria and standards.

- *Creating:* Putting elements together to form a coherent or functional whole, reorganizing elements into a new pattern or structure.

- *Being metacognitive:* Being aware of one's own comprehension and being able and willing to repair comprehension breakdowns when they occur. (p. 31)

As is the case with the concept of higher level thinking, many scholars have contributed to our concept of deep understanding. They include Howard Gardner (2000), Grant Wiggins and Jay McTighe (1998), and Martha Stone Wisk (1998). However, the most notable influence on our thinking here comes from David Perkins (1992, 1995; Perkins & Tishman, 1998).

As part of considering how to develop students' higher level thinking, it is important to keep in mind that knowledge and understanding are the raw materials needed to engage in higher level thinking. The more information students have about a topic and the deeper their understanding of that information, the better able they are to think critically about the topic. Perkins (1992, 1995) has developed and articulated the concept of "teaching for understanding," teaching in such a way that students understand topics deeply, retain important information, and actively use the knowledge they gain. We believe that these are extremely important goals and that they should frequently be among the goals of SREs.

In addition to developing the cognitive dimension of the teaching for understanding perspective, Perkins (Perkins & Tishman, 1998) has stressed the importance of cultivating in students a disposition toward thinking critically. The importance of such a disposition is widely endorsed, and we too endorse it. To fully develop higher level thinking skills and to be willing to put in the effort it takes to read for deep understanding, students need to be disposed to think critically about what they are reading and to seek deep understanding. Leading students toward such a disposition is, we believe, one of the most important and rewarding opportunities teachers face.

Assessing Students, Texts, and the Effects of SREs

Matching students to texts and assessing the effects of SREs are both extremely important aspects of working with SREs in ways that lead students to successful reading experiences and long-term success at reading. However, we do not believe that assessment should occupy anywhere near the amount of time and attention given to instruction. Moreover, there are a plethora of entire books on assessment available (for example, Graves, Juel, & Burns, 2001; Harp, 2000; Hill, 2001). Consequently, we treat assessment rather briefly here, considering only the kinds of assessment that are necessary to match students and texts and to assess the effects of SREs.

Matching Students and Texts

In order to match students with appropriate texts, it is necessary to get some indication of the students' competence and to get some indication of the texts' difficulty. At the beginning of the year and as a first approximation, we would use standardized test scores as an indication of students' competence; and we would focus on those students who we suspect may be noticeably below grade level. If your reading selections are generally appropriate for the grade you teach, then students who score nearly at, at, or above grade level can probably deal competently with them. Students more than one level below grade, however, may experience some problems with grade-level texts, which means asking yourself if these are the right texts for those students and providing students with sturdy scaffolds if you do use them.

Of course, standardized tests do not have to be the only information you have when the year begins; nor should they be the only measure you use as the year progresses. Evaluations done by your students' previous teachers are tremendously valuable, if available. Also, as the year progresses, it makes good sense to do some of your own informal assessments. Our preference is for some form of informal reading inventory. This could be a traditional inventory made up of a set of passages and questions representing a range of difficulty, either a published inventory (Burns & Roe, 2002) or one you construct yourself (Graves, Watts-Taffe, & Graves, 1999).

Alternately, you could create an inventory by simply taking a short passage (perhaps 250 words or so) out of a selection you are planning to read, constructing a short set of comprehension questions on the passage, and having students read the passages orally and answer the questions. In general, in considering the results of such inventories, we would follow the traditional standards and consider the selection at students' instructional level when they correctly pronounce about 95 percent of the words and answer at least 75 percent of the comprehension questions correctly. However, if you have students somewhat below these broad guidelines, you may be able to use the selection with them if you construct a sturdy SRE to support their reading.

As with standardized test scores, we suggest that you begin using these informal measures with students who you suspect may be challenged by the selections you are using. Over time, however, you should also gather information on your stronger readers, paying particular attention to the need to challenge and stretch able readers with more challenging tasks. As you begin to accumulate information on students' performance with different selections, you can better predict how they will do on other selections on which you have not tested them. This is particularly the case if you keep anecdotal records on their performance with the passages, making notes on such matters as their fluency as they read, their reading rates, and their interest in various topics. Measuring rate in words per minute is particularly helpful, as it gives you an idea of how much class time you need to allot to various selections or to how much homework you are requiring if you assign a selection to be read at home. Measuring students' interest in various topics is critical to discovering what engages students. Bill Harp's handbook on assessment (2000) contains useful suggestion on informal assessments on attitudes toward reading and informal interest inventories.

In order to effectively match students with texts, you also need information on the texts. Here we recommend two things. First, use a readability formula. Although readability formulas have received a good deal of criticism and certainly deserve some criticism, they serve one extremely useful purpose. They are very useful in avoiding mismatches in which the text is markedly too difficult for the students. We currently use the New Dale-Chall Readability Formula (Chall & Dale, 1995) for this purpose. It has several features to recommend it. It has been revised fairly recently, it has better than average instructions and explanations, it is as accurate as any formulas, and it is easy to use. It is, however, a bit time consuming. For this reason, you may prefer to use Edward Fry's readability graph (Fry, 1977; Fry, Polk, & Fountoukidis, 2000), which is probably a bit less accurate but definitely less time consuming. Whatever formula you use, we recommend that if you assess a text and find that it is two grade levels or more above the reading level of some of your students, you seriously consider if it is the right text for those students. If after such reflection you decide that it is, or if you have no alternative, then you will once again have to count on a particularly sturdy SRE for these students.

In matching students and texts, we recommend that you also consider 10 factors that research and theory have shown to influence both the difficulty of text and its accessibility. In chapter 9, we describe these factors and how to use them in some detail, so we will say just a word about them here. They fall into two groups. In the first group are six factors that are fairly easily defined, fairly easily identified, and largely inherent in the text itself. These six factors are vocabulary, sentence structure, length, elaboration, coherence and unity, and text structure. In the second group are four factors that are less easily defined, less easily identified, and very definitely involve both the reader and the text. These are familiarity of content and background knowledge required, audience appropriateness, quality and verve of the writing, and interestingness. We should emphasize that these factors do not constitute a readability formula and yield a tidy grade level for a text. However, in the hands of skillful teachers they can be enormously useful.

Assessing the Effects of SREs

The second factor we consider in this section is assessing the effects of SREs on students' understanding and learning from the selections they read. For this we offer a single tool, but we believe it is an enormously valuable tool: the story map developed by Isabel Beck and Margaret McKeown (1981). As we noted in chapter 6, a story map is a listing of the major events and ideas in a selection in the order in which they occur. To create a story map, you first identify the major elements, both explicit and implicit, of a selection. Then you generate a question for each major element for the students to answer. These questions elicit information that is central to understanding the selection, and the answers to the questions constitute the essence of the meaning of the selection. Table 8-1 shows the major elements of a Russian folktale, *Baba Yaga*, by Margaret Phinney in the left column and the corresponding questions for students in the right column.

The answers to the story map questions are an important part of what we would expect students to know after reading a selection. As Beck and McKeown note, however, story map questions are not the only questions to ask about a reading selection. Once students understand the essence of the selection, then interpretive, analytical, and creative questions are appropriate and important to pursue. For example, with competent third or fourth graders reading *Baba Yaga*, you might add extension questions such as these: "Have you ever been warned not to do something, as Katrina was? What were you warned not to do? What happened?" Typically, we would include two or three questions of this sort.

Once you have created the story map and extension questions, there are several ways to use them in assessing students' comprehension and learning following an SRE. One is to have students study and answer the story map and extension questions individually and then have them, or some of them, come up and discuss their responses with you. Another is to have students write out the answers to the questions and turn them into you. A third is to have students discuss their responses in small groups as you sit in and consider the contributions of individual students. You are trying to find out if

Table 8-1. Story Map and Extension Questions for *Baba Yaga*

Event	Corresponding Question
Event 1: Katrina's father warns her not to go into the woods where the witch Baba Yaga lives.	Why did Katrina's father warn her not to go into the woods?
Event 2: The cruel housemaid sends Katrina into the woods to take food to a sick aunt.	What did the cruel housemaid ask Katrina to do?
Event 3: Katrina finds a dying dog in the woods and revives it with milk from her jug.	What did Katrina do to help the dog she found in the woods?
Event 4: A bit farther, Katrina stops to grease the squeaky hinges of a rusted gate.	Why did Katrina stop to grease the gate?
Event 5: Deep in the forest, Katrina comes upon Baba Yaga's hut, not the sick aunt's, and realizes the housemaid has betrayed her.	Whose hut did Katrina reach deep in the woods?
Event 6: Baba Yaga takes Katrina as a prisoner and slave.	What did Baba Yaga do to Katrina?
Event 7: Katrina shows kindness to Baba Yaga's cat by combing its matted fur, and the cat tells her to flee from Baba Yaga at midnight.	Why did Baba Yaga's cat tell Katrina she should escape?
Event 8: Katrina flees with Baba Yaga pursuing her but is able to escape with the aid and magic of those she was kind to—the cat, the gate, and the dog.	Who helped Katrina escape from Baba Yaga and why?
Event 9: Katrina throws the rag she had greased the gate with at Baba Yaga; it turns into a lake, and Baba Yaga drowns.	What happened when Katrina threw the rag at Baba Yaga?
Event 10: Katrina returns home and her father sends the evil housemaid packing.	Why did Katrina's father "send the housemaid packing"?

Extension Questions

Question 11: One frequent component of folktales such as *Baba Yaba* is magic. Note some instances of magic in *Baba Yaba* and some instances in other folktales.

Question 12: Another frequent component of folktales is characters who are distinctly evil. Think of some other folktales with evil characters. Why do you think folktales often contain such evil characters?

students understood and learned from reading the selection and participating in the SRE activities you created, and if they can make valid inferences and generalizations based on the selection. If they can, that's terrific; your SREs are assisting students in effectively dealing with texts. If they cannot, you will need to make modifications—creating stronger SREs, using different texts, giving students more time with the selections, or whatever it takes to lead students to successfully reading and learning from what they read.

The Place of SREs in a Comprehensive Literacy Program

In chapter 2 we specifically pointed out that an SRE is not a complete plan for a reading program. Here, as we approach the end of this book, we want to amplify on that point, saying a bit more about what we believe a comprehensive reading program should include. Our beliefs are essentially what they were at the beginning of the book, but they have been enriched and broadened by writing and revising this book and, with Connie Juel, writing and revising a book that does describe a comprehensive reading program—*Teaching Reading in the 21st Century* (Graves, Juel, & Graves, 2001).

In the remainder of this chapter, we take a paragraph to describe each of nine components, which together constitute a program we believe would serve students well. For those who want more information on these and other components of a truly comprehensive reading program, we suggest our *Teaching Reading in the 21st Century*.

Building Positive Perceptions and Attitudes About Reading

We list building positive perceptions and attitudes about reading first because unless children learn to love reading and the enjoyment and knowledge it can give them, no amount of expertise in reading can be considered adequate learning. As Fielding, Wilson, and Anderson (1986) point out in introducing their study of children's reading of trade books, in most cases "the problem is not that students cannot read, but that on most days they do not choose to do so." This, they go on to say, is a real pity because they found that "among all the ways that children can spend their leisure time, average minutes per day reading books was the best and most consistent predictor of standardized comprehension test performance, size of vocabulary, and gains in reading achievement." We must do everything possible to encourage children to truly love and value reading, because only by loving and valuing reading—and therefore choosing to read frequently—will children reach their full potential as readers.

Building Knowledge About Print and Sounds

Although this book does not deal with the very beginnings of reading instruction, a comprehensive literacy program must do so. As part of learning to read, students need to internalize a substantial body of knowledge about print and about the relationship between print and speech. That knowledge includes such matters as recognizing that the written language they are just beginning to learn about is in many ways similar to the oral language they are already quite proficient at, or recognizing that words are closely grouped sets of letters with white space at both ends. That knowledge also includes being able to do things such as tracking from left to right and from the top of the page to the bottom. Finally, it includes phonemic awareness, the insight that spoken words are composed of somewhat separable sounds (National Reading Panel, 2000; Snow, Burns, & Griffin, 1998).

Instruction in Word Identification Strategies

As they read, children often encounter words they do not immediately recognize, and at least some of the time they need to apply strategies to pronounce these words. One word identification strategy they need to learn is phonic analysis, which includes using letter-sound correspondences, decoding by analogy, and blending sounds to form words. Another word-identification strategy they need to learn is structural analysis, which includes using roots, prefixes, and suffixes in arriving at the pronunciation as well as the meaning of words. Students need to respond automatically to most words they encounter, and thus they will not constantly be using their word identification strategies, but they do need to have the strategies available.

Systematic Vocabulary Instruction

Most children enter school with very small reading vocabularies, perhaps numbering only a few dozen words. Each year, however, the average student's reading vocabulary grows by something like 3,000 to 4,000 words (White, Graves, & Slater, 1990), and by the sixth grade the average student is likely to have a vocabulary of approximately 20,000 words that he or she can both read and understand (Nagy & Herman, 1987). Clearly, students need help with this monumental learning task (Biemiller, 2001). Such help should include direct teaching of individual words—primarily the important words and concepts in materials students are reading—as well as instruction in using context, word parts, the dictionary, and the thesaurus.

Instruction That Fosters Comprehension of Specific Selections

This is the part of a comprehensive literacy program that this book does cover. The SRE is our approach to fostering comprehension of specific selections.

Instruction in Reading Strategies

In addition to receiving the assistance with individual selections that SREs provide, students need to become adept at independently using reading comprehension strategies. As David Pearson and his colleagues (Pearson, Roehler, Dole, & Duffy, 1992) note, reading comprehension strategies are "conscious and flexible plans that readers apply and adapt to a variety of texts and tasks." They are deliberate processes that readers use in order to understand and remember what they read. Among the strategies that Pearson and his colleagues have identified as particularly important are using prior knowledge, asking and answering questions, determining what is important, summarizing, making inferences, dealing with graphic information, imaging, and monitoring comprehension. One approach to teaching these strategies, the approach we tend to favor, is to systematically provide focused, explicit instruction in each of them (Graves, Juel, & Graves, 2001). Another approach, one advocated by Michael Pressley and his colleagues (Pressley, 2000; Pressley, El-Dinary, Wharton-McDonald, & Brown, 1998), is to embed instruction in these strategies within the normal reading activities students undertake from day to day. Whichever approach is used, it is vital that the strategies are taught and learned.

Fostering Deep Understanding and Teaching Critical and Creative Thinking

Too often, we believe, schools concentrate on one sort of learning at the expense of others. Usually the charge is that there is too much attention to factual information and too little attention to higher level thinking, and this may well be the case. However, the point we wish to make—by including instruction that fosters deep understanding, critical thinking, and creative thinking as part of a comprehensive literacy program—is that various sorts of learning, thinking, doing, and feeling are important to a student becoming independent, competent, productive, caring, fulfilled, and a happy member of our adult society.

Integration of Reading, Writing, Speaking, and Listening

We have addressed directly the matter of the close relationship between reading and writing, the fact that instruction in reading and writing frequently ought to be coupled, and the fact that instruction and practice in one of these modalities reinforces learning in the other. Here we simply add that this close and reciprocal relationship holds among all four language modalities. Experiences in reading, writing, speaking, and listening go hand in hand, reinforce each other, occur together in the world outside school, and should frequently be integrated in the classroom as well. We have attempted to take advantage of these interrelationships and highlight them in the sample SRE activities we have presented.

Independent Reading

When using SREs, teachers are generally working with the whole class or relatively large groups of students in order to ensure understanding and success on the part of all students. SREs can also be used with small groups, and their use with such groups is frequently appropriate. Obviously, we believe that such experiences play a crucial part in students developing literacy. So does independent reading, however. Eventually, if students are to continue reading, they need to become independent readers. Schools need to start them on this road to independence.

Incorporating SREs Into
Your Classroom: A Final Word

In this chapter, we have attempted to provide practical advice and some closure by discussing some of the principal decisions you will need to make in implementing SREs, the use of SREs to foster higher level thinking and deep understanding, how to match students and texts and how to assess the effects of SREs, and what should be included in a comprehensive literacy program.

Becoming literate grew increasingly important to virtually every individual in our society throughout the second half of the 20th century. Today, in the first decade of the 21st century, literacy is more important than ever, and beginning reading instruction is currently receiving more emphasis than ever before. As we write, however, not nearly as much is being done to improve students' reading beyond the beginning years, to improve their comprehension and their learning from the increasingly complex texts they encounter as they move through school. This is a real tragedy. The diversity of cultures, languages, and values in today's society—along with the increasing number of challenges we face each year—makes high levels of literacy a must for each and every student. SREs can play only a small role in meeting this challenge, but we believe that they can play a significant role. By considering your students, the selections they are reading, and the outcomes that you and they seek, and then constructing SREs specifically designed to allow those students to use those texts to achieve those outcomes, you will make those experiences successful ones—experiences that build students' sense of accomplishment, their competence in reading, and their readiness to become responsible contributors to today's world.

References

Anderson, L. W., & Krathwohl, D. R. (2001). *A taxonomy for learning, teaching, and assessing. A revision of Bloom's Taxonomy of Educational Objectives.* New York: Addison Wesley Longman. A substantially updated revision of Bloom's widely used taxonomy.

Beck, I. L., & McKeown, M. G. (1981). Developing questions that promote comprehension: The story map. *Language Arts, 58,* 913–918. A brief description of the authors' plan for choosing questions to ask on reading selections.

Biemiller, A. (2001, Spring). Teaching vocabulary: Early, direct, and sequential. *American Educator,* pp. 24–28, 47. An argument for direct instruction in vocabulary, particularly in the early grades.

Block, C. C., & Dellamura, R. J. (2000–2001). Better book buddies. *The Reading Teacher, 54,* 364–370. Some very useful advice on children helping other children in their reading.

Bransford, J. D., Brown, A. L., & Cocking, R. R. (Eds.). (2000). *How people learn: Brain, mind, experience, and school* (expanded edition). Washington, DC: National Academy Press. Presents the results of a two-year review of the research on teaching and learning conducted by the National Research Council.

Burns, P. C., & Roe, B. D. (2002). *Burns/Roe informal reading inventory: Preprimer to 12th grade* (6th ed.). Boston: Houghton Mifflin. Widely used informal reading inventory.

Chall, J. S., & Dale, E. (1995). *Readability revisited: The new Dale-Chall readability formula.* Cambridge, MA: Brookline Books. Explanation and instructions for using the new Dale-Chall readability formula.

Cohen, P. A., Kulik, J. A., & Kulik, C. C. (1982). Educational outcomes of tutoring: A meta-analysis of findings. *American Educational Research Journal,* 19, 237–248. Major review showing the very positive effects of tutoring.

Cooke, C. L. (2001). *The effects of scaffolded multicultural short stories on students' comprehension, response, and attitudes.* Unpublished doctoral dissertation, University of Minnesota, Minneapolis. Experimental study showing the effects of SREs with multicultural texts.

Costa, A. L., & Kallick, B. (Eds.). (2000). *Discovering and exploring habits of mind.* Alexandria, VA: Association for Supervision and Curriculum Development. Includes a discussion of Costa's concept of higher level thinking.

Ennis, R. H. (1985). Critical thinking and the curriculum. *National Forum,* 65 (1), 28–31. A brief but insightful statement about the place of critical thinking in schools.

Fielding, L. G., Wilson, P. T., Anderson, R. C. (1986). A new focus on free reading: The role of trade books in reading instruction. In T. E. Raphael (Ed.), *The contexts of school-based literacy.* New York: Random House. A forceful plea for using trade books.

Fournier, D.N.E., & Graves, M. F. (In press). Scaffolding adolescents' comprehension of short stories. *Journal of Adolescent and Adult Literacy.* Experimental study demonstrating the positive effects of SREs.

Fry, E. (1977). Fry's readability graph: Clarifications, validity, and extension to level 17. *Journal of Reading,* 21, 242–52. Original source of the formula also found in the following reference.

Fry, E. B., Polk, J. K., & Fountoukidis, D. (2000). *The reading teacher's book of lists* (4th ed.). Englewood Cliffs, NJ: Prentice-Hall. Contains complete instructions for use of the Fry Readability Graph, also a very handy source of word lists and other lists helpful in the classroom.

Gardner, H. (1999). *Intelligence reframed: Multiple intelligences for the 21st century.* New York: Basic Books. An updated presentation of Gardner's theory.

Gardner, H. (2000). *The disciplined mind: Beyond facts and standardized tests, the K–12 education that every child deserves.* New York: Penguin Books. Gardner's conception of the education students deserve.

Graves, M. F. (1998, October/November). Beyond balance. *Reading Today,* p. 16. An essay on what constitutes a balanced and effective reading program.

Graves, M. F. (1999, October). Fostering high levels of reading and learning in secondary students. *Reading Online.* Available: online at http://www.readingonline.org/articles/graves1/. An essay describing the importance of fostering high level reading and learning and some ways of doing so.

Graves, M. F., Juel, C., & Burns, B. (2001). *Rubrics and other tools for classroom assessment.* Boston: Allyn & Bacon. A brief set of suggestions and materials for classroom assessment with an emphasis on assessing beginning reading skills.

Graves, M. F., Juel, C., & Graves, B. B. (2001). *Teaching reading in the 21st century* (2nd ed.). Boston: Allyn & Bacon. A comprehensive elementary reading methods text focusing on research-based teaching practices.

Graves, M. F., & Liang, L. A. (in press). Online resources for fostering understanding and higher-level thinking in senior high school students. *National Reading Conference yearbook.* Chicago: National Reading Conference. Describes our evaluation of a Web-site containing SREs. Data include the results of surveys and interviews of teachers as well as multiple-choice and short-answer tests of student learning.

Graves, M. F., Watts-Tafte, S., & Graves, B. B. (1999). *Essentials of elementary reading* (2nd ed.). Boston: Allyn & Bacon. A compact reading methods text. We include it because it includes a description of informal reading inventories.

Harp, B. (2000). *The handbook of literacy assessment and evaluation* (2nd ed.). Norwood, MA: Christopher-Gordon. A compendium of teacher-made and published assessment and evaluation tools.

Herber, H. L. (1970). *Teaching reading in content areas.* Englewood Cliffs, NJ: Prentice-Hall. One of the first books on content area reading.

Hill, B. C. (2001). *Developmental continuums: A framework for literacy instruction and assessment K–8.* Norwood, MA: Christopher-Gordon. A detailed set of materials and procedures for assessing a developmentally oriented literacy program.

Juel, C. (1996). What makes literacy tutoring effective? *Reading Research Quarterly, 31,* 268–289. Careful examination of factors making tutoring effective.

McKeachie, W. J., & Gibbs, G. (1999). *McKeachie's teaching tips: Strategies, research, and theory for college and university teachers* (10th ed.) Boston: Houghton Mifflin.

Nagy, W. E., & Herman, P. A. (1987). Breadth and depth of vocabulary knowledge: Implications for acquisition and instruction. In M. G. McKeown & M. E. Curtis (Eds.), *The nature of vocabulary acquisition.* Hillsdale, NJ: Erlbaum. Provides an accurate estimate of vocabulary size and growth.

National Reading Panel. (2000), *Report of the National Reading Panel: Teaching children to read.* Bethesda, MD: National Institute of Child Health and Human Development. Documents findings of a national panel established to review the scientific research on teaching reading.

Pearson, P. D., Roehler, L. R., Dole, J. A., & Duffy, G. G. (1992). Developing expertise in reading comprehension. In S. J. Samuels & A. E. Farstrup (Eds.), *What research has to say about reading instruction* (2nd ed., pp. 145–199). Newark, DE: International Reading Association. An important perspective on reading comprehension instruction, with particular emphasis on teaching comprehension strategies.

Perkins, D. (1992). *Smart schools: From training memories to educating minds.* New York: Free Press. An explanation of and rationale behind teaching for understanding.

Perkins, D. (1995). *Outsmarting IQ: The emerging science of learnable intelligence.* New York: Free Press. Discussion of the many ways in which intelligence can be improved through instruction.

Perkins, D. N., & Tishman, S. (1998). *Dispositional aspects of intelligence.* Available online at http://learnweb.harvard.edu/alps/thinking/docs/ Plymouth.htm. Examines the importance of giving students a disposition toward higher level thinking and deep understanding.

Pressley, M. (2000). What should reading comprehension instruction be the instruction of? In M. Kamil, P. Mosenthal, P. D. Pearson, & R. Barr (Eds.), *Handbook of reading research* (Vol. 3, pp. 545–561). Mahwah, NJ: Erlbaum. Consideration of a variety of component parts that constitute a comprehensive instructional program aimed at developing reading comprehension.

Pressley, M., El-Dinary, P. B., Wharton-McDonald, R., & Brown, R. (1998). Transactional instruction of comprehension strategies in the elementary grades. In D. H. Schunk & B. J. Zimmerman (Eds.), *Self-regulated learning: From teaching to self-reflective practice* (pp. 42–56). New York: Guilford Press. A concise summary of the authors' work on transactional strategies instruction.

Resnick, L. G. (1987). *Education and learning to think.* Washington, DC: National Academy Press. Also available online at http://books.nap.edu/catalog/1032.html. Brief but excellent discussion of critical thinking.

Sales, G. C., & Graves, M. F. (2001). *On-line resources for teaching higher-order reading and comprehension skills.* Unpublished report submitted to the Office of Vocational and Adult Education. Describes a Web site and provides a variety of test data on it and on the effectiveness of SREs.

Snow, C. E., Burns, S. M., & Griffin, P. (1998). *Preventing reading difficulties in young children.* Washington, DC: National Academy Press. Very influential review of research sponsored by the National Research Council.

Sternberg, R. J., & Sperling, L. S. (1996). *Teaching for thinking.* Washington, DC: American Psychological Association. Clear and teacher-oriented explanation of Sternberg's triadic theory and suggestions for using it in the classroom.

Watts, S. M., & Rothenberg S. S. (1997). Students with learning difficulties meet Shakespeare: Using a scaffolded reading experience. *Journal of Adolescent & Adult Literacy, 40,* 532–539. Classroom study of using a scaffolded reading experience.

White, T. G., Graves, M. F., & Slater, W. H. (1990). Growth of reading vocabulary in diverse elementary schools: Decoding and word meaning. *Journal of Educational Psychology, 82* (2), 281–290. Details on the size of first through fourth graders' vocabularies.

Wiggins, G., & McTighe, J. (1998). *Understanding by design.* Alexandria, VA: Association for Supervision and Curriculum Development. The basic description of the authors' approach to teaching for understanding.

Wiske, M. S. (Ed.). (1998). *Teaching for understanding: Linking research with practice.* San Francisco: Jossey-Bass. Describes the specifics of the teaching for understanding approach and how it looks in the classroom.

Children's Literature

Bauer, M. D. (1986). *On my honor.* Boston: Clarion. 90 pages.

Carrick, C. (1999). *Upside-down cake.* New York: Clarion. 64 pages.

Collier, J. L., & Collier, C. (1974). *My brother Sam is dead.* New York: Four Winds. 216 pages.

Forbes, E. (1971). *Johnny Tremain.* New York: Dell. 256 pages.

Giddens, S. (2000). *Coping with grieving and loss.* New York: Rosen. 122 pages.

Graves, B. (2002). *California condor: Flying free.* Logan, IA: Perfection Learning. 62 pages.

O'Dell, S. (1960). *The island of the blue dolphins.* Boston: Houghton Mifflin. 181 pages.

Paterson, K. (1977). *Bridge to Terabithia.* New York: Crowell. 128 pages.

Phinney, M. Y. (1995). Baba Yaga: A Russian folk tale. Greenvale, NY: Mondo. 38 pages.

Sprung, B. (1998). *Death.* Austin, TX: Steck-Vaughn. 48 pages.

Walker, P. (2001). *Pray hard.* New York: Scholastic. 172 pages.

Chapter

9

Assessing Text
Difficulty and Accessibility

One hugely important factor to take into account in planning a Scaffolded Reading Experience is of course the text itself. As part of matching your students with appropriate texts, you need to assess the difficulty of the texts you consider using, as well as the likelihood that your students will be motivated to read them. Up until a few years ago, text difficulty was typically assessed with readability formulas, mathematical equations that took into account vocabulary difficulty and sentence complexity and then assigned a grade level to a text. In recent years, however, readability formulas have been severely criticized. In 1984, for example, the presidents of IRA and NCTE issued a joint statement decrying the use of readability formulas as the sole criterion for measuring text difficulty and matching students with texts (Cullinan & Fitzgerald, 1984–1985).

In the years that have passed since Cullinan and Fitzgerald issued their statement, textbooks and text difficulty have been the topic of a substantial body of research and writing (Alexander & Jetton, 2000; Britton & Black, 1985; Britton & Guelgoez, 1991, Chall, Bissex, Conard, & Harris-Sharples, 1996; Chambliss & Calfee, 1998; Goldman & Rakestraw, 2000; Linderholm et al., 2000; Muth, 1989; Rouet, Vidal-Abarca, Erboul, & Millogo, 2001; Sawyer, 1991), and evidence that factors beyond those considered in readability formulas influence text difficulty has continued to accrue. Several authors have discussed factors to consider in assessing the difficulty of texts. The best known articles on the topic are those of Thomas Anderson and Bonnie Armbruster (1984) and of Isabel Beck and Margaret McKeown and their colleagues (Beck & McKeown, 1989; Beck, McKeown, & Gromoll, 1989; Beck, McKeown, & Worthy, 1995; McKeown, Beck, Sinatra, & Loxterman, 1992). Other important studies have been reported by Bruce Britton and Sami Guelgoez (1991) and Tracy Linderholm and her colleagues (2000). And Richard Allington (2001) has made some very practical observations.

The suggestions made here draw heavily on this work, on our experiences as English and reading teachers, and on other work that suggests characteristics of the material that children can and will read. Our intent is to provide you with a reasonably comprehensive yet manageable set of factors to consider in selecting appropriate reading materials for your students. In this chapter, we discuss a set of factors for you to consider carefully, along with considering the students who will be reading the selection, your purposes and their purposes in reading it, and the assistance you will give them in dealing with it.

In all, we consider 10 factors that influence text difficulty and accessibility. These are divided into two groups. The first group includes six factors that are fairly easily defined, fairly easily identified, and largely inherent in the text itself. Because reading is an interactive process that involves both the reader and the text, no text factors are fully independent of the reader. The second group includes four factors that are less easily defined, less easily identified, and very definitely involve both the reader and the text. The 10 factors are shown here.

> Vocabulary
> Sentence structure
> Length
> Elaboration
> Coherence and unity
> Text structure
>
> Familiarity of content and background knowledge required
> Audience appropriateness
> Quality and verve of the writing
> Interestingness

These factors reflect both the ease or difficulty young readers are likely to have in comprehending a text and how interesting and accessible the material will be for them. Of course, the more interesting and accessible the material is, the better the chance that students will pursue it, understand it, learn from it, and enjoy it.

Factors Largely Inherent in the Text Itself

The six factors we consider here are vocabulary, sentence structure, length, elaboration, coherence and unity, and text structure. The first two, vocabulary and sentence structure, are ones you are probably familiar with because they are the two factors considered in readability formulas. However, we want to stress that, although these two factors deserve consideration, they should not be relied on too heavily or to the exclusion of the other factors we consider. All 10 factors are worth considering, and some of them—for example, familiarity of content and background knowledge required—are hugely important.

Vocabulary

We list vocabulary as the first matter to consider because it is one of the most easily identifiable characteristics suggesting text difficulty and because it is a very influential factor. A substantial body of research testifies to the fact that texts containing many difficult words are likely to be difficult texts. However, this does not mean that such texts can necessarily be simplified by replacing the difficult words with easier ones. It appears that vocabulary is an excellent predictor of difficulty because vocabulary reflects difficulty; a difficult or unfamiliar topic frequently needs to be conveyed using the difficult and unfamiliar vocabulary that is inherent to the topic (Anderson & Freebody, 1981). Because of this, simply replacing difficult words with easier ones may do little to simplify a text; in fact, it can even make a text more difficult.

In addition, in considering vocabulary, you need to think about more than just difficulty; simpler words are not necessarily better words. The words used in a selection need to be appropriate to the selection and to convey the intended meaning precisely. If, for example, the intended meaning is *petrified*, the simpler substitutes *afraid* or *scared* do not convey quite the same meaning. These latter terms do not describe a fear so great that the person becomes immobilized and cannot react. This is another reason that replacing less frequent words with more frequent ones often fails to simplify a text; the words used to replace the originals frequently do not mean exactly the same thing and do not fit the context nearly as well.

Finally, we want to stress that a few difficult words are unlikely to pose serious barriers to comprehension. In fact, research has shown that it takes a substantial proportion of difficult words to affect students' comprehension (Freebody & Anderson, 1983). In addition, if students read only texts in which all the words are familiar, they will be denied a major opportunity for enlarging their vocabularies. Wide reading in texts that include varied and novel words is, in fact, the main route to vocabulary growth.

Sentence Structure

Sentence structure, another text characteristic that is fairly easy to assess and the other factor considered in readability formulas, is a second factor that reflects difficulty. Very long, complex, and convoluted sentences make texts more difficult to read. However, sentence structure does not have nearly as strong an effect as vocabulary (Coleman, 1971). Moreover, the sentences in a text should be complex enough to clearly convey the meaning of the text (Pearson, 1974–1975). If the intended meaning is something like "Ted failed to win the award because neither his test scores nor his grades were high enough," breaking that sentence up into something like "Ted failed to win the award. His test scores were not high enough. His grades were not high enough." is not going to result in more comprehensible text. Texts that lack logical connectives require students to infer relationships that could have been stated explicitly, and inferring relationships may cause problems for some students.

On the other hand, some sentences are clearly difficult. Here is one from "Shooting an Elephant" by George Orwell. "Its mahout, the only person who could manage it when it was in that state, had set out in pursuit, but had taken the wrong direction and was now twelve hours' journey away, and in the morning the elephant had suddenly reappeared in the town." Materials that contain a very large percentage of complex sentences are likely to present difficulties for younger and less proficient readers.

At the same time, texts that employ artificially short sentences, the kind sometimes written for beginning or remedial readers, do not have the sound of real language. Here is a paragraph from a high interest-easy reading book. To our ears, at least, it sounds unnatural, and we suspect that the author deliberately used this series of short sentences to keep the readability score down.

> Payton's training paid off. He rushed for 1,421 yards in 1983. He caught passes for 607 yards. That was the most passes (53) of any Bear. He passed for 95 yards. He gained a total of more than 2,000 yards for the second time in his career. His yardage was thirty-six percent of the Bear's total yardage. He was almost a one man team.

Many readers, even remedial ones, would do better with a more natural sounding text; and at least one study (Green & Olsen, 1988) has shown that readers, particularly less able ones, comprehend original texts just as well as simplified ones and actually prefer original texts to simplified ones.

Length

Length is an obvious but sometimes overlooked factor that influences the difficulty of a selection and the likelihood that a less avid reader will make a real stab at finishing it. Particularly for students who do not read fluently, length alone can be a very formidable obstacle (Grobe, 1970). Research has shown that in some cases shorter texts—summaries or much reduced versions of complete texts—can actually produce better comprehension and memory than longer ones (Carroll, 1990; Reder, 1982). If the intent of a reading assignment is to have students retain key information, then short summaries specifically designed to convey that key information may be more effective than longer, less focused selections. Fortunately, how much material and what parts of the material we ask students to read is usually directly under our control as teachers.

However, as we discuss in the next section, shorter is not always better. In making a point, verbal illustrations and examples are often useful, but they also increase the length of a piece.

Elaboration

Texts can be written so that they present concepts without much explanation or so that they present concepts along with a good deal of explanatory material—examples, analogies, and linkages.

Elaboration refers to a certain type of explanatory material. Elaborative information explains the reasons behind the bare-bones information presented. Elaboration makes information more meaningful and understandable, and information that is more understandable is more memorable. The concept is an important one and worth some examples. Here are two examples, one from a psychological experiment on elaboration (Bransford & Johnson, 1972) and one from an elementary social studies text.

In the experiment, some students were given unelaborated statements such as "The tall man bought the crackers," "The bald man read the newspaper," and "The funny man liked the ring," and other students were given elaborated statements such as "The tall man purchased the crackers that had been lying on the top shelf," "The bald man read the newspaper in order to look for a hat sale," and "The funny man liked the ring that squirted water." Then both groups were given questions such as "Who bought the crackers?" "Who read the newspaper?" and "Who liked the ring?" Students who read the unelaborated statements could answer almost no questions, while those who read the elaborated text could answer nearly all of them.

The passage from a social studies textbook concerned American Indian houses. It consisted of statements such as "The Indians of the Northwest Coast lived in slant-roofed houses made of cedar planks," "Some California Indian tribes lived in simple, earth-covered or brush shelters," and "The Plains Indians lived mainly in tepees." The textbook contained nothing to explain these facts and make them something other than arbitrary pieces of information. For example, it said nothing about the relationships between the types of houses and the climates of the areas, the types of building materials available in the area, or the lifestyles of the various groups. Unelaborated information is difficult to remember and not very interesting.

The idea that elaborations facilitate comprehension and recall makes good sense, and the facilitative effects of elaborated text have been empirically documented (Bransford & Johnson, 1972; Reder, Charney, & Morgan, 1986). However, as we noted above, shorter texts sometimes produce better comprehension and memory than longer ones. The matter of just when elaborations help and when they hinder is not yet resolved. It appears to be the case, though, that shorter texts may be more effective if the goal is simply to remember material, while elaborated texts may be more effective if one needs to thoroughly understand material—for example, to write about what he or she has read or apply it in some real-world context such as operating computer software (Charney & Reder, 1988).

Coherence and Unity

Coherence refers to the integration of material, to how each topic and subtopic is defined and to how well the parts relate to each other (Anderson & Armbruster, 1984; Beck & McKeown, 1989). With young and inexperienced readers and with material that is unfamiliar to students, it is particularly important that authors be explicit about how each piece of information fits with the other information in the text and about how each piece of information helps to explain the event or idea the text presents. Coherence is another text factor that can be adversely affected by undue attention to readability requirements. Rigid adherence to readability requirements often results in the deletion of connectives and clauses that explain how the parts of a topic fit together, and the deletion of such material is likely to make a text less coherent.

Unity refers to oneness of purpose. Good texts are directed toward particular topics, particular points, particular themes, and particular concepts. After reading a selection, the reader should be able to summarize the content of the text and explain its purpose fairly succinctly because the text has not dealt with a myriad of topics. Texts that wander, take up too many topics, or contain pockets of irrelevant material are difficult to read, summarize, and remember.

Beck and McKeown (1989) give a number of specific examples of elementary texts in which coherence and unity have been obscured. Here are three of them. In one fourth-grade text, an 800-word expository selection on subways is introduced with a 100-word anecdote in which the reader is asked to imagine that he or she is at home alone and needs to get someplace quickly: "It is Saturday morning. You are alone in the house when the phone rings. A friend of yours needs help" (p. 52). In this case, the reader may well be riveted, but unfortunately he or she is likely to be riveted on the wrong topic. The reader is focused on an adventure, while the text is intended to provide information about subways. In another fourth-grade text, a 950-word selection about volcanoes, a description of the volcano Mt. Fuji is interrupted with a 60-word digression about Mt. Fuji as a summer resort. It may be interesting to know that Mt. Fuji is a popular vacation spot, but the digression does nothing to further the reader's knowledge about volcanoes, the topic the passage is intended to present. As a third example, Beck and McKeown cite a 900-word, third-grade selection on the brain, which attempts to describe diverse functions such as "neural impulse, memory and dreaming in addition to the brain's physical appearance." Such an attempt at presenting a huge and diverse body of information in so few words, Beck and McKeown note, "absolutely prohibits both supportive elaboration . . . and development of logical connections necessary for coherent presentation" (p. 56).

Two studies that involve the coherence and unity of text are particularly worth considering because they offer guidelines for writing or identifying coherent text. In the earlier of these, Britton and Guelgoez (1991) successfully revised text to avoid barriers to comprehension and developed four guidelines for doing so: (a) making implicit referents explicit, (b) repeating a linking word from the previous sentence, (c) using the same terms for the same concepts, and (d) constructing sentences in keeping with the given-new format. In the given-new format, information that has already been given in the text comes first in a sentence, and information to be added to that given information comes later. In a more recent study, Linderholm and her colleagues (2000) successfully revised difficult texts to improve coherence and developed three guidelines for doing so: (a) arranging text events in temporal order, (b) making implicit goals explicit, and (c) repairing coherence breaks caused by inadequate explanations, multiple causality, or distant causal relationships.

Text Structure

Text structure refers to the organization of a text. The majority of texts students encounter in school can be categorized as belonging to one of two broad categories, narratives or exposition, and these two types of texts are organized very differently (Drum, 1984; Ogle & Blachowicz, 2002; RAND Reading Study Group, 2002). Typical narratives reflect the temporal order of real-life events in which motives, actions, results, and reactions occur in sequence, and episodes in the main character's life are integrated by goals and subgoals. Time thus provides a natural structure for remembering episodic information. Most children's books are narratives, most of the material parents read to children are narratives, and most of the selections in primary grade basal readers are narratives. Although there are certainly easier and more difficult narratives and ones that do not follow the prototypical structure, children generally do fairly well with narratives.

Exposition is another matter. Expository text, even well-written expository texts, can have a variety of organizations, and different authors have created different lists of the organizational patterns of expository writing. Anderson and Armbruster (1984), for example, list description, temporal sequences, explanation, compare-contrast, definition-examples, and problem-solution as typical organizational patterns. Calfee and Chambliss (1988), on the other hand, identify description and sequence as the two major rhetorical patterns and then further divide each of these categories. In addition to these rhetorical patterns, Calfee and Chambliss identify several functional devices—introductions, transitions, and conclusions—that serve to link the various parts of a text. Unfortunately, in surveying social studies texts, Calfee and Chambliss found that authors frequently employed weak rhetorical patterns such as lists or simply presented material without any apparent pattern. In addition, the texts employed few effective functional devices to aid the reader. What is needed is expository texts that are clearly organized and that make that organization apparent to the reader (Chambliss & Calfee, 1998), and it appears that many of the expository texts used in schools fail to meet these criteria.

Moreover, since there is no single prototypic structure for exposition, previous reading of exposition, even well-written exposition, does not provide clues to the structure of upcoming expositions in the way that previous reading of narratives provides clues to the structure of upcoming narratives. Also, little children's literature is exposition, parents seldom read expository material to preschoolers, and primary grade basal readers and even some intermediate grade basals contain little exposition. For these reasons, many students find expository text difficult.

Factors Involving the Reader and the Text

The factors considered here are familiarity of content and background knowledge required, audience appropriateness, the quality and verve of the writing, and interestingness. As we have already noted, each of these factors definitely involves both the reader and the text; for example, one reader may find the content of a particular text quite familiar, while another might find it largely unfamiliar. It also should be recognized that assessing texts along these dimensions is very much a subjective task.

Familiarity of Content and Background Knowledge Required

As we already noted, vocabulary is probably the excellent predictor of difficulty that it is because it is an index of how familiar students are with the content of the material. Reading a selection on a topic with which we have little familiarity is difficult. Reading a selection on a topic that is totally unfamiliar to us is simply impossible (Adams & Bruce, 1982). It is for this reason that the language experience approach in which children dictate their own stories and then read them offers some real advantages when used with children just beginning to read. The content of a story that a child dictates is totally familiar to the child.

Of course, children read a great deal besides experience stories, but much of this material contains familiar content. A descriptive piece about a zoo will contain a good deal of content familiar to students who have visited zoos. Similarly, a narrative set in a suburban community and focusing on the adventures and misadventures of a Cub Scout will contain a lot of material familiar to a Cub Scout from the suburbs. However, the same narrative may contain much less material familiar to a young Chicano living in the Los Angeles barrio. Still, even when placed in unfamiliar settings, narratives are likely to contain familiar themes. Most children are raised by parents, a parent, or a parent substitute; situations that arise between adults and children, between authority figures and youngsters, occur everywhere. Children have peers with whom they play, fight, and engage in a host of other pleasant and unpleasant human interactions. They go to school, shop at a store, and sleep at night. These commonalities result in a good deal of familiar content in most short stories and novels.

Not only must the reader have some familiarity with the contents of a selection, he or she must also have the background knowledge assumed by the author (Adams & Bruce, 1982; Anderson, 1984, Pressley & Block, 2002). In some cases, the general knowledge that one picks up from day-to-day living is sufficient. This is true of many short stories and novels. In other cases, much more specific knowledge is required to understand the text. This is particularly the case in technical and scientific areas; many of us could deal with a calculus text about as well with the cover closed as with it open. However, many humanities and social science texts also require extensive background knowledge for comprehension and thus pose problems for some students.

An example from a television serial, an example in which the content is not difficult but for which those of you not familiar with the serial will lack relevant background knowledge, will perhaps illustrate the point. The serial is *Dr. Who,* a fantasy series that was popular with many preteens and teens some years ago.

Imagine that you are watching the beginning of the show and see a barren, desertlike scene, obviously hot and evidently devoid of life. Suddenly, a red British phone booth appears in the desert. The camera zooms in to what should be the inside of the phone booth, but what you see is the cabin of some sort of spaceship, and it is much larger than the inside of a phone booth. In the cabin are a tall, lanky man wearing a long coat and a wool muffler reaching nearly to the floor and a young woman in contemporary clothes. The camera zooms out and you are again looking at the British phone booth in the desert, yet out of it walk the tall man and the young woman. The man then turns to the woman and says in a very solemn voice, "As the fourth doctor, I am of course responsible for the tardis." The woman nods, showing her full understanding of the fourth doctor's evidently poignant message.

What are the uninitiated to think? What is a phone booth doing in the middle of a desert? Is the large cabin supposed to be inside that little phone booth? Why does the man wear a long coat and an even longer muffler in the middle of a desert? In what sense is he the *fourth* doctor? Is there a third doctor? A fifth? What is a *tardis*?

The answers to these questions and a host of others are readily available to *Dr. Who* fans, but totally unavailable to those who know nothing of the show; and although in this case one could acquire the background knowledge rather readily, in many cases there are myriad facts, concepts, and relationships that a reader must know in order to approach a particular text.

Audience Appropriateness

Obviously, the topic of a selection and the sophistication with which the topic is treated need to be appropriate for the students reading the selection. Consider, for example, two human interest pieces, both out of periodicals and both written for adults, but both readily interpretable by fifth or sixth graders. The first is by William Geist, a columnist for *The New York Times*. It is entitled "The Friends of Trees," and it begins like this.

> Marianne Holden could not restrain herself any longer. She whipped out her trusty 12 inch folding saw and attacked a Japanese pagoda tree.
>
> "It feels so-o-o good," she said, standing on her tiptoes while she removed a limb the tree did not need. A wise guy

> walking by yelled "Timberrrr!" when the little branch dropped
> to the ground.

The sketch goes on to describe a group of New Yorkers who help the city to care for boulevard trees. It is well written, and we like it because it shows people doing something positive and caring, behaving in a way we don't often think of as typical of New Yorkers, perhaps in a way we don't often think of as typical of these times. But how appropriate is it for fifth or sixth graders? Will they appreciate it, relate to it, be interested in it? We are not sure, but it seems likely that many students will not find it engaging.

Now consider another human interest piece. This one is by Charles Kuralt, the CBS journalist. It is titled "The Butterfly Mystery," and it begins like this:

> Monarch butterflies spend the winter in Pacific Grove, Cali-
> fornia. In early spring, the monarchs migrate north. This
> fact is part of a mystery that suggests all kinds of troubling
> questions.
>
> In the first place, the monarchs are confused by radio, tele-
> vision, and radar waves. And they are destroyed by fertil-
> izer, insect sprays, and air pollution. So how do they survive
> at all?
>
> In the second place, after they leave Pacific Grove, they fly
> as far as 2,000 miles into Canada. They fly through storms
> and across mountains and deserts, even though they are
> as fragile as feathers. How do they do it?

The sketch goes on to describe some of the other mysteries of the butterflies' annual visit to Pacific Grove, never really explaining them but describing some of the folktales about the monarchs' visits and, all in all, presenting the visits as a rather magical and wonderful annual event. It too is well written, and we like it because we find the phenomenon an interesting one. Is it appropriate for fifth and sixth graders? Will they appreciate it, relate to it, and be interested in it? It seems likely that they will. It seems likely that of the two pieces, both about the same length, both about the same difficulty, and both well written, "The Butterfly Mystery" will be more appropriate for many fifth and sixth graders.

Quality and Verve of the Writing

In addition to the factors that have been presented thus far, one must consider the quality of the writing, the flair of the writing, the particular blend of topic, organization, and style that makes one piece of writing intriguing and memorable and another piece mundane.

There has been very little research on the effects of the quality and verve of writing. However, in one very relevant study, Beck, McKeown, and Worthy (1995) found that modifying textbook passages by giving them "voice" significantly increased fourth graders' comprehension of the passages. In revising the passages to give them voice, Beck and her colleagues attempted to make text situations more dynamic, make the language more conversational, and highlight connections between the reader and the text. Although voice is only part of what we mean by quality and verve, it is certainly an important part of it.

Of course, quality and verve is not the only aspect of writing to consider. Certainly the texts we ask students to read should be lucid, but clarity is only one criterion for good prose. Joseph Williams (1985), author of a wonderful little book entitled *Style: Ten Lessons in Clarity and Grace*, addresses the topic in this way:

> Let us assume that you can now write clear [and] cohesive . . . prose. That in itself would constitute a style of such singular distinction that most of us would be more than satisfied to achieve so much. But even though we might prefer bald clarity of the complexity of [much] . . . prose, the unrelenting simplicity of the plain style can finally become very flat and dry indeed, eventually arid. Its plainness invests prose with the blandness of unsalted meat and potatoes—honest fare to be sure, but hardly memorable and certainly without zest. Sometimes a touch of class, a flash of elegance can make the difference between forgettable Spartan plainness and a well-turned phrase that fixes itself in the mind of the reader. (p. 153)

Exposing young readers to the power and beauty of the language ought to be one of our aims in selecting texts.

Interestingness

We left this factor for last because it is the most subjective factor and the factor most dependent on the reader. A poorly written piece on dogs is likely to be of great interest to a child who loves dogs, while even a very well written article on the topic will not capture the interest of a child who doesn't care much about animals. Moreover, the results of studies of interesting material on children's comprehension are mixed. Some studies have shown positive effects of interesting material (Anderson, Shirey, Wilson, & Fielding, 1987; Asher, 1980). Others have failed to show such effects and have even found that interesting anecdotes in textbooks can sometimes focus children's attention away from more important parts of a selection (Duffy et al., 1989; Garner, 1992; Graves et al., 1991). Garner has aptly labeled interesting but tangential topics that detract from comprehension "seductive details." Like the Sirens of Greek mythology, they lure unsuspecting readers from their true course with their arresting call. Recall, for example, the adventure narrative that begins the fourth-grade expository selection on subways, a passage we mentioned in the section on coherence and unity. The narrative is very likely to capture students' interest, but their attention will be focused on solving the problem of helping a friend and not on the information about subways.

In general, it appears that texts with material a child finds interesting as an integral part of their makeup are likely to facilitate comprehension, while texts in which the interesting material is an add-on are likely to impede comprehension. The implications for teaching are threefold. First, although there is a good deal written about children's interests, the best way to find out about what interests your particular students is to spend time with them, sharing your interests and seeking to learn about and share theirs. Second, annotated bibliographies and other discussions of children's books abound, and we encourage you to use them. We also encourage you to spend time reading children's books and periodicals themselves. Finally, be particularly aware of seductive details in expository writing for children. Try to choose writing that makes the subject matter itself interesting rather than writing that relies on irrelevant asides to gain its readers' interest. Alert students to the presence of irrelevant details in some texts; learning to deal with such matters is part of becoming genuinely metacognitive in reading.

Concluding Comments

In all, we have listed 10 factors likely to influence text difficulty. Six of the factors—vocabulary, sentence structure, length, elaboration, coherence and unity, and text structure—are largely inherent in the text itself. Four factors—familiarity of content and background knowledge required, audience appropriateness, the quality and verve of the writing, and interestingness—definitely involve both the reader and the text.

This set of factors is not a checklist in the sense that you can simply tag each factor as present or absent and then tally the checkmarks to arrive at a score. Instead, it is a set of factors to consider carefully, to ponder as you try to decide whether or not a particular text ought to be used with a particular group of students.

We also want to point out that the factors are not presented in order of their importance. In fact, the first factor, vocabulary, is seldom the single most important factor to consider, and the second factor, sentence structure, is virtually never the most important one.

We should further note that a factor may be critically important with one text or situation but not very important with another. As one example, consider length. Length may be critically important in considering an expository selection that requires a great deal of background knowledge, that is not very interesting, and that is going to be used as a required reading for students who are not particularly good readers. Conversely, length may be unimportant in considering an interesting narrative selection that you plan to recommend as recreational reading for an adept reader.

As another example, consider quality and verve. Quality and verve are likely to be extremely important when considering a lengthy social science selection to be given to less-than-avid readers as a required assignment. On the other hand, quality and verve are not very important considerations in choosing documentation for some computer software that a student really wants to learn to use. In fact, straightforward and unadorned prose may well be preferable for the software documentation.

We should also note that with some texts you will probably consider only some of the factors before making a decision. For example, you might choose to discard a poorly organized selection on an unfamiliar and uninteresting topic without examining the piece in great detail. Or, you might plan to use a particularly interesting piece even though it displays a number of difficult features. Of course, in the latter case, you will probably decide to give students a good deal of scaffolding to be sure they are successful with the piece.

Before concluding, we want to return to the subject of readability formulas. As we and many others have noted, readability formulas have many drawbacks. This is why we developed and presented this list of 10 factors to consider in assessing text difficulty. We believe that using it will generally result in better matches of texts and students than will readability formulas. However, we also think that for beginning teachers, teachers not familiar with a range of children's texts, and situations in which there is very little time available, a readability formula is a useful tool for estimating the difficulty level of a text. For these purposes, we suggest either the New Dale-Chall Readability Formula (Chall & Dale, 1995) or Edward Fry's readability graph (Fry, 1977; Fry, Polk, & Fountoukidis, 2000). However, if you do use a readability formula, we suggest strongly that you always consider the difficulty level you obtain from it as supplementry and tentative.

Another tool that some of you will find useful is Jeanne Chall and her colleagues *Qualitative Assessment of Text Difficulty* (Chall et al., 1996). In addition to other valuable contents, one section of this guide contains short selections of literature, popular fiction, life science, physical science, narrative social studies, and expository social studies material ranging from the first-grade level to the college level. These passages are a very handy source for getting a beginning concept of what selections at various grade levels look like.

In concluding, we want to note again that the text is just one important element to consider in matching texts and students. Other elements—the students who will be reading the selection, your purposes and their purposes in reading the selection, and the scaffolding you will provide to help them deal successfully with the selection—also deserve and require your consideration.

References

Adams, M. L., & Bruce B. (1982). Background knowledge and reading comprehension. In J. A. Langer & T. M. Smith Burke (Eds.), *Reader meets author: Bridging the gap* (pp. 2–25). Newark, DE: International Reading Association. A very readable introduction to the importance of background knowledge.

Alexander, P. A., & Jetton, T. L. (2000). Learning from text: A multidimensional and developmental perspective. In M. Kamil, P. Mosenthal, P. D. Pearson, & R. Barr (Eds.), *Handbook of reading research* (Vol. 3, pp. 285–310). Mahwah, NJ: Erlbaum. Review of research on learning from text.

Allington, R. L. (2001). *What really matters for struggling readers: Designing research-based programs.* New York: Longman. Some very practical suggestions for working with struggling readers.

Anderson, R. C. (1984). The role of the readers' schema in comprehension, learning, and memory. In R. C. Anderson, J. Osborn, & R. J. Tierney (Eds.), *Learning to read in American schools* (pp. 243–257). Hillsdale, NJ: Erlbaum. Another readable introduction to the importance of background knowledge.

Anderson, R. C., & Freebody, P. (1981). Vocabulary knowledge. In J. Guthrie (Ed.), *Comprehension and teaching* (pp. 77–117). Newark, DE: International Reading Association. An intriguing examination of three hypotheses about the relationship between vocabulary knowledge and reading comprehension.

Anderson, R. C., Shirey, L. L., Wilson, P. T., & Fielding, L. G. (1987). Interestingness of children's reading material. In R. Snow & M. Farr (Eds.), *Aptitude, learning and instruction: Cognitive and affective process analyses.* Hillsdale, NJ: Erlbaum.

Anderson, T. H., & Armbruster, B. B. (1984). Content area textbooks. In R. C. Anderson, J. Osborn, & R. J. Tierney (Eds.), *Learning to read in American schools* (pp. 193–226). Hillsdale, NJ: Erlbaum. Influential chapter on what is wrong with textbook writing and how it can be improved.

Asher, S. (1980). Topic interest and children's reading comprehension. In R. J. Spiro, B. C. Bruce, & W. F. Brewer. *Theoretical issues in reading comprehension.* Hillsdale, NJ: Erlbaum. Brief review of research suggesting that interest does positively affect reading comprehension.

Beck, I. L., & McKeown, M. G. (1989). Expository text for young readers: The issue of coherence. In L. Resnick (Ed.), *Essays in honor of Robert Glaser* (pp. 47–66). Hillsdale, NJ: Erlbaum. Insightful overview of text characteristics that reduce coherence.

Beck, I. L., McKeown, M. G., & Gromoll, E. W. (1989). Issues that may affect social studies learning: Examples from four commercial programs. *Cognition and Instruction, 6,* 99–158. An extended and sophisticated examination of text factors affecting learning.

Beck, I. L., McKeown, M. G., & Worthy, J. (1995). Giving a text voice can improve students' understanding. *Reading Research Quarterly, 30,* 220–238. Empirical study of the effects of giving a text "voice," including sample materials illustrating the concept.

Bransford, J. D., & Johnson, M. K. (1972). Contextual prerequisites for understanding: Some investigations of comprehension and recall. *Journal of Verbal Learning and Verbal Behavior, 11,* 717–726. A classic article on the effects of elaboration.

Britton, B. K., & Black, J. B. (Eds.). (1985). *Understanding expository text: A theoretical and practical handbook for analyzing explanatory text.* Hillsdale, NJ: Erlbaum. A comprehensive and fairly technical collection on expository text.

Britton, B. K., & Guelgoez, S. (1991). Using Kintsch's computational model to improve instructional text: Effects of repairing inference calls on recall and cognitive structures. *Journal of Educational Psychology, 83,* 329–345. Empirical study demonstrating the effects on comprehension of certain sorts of revision.

Calfee, R. C., & Chambliss, M. (1988, April). *Structure in social studies textbooks: Where is the design?* Paper presented at the meeting of the American Educational Research Association, New Orleans. Analysis showing that many social studies texts are poorly designed.

Carroll, J. M. (1990). *The Nurnberg funnel: Designing minimalist instruction for practical computer skills.* Cambridge, MA: MIT Press. Advances the intriguing concept that less detail is sometimes preferable for learning.

Chall, J. S., Bissex, G. L., Conard, S. S., & Harris-Sharples, S. (1996). *Qualitative assessment of text difficulty: A practical guide for teachers and writers.* Cambridge, MA: Brookline Books. A good source of passages representing various grade levels and several subject areas.

Chall, J. S., & Dale, E. (1995). *Readability revisited: The new Dale-Chall readability formula.* Cambridge, MA: Brookline Books. Explanation and instructions for using the new Dale-Chall readability formula.

Chambliss, M., & Calfee, R. C. (1998). *Textbooks for learning: Nurturing children's minds.* Cambridge, MA: Basil Blackwell. An in-depth and insightful look at textbooks and textbook adoption.

Charney, D. H., & Reder, L. M. (1988). Studies in elaboration of instructional texts. In S. Doheny-Farina (Ed.), *Effective documentation: What we have learned from research* (pp. 47–72). Cambridge, MA: MIT Press. A summary of the authors' research on elaboration.

Coleman, E. B. (1971). Determining a technology of written instruction: Some determiners of the complexity of prose. In E. Z. Rothkopf & P. E. Johnson (Eds.), *Verbal learning research and the technology of written instruction.* New York: Teachers College Press. An early look at factors affecting text difficulty.

Cullinan, B., & Fitzgerald, S. (1984–1985). Background information bulletin on the use of readability formulae. *Reading Today, 2* (3) 1–2. The source of the joint IRA/NCTE pronouncement against over-reliance on readability formulas.

Davison, A., & Green, G. M. (Eds.). (1987). *Linguistic complexity and text comprehension.* Hillsdale, NJ: Erlbaum. Another sophisticated collection on text characteristics and comprehension.

Drum, P. (1984). Children's understanding of passages. In J. Flood (Ed.), *Promoting reading comprehension* (pp. 61–78). Newark, DE: International Reading Association. A very lucid examination of what children understand from narrative and expository texts.

Duffy, T. M., Higgins, L., Mehlenbacher, B., Cochran, C., Burnett, R., Wallace, D., Hill, C., Haugen, D., McCaffery, M., Sloane, S., & Smith, S. (1989). Models for the design of instructional text. *Reading Research Quarterly, 24,* 434–457. Study showing the superiority of less-adorned text.

Freebody, P., & Anderson, R. C. (1983). Effects on text comprehension of differing proportions and locations of difficult vocabulary. *Journal of Reading Behavior, 15,* 19–39. Study indicating that a very large proportion of difficult vocabulary must be present to affect comprehension.

Fry, E. (1977). Fry's readability graph: Clarifications, validity, and extension to level 17. *Journal of Reading, 21,* 242–252. Original source of the formula.

Fry, E. B., Polk, J. K., & Fountoukidis, D. (2000). *The reading teacher's book of lists* (4th ed.). Englewood Cliffs, NJ: Prentice-Hall. Contains complete instructions for use of the Fry readability graph, also a very handy source of word lists and other lists helpful in the classroom.

Garner, R. (1992). "Seductive details" and learning from text. In K. A. Renninger, S. Hidi, & A. Krapp (Eds.). *The role of interest in learning and development.* Hillsdale, NJ: Erlbaum. Review of research showing the negative effects of seductive details.

Goldman, S. R., & Rakestraw, J. A., Jr. (2000). In M. Kamil, P. Mosenthal, P. D. Pearson, & R. Barr (Eds.), *Handbook of reading research,* (Vol. 3, pp. 311–335). Mahwah, NJ: Erlbaum. Review of research of structural aspects of text broadly conceived.

Graves, M. F., Prenn, M. C., Earle, J., Thompson, M., Johnson, V., & Slater, W. H. (1991). Improving instructional text: Some lessons learned. *Reading Research Quarterly, 26,* 110–120. Reports a study and reviews a series of studies indicating the negative effects of seductive details.

Green, G. M., & Olsen, M. D. (1988). Preferences and comprehension of original and readability adapted materials. In A. Davison & G. M. Green (Eds.), *Linguistic complexity and text comprehension* (pp. 115–140). Hillsdale, NJ: Erlbaum. Study showing that students prefer original text to supposedly more readable adapted versions.

Grobe, J. A. (1970). Reading rate and study time demands on secondary students. *Journal of Reading, 13,* 286–288, 316. Illustrates the huge task that lengthy readings pose for slow readers.

Linderholm, T., Everson, M. G., van den Broek, P., Mischinski, M., Crittenden, A., & Samuels, J. (2000). Effects of causal text revisions on more- and less-skilled readers' comprehension of easy and difficult texts. *Cognition & Instruction, 18,* 525–556. Empirical study demonstrating the effects on comprehension of certain sorts of revision.

McKeown, M. G., Beck, I. L., Sinatra, G. M., & Loxterman, J. A. (1992). The contribution of prior knowledge and coherent text to comprehension. *Reading Research Quarterly, 27*, 78–93. Study showing that both of these factors have significant effects on comprehension.

Muth, K. D. (Ed.). (1989). *Children's comprehension of narrative and expository text: Research into practice.* Newark, DE: International Reading Association. A teacher-oriented collection of articles on text comprehension.

Ogle, D., & Blachowicz, C.L.Z. (2002). Beyond literature circles: Helping students comprehend informational text. In C. C. Block & M. Pressley (Eds.), *Comprehension instruction: Research based best practices* (pp. 259–274). Suggestions for the sort of assistance students frequently need with expository text.

Orwell, G. (1950). Shooting an elephant. In *Shooting an elephant, and other essays.* New York: Harcourt. Challenging and fascinating essay.

Pearson, P. D. (1974–1975). The effects of grammatical complexity on children's comprehension, recall, and conception of certain semantic relations. *Reading Research Quarterly, 10*, 155–192. Probably the first study to show that syntactically more complex text can sometimes be comprehended better than syntactically less complex text.

Pressley, M., & Block, C. C. (2002). Summing up: What comprehension could be. In C. C. Block & M. Pressley (Eds.), *Comprehension instruction: Research based best practices* (pp. 383–392). Summary of both research-based evidence and somewhat less certain understandings about comprehension instruction.

RAND Reading Study Group. (2002). *Reading for understanding: Toward an R&D program in reading comprehension.* Santa Monica, CA: RAND Education. Also available online at http://www.rand.org/multi/achievementforall/reading/. A review of our existing knowledge about reading comprehension and a plan for future research.

Reder, L. M. (1982). Elaborations: When do they help and when do they hurt? *Text, 2*, 211–224. Study indicating that elaboration does not always facilitate learning.

Reder, L. M, Charney, D. H., & Morgan, K. I. (1986). The role of elaborations in learning a skill from an instructional text. *Memory and Cognition, 14*, 64–78. Study indicating cases in which elaboration does facilitate learning.

Rouet, J. F., Vidal-Abarca, E., Erboul, A. B., & Millogo, V. (2001). Effects of information search tasks on the comprehension of instructional text. *Discourse Processes, 31,* 163–186. Experimental study investigating effects of search tasks given to readers.

Sawyer, M. H. (1991). A review of the research in revising instructional text. *Journal of Reading Behavior, 23,* 307–333. Comprehensive review of the literature on revising text to facilitate learning.

Williams, J. M. (1985). *Style: Ten lessons in clarity & grace.* New York: Scott, Foresman and Company. Wonderful essay on writing with style.

Children's Books Index

Grade Level Index

Grades 3-6——

Grades 5-6———

Grades 5-8———

Grades 6-8———

Grades 6 and Up———

Subject Index

L = Literature
SS = Social Science
ST = Science and Technology

Academic Author Index

Y——

Academic Subject Index

About the Authors

Bonnie Graves is a former elementary school teacher and full time author—both of children's books and books on teaching reading. She received a B.A. in English Literature and an Elementary teaching credential from California State University at Long Beach and has taken advanced coursework on reading and instructional design at the University of Minnesota. Currently, she has thirteen published books for young readers, the most recent being *Taking Care of Trouble* (Dutton, 2002) and *California Condor: Flying Free* (Perfection, 2002). In addition to her children's books, Graves has written instructional materials for numerous publishers, including Scholastic, NCTE, IRA, Capstone Press, Minnesota Public Television, Science Research Associates, and Glencoe/McGraw-Hill. She has also co-authored two reading textbooks and several articles on teaching reading with her husband Michael Graves. In addition to visiting classrooms throughout the year as a children's author, Ms. Graves is currently working on two middle grade novels and a sequel to *The Whooping Crane*. She can be reached through the website www.childrensliteraturenetwork.org.

Michael Graves is Professor of Literacy Education and the Guy Bond Fellow in Reading at the University of Minnesota. He received his Ph.D. in Education from Stanford University and his MA and BA in English from California State College at Long Beach, and he has taught in both the Long Beach and Huntington Beach Public Schools. His research, development, and writing focus on comprehension development, vocabulary development, text difficulty, and effective instruction. His recent books include *Reading and Learning in Content Areas* (2003, with Randall Ryder, Wiley), *Teaching Reading in the Twenty-first Century* (2001, with Connie Juel and Bonnie Graves, Allyn & Bacon), *Reading for Meaning: Fostering Comprehension in the Middle Grades* (2000, edited with Barbara

Taylor and Paul van den Broek, Teachers College Press). He has also published widely in journals such as *Reading Research Quarterly, Research in the Teaching of English, Journal of Reading Behavior, Journal of Adolescent and Adult Literacy, Elementary School Journal, American Educator, and Educational Leadership*. Dr. Graves is the former editor of the *Journal of Reading Behavior* and the former associate editor of *Research in the Teaching of English*. He is currently developing a federally-funded website of Scaffolded Reading Experiences, www.onlinereadingresources.com, and completing a book on *Scaffolding Reading Experiences for English-Language Learners* with Jill Fitzgerald.